Tracks of San Jose

Berryessa

FELTER

SWEIGERT RD.
KAHLER CT.
KAHLER CT.

RD.

SIERRA RD.

FELTER RD.

Creek

Penitencia Creek

Speedway

Alum Rock Pk.

CREEK RD.
Upper

TENCIA CREEK RD.

WHITE RD.

TOYON AV.

21

Alum Rock Hill Climb

130

MOUNT

ROCCA RD.

HAMILTON

Arroyo

FLEMING AV.

ROCK ROAD

STORY RD.

East Side Speedway

Cherry Flat Reservoir

LS RD.

130

Joseph D. Grant County Park

Aguague ROAD

QUIMBY RD.

130

UM

ANTONIO

29

JACKSON AV.

RD.

MARTEN AV.

WHITE RD.

Little Bonneville Drag Strip

CUNNINGHAM AV.

Reid - Hillview Airport

NORWOOD AV.

QUIMBY

RD.

ROAD

BAYSHORE ROAD

UGHLIN RD.

Coyote AV.

ROAD

CAPITOL EXPWY.

101

ABORN

LOUPE AV.

SILVER

San Jose Speedway

FOWLER

Evergreen Valley College

YERBA BUENA RD.

SAN FELIPE

THE VILLA

CREEK

San Jose Driving Park

Metcalf Raceway Park

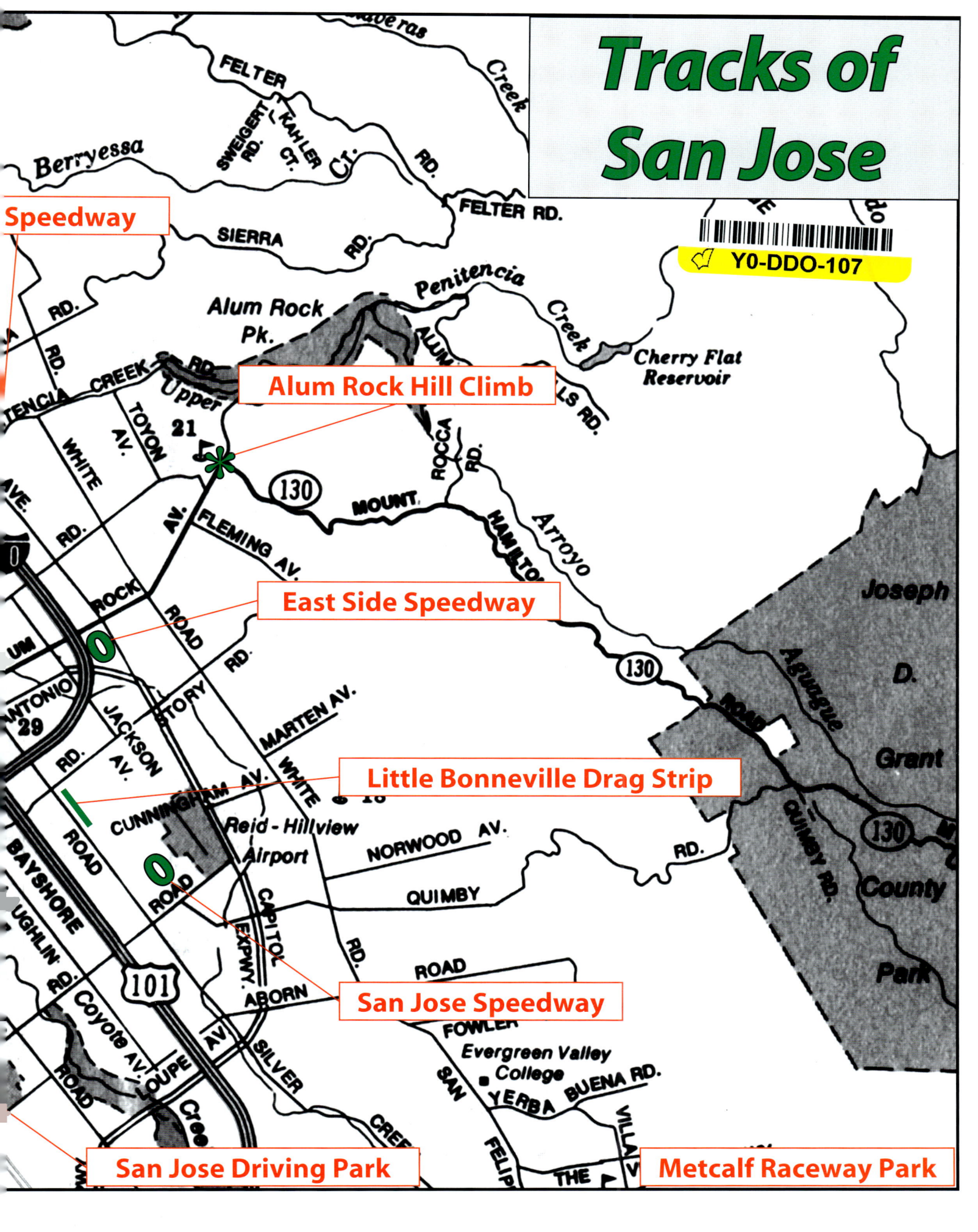

History of
San Jose Auto Racing
1903 - 2007

by Dennis Mattish

Published by

DENNIS MATTISH PHOTOS
SAN JOSE, CA.

Website: historysanjoseautoracing.com

Copyright 2009 by
Dennis Mattish

First Edition
First Printing 2009
Second Edition
First Printing 2013

ISBN 978-0-9881861-1-8 (Limited Edition)

Library of Congress Control Number: 2009908776

Layout and design by
Dennis Mattish

Printed in the USA by
Walsworth Publishing Company
Marceline, Missouri 64658

Table of Contents

Acknowledgements

Many people assisted me in this project, some without realizing it. Without their help, this book would never have come together. I would like to acknowledge:

Historians

Ken Clapp
Jim Montgomery
Tom Motter
Don Radbruch
Jim Chini
Jerry Santibanes

I would like to thank these people for letting me scan their collections

Don Bishop
Al Soto
Tom Henry
Dick Slate
Mike Manthey

Also providing me with much needed information and help were:

Jim Arbuckle
Steve Gregory
Tony Iacobitti
Jim Burns
Karl Laucher
Gordon White
Burt Foland
Wanda Sargent
Steve Lafond
Richard Davis
Stacy Lynne
Toastmasters

The early chapters would not have been possible if it were not for
San Jose Public Library/Martin Luther King Library (Ralph Pearce)
Sourisseau Academy, San Jose State University
(Charlene Devul, Thomas Layton & Leilani Marshall)
History San Jose (Jim Reed & Sarah Puckitt)
CH Motorcars, LLC (Paul Kierstein)

And of course, my editor Andy Weltch www.weltchmedia.com

Special thanks are in order for fellow photographers who contributed to this book.

Nice cameras. Dennis Arnold (left) and Jim Abreu were major contributors to the early years of the Tully Road San Jose Speedway chapter.

Bob Mize and his son Don (pictured) contributed to three different chapters.

Ken Clapp
Promotor/historian

Jim Montgomery (left)
Midget car owner and historian

Mykeal Clark - San Jose Speedway and SJ Fairgrounds contributing photographer

Foreword

By Joe Leonard

Joe Leonard is the only racing personality in United States history to win both the USAC National Indianapolis Car Championship and the AMA National Championship. Joe was the AMA Grand National Flat Track Champion in 1954, 1956 and 1957. He won the USAC National Championship in 1971 and 1972. Only the great Sir John Surtees of Great Britain can lay claim to this kind of accomplishment.

Joe gained notoriety when he won the pole position for the 1968 Indianapolis 500 driving the controversial "Turbine Powered" car sponsored by STP. Leonard is also the only motor sports personality to be inducted into the San Jose Sports Hall of Fame.

Do you know the way to San Jose? Well I found my way to San Jose in 1951 when I moved up here from my hometown of San Diego.

Although baseball was my first sporting love, a shoulder injury on my pitching arm ended that, and motor sports soon became my passion.

I truly believe motor sports to be the greatest sport in the world, and San Jose was always a hot bed of racing activity. Unfortunately, today we can no longer say that.

I first raced in San Jose at an AMA National event on the one-mile oval at the Santa Clara County Fairgrounds during the 1951 season.

Five years later, I had my first car race in San Jose–the Little Indy 500-lap Midget race at San Jose Speedway in 1956. That was one of the most grueling races I have ever been in – I even had to tie a rope to my helmet to keep my head from falling over on my shoulder because of the g-forces from 1,000 left turns.

I have many fond memories of racing on the high-banked Tully Road track. I raced in many USAC and BCRA Midget races as well as the NASCAR Modifieds. My most memorable race in the Modifieds was racing wheel to wheel with Al Pombo and winning on opening day in 1964. Over the years, I have had the pleasure to race against the finest drivers to ever grace the high-banked San Jose Speedway – guys like A.J. Foyt, Parnelli Jones, Al Unser, Bill Vukovich, Gary Bettenhausen, Dan Gurney, Johnnie Parsons, Art Pollard, George Snider, George Benson, Marshall Sargent, Howard Kaeding, Burt Foland and a host of others. The latter two, if given the chance, would certainly have done well at Indianapolis. Although these gentlemen never raced in San Jose, I must acknowledge my good friends Lloyd Ruby and Johnny Rutherford.

San Jose missed its greatest opportunity at the big time when politics shot down the NASCAR plan to turn the Fairgrounds Mile into a super speedway back in the 1980s. We have all seen how big NASCAR has become since then; sadly, San Jose missed out on being part of it. Although the San Jose Grand Prix was a positive development, once again I feel that due to local politics and the declining economy, it was doomed to be a lost cause.

There have certainly been some highs and lows in the story of motor sports in San Jose, and this book offers a unique opportunity to relive them in a true celebration of more than a century of auto racing history.

Joe Leonard

Indianapolis - 1968

AMA - 1954

Preface

In the early part of the 1950s my parents, two brothers and I would pile into the family car and head out to San Jose Speedway and watch the Hardtops. The sights, sounds and smells of those evenings made an impression on my young mind. I have been hooked on the sport of auto racing since then.

My father started an automotive business (Mattish Automotive) in 1958. Within a year we had three Hardtops that were racing at Alviso Speedway stationed there. I would spend part of my weekend cleaning the mud off the cars as a favor to the drivers. It was also at this time that I took my first race car photos with my Kodak Brownie camera. Ten years later, I was taking our tow truck out to the track and helping with the clean-ups after accidents. I also kept my camera (now a 35mm) with me and would photograph the races.

During 1972 I had my first photos published in a magazine called *Cavalcade of Auto Racing*. Soon after, I was shooting for *National Speed Sport News*, *Racing Wheels Newspaper* and eventually *Open Wheel* and *Flat Out* magazines. I became a member of the Motor Sports Press Association in the 1980s and served on the Board as VP of Photography. Nowadays, besides shooting motor sports events in the Bay area, I occasionally travel through America and England photographing races.

About 15 years ago, Andy Weltch, a British journalist, started encouraging me to write a book on San Jose Speedway. I told him I wasn't ready to take on a project like that. Then in 2005, I read a very brief History of San Jose racing in *National Speed Sports News*, written by Don Radbruch. The moment I finished reading that, I thought to myself, "Hey! I can do this." Having been a motor sports photographer for over 35 years and having written stories

for a third of that time, I was ready to take it to the next level. I then started the five-year journey of intensive microfilm research, photo gathering, writing, editing and page-layout.

At the beginning of this journey I asked Radbruch about writing a book, and this is what he wrote me. "There are several stages to writing a book. First off it is 'the book'---from here it moves on to 'THE BOOK' and the final stage is 'That &&^^%$$$$$$$##**&&^^^ book. ' I know that my books took about five years from the beginning to publication." You know what, he was right.

I do not sugar-coat anything. Everything is written according to facts as I found them during my research.

If a phrase like "dynamite under the hood" or "wind burners" (meaning race cars) sounds corny, it is because I took these quotes straight from the newspaper articles that were written during that era.

I spend only a limited time talking about motorcycles because they have so much history in San Jose that I feel the subject should be reserved for another book, written by a motorcycle historian.

It would be impossible to cover every driver who ever raced in San Jose. I did my best to cover the history of San Jose racing in words and photos. I am sorry if your favorite driver is not included.

This was a massive project for me and I did my best to assure everything is accurate. If the information in the newspapers was wrong, as it sometimes was, then I apologize if it made its way into this book.

Primary sources of information for this book were microfilm, newspaper articles, books, magazines, programs and interviews.

And here you have it, my labor of love.

1959: Mattish Automotive. *Dennis Mattish Photo*

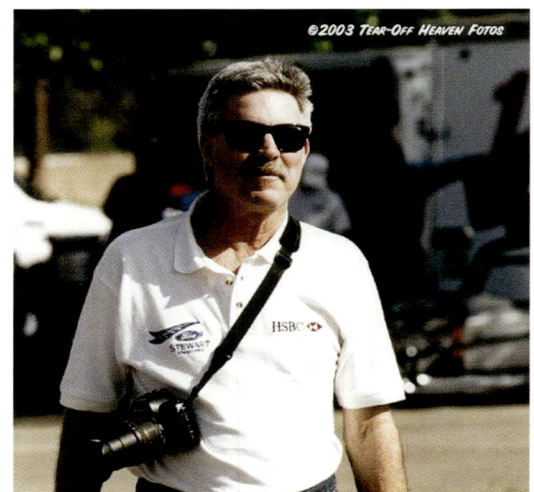

Dennis Mattish - *Photo by Steve Lafond*

Introduction

On November 28, 1895, a cold day in Chicago, America's first automobile race was run. The six-car field would race a 52-mile round trip from Jackson Park to Evanston. Frank Duryea powered his own car to victory at the blazing average speed of 5.1 mph. The importance of this event cannot be overstated. All the different types of automotive events would grow out of this one occasion–road racing, oval racing, car shows and a host of other types of motoring events.

For over 100 years Americans have loved both the automobile and sports. Put the two together and you have a sport that has been among the top three in attendance for more than seven decades. The largest single-day spectator sport in the world is the Indianapolis 500. In more than 10 states, auto racing has produced the largest sports crowds ever assembled there.

San Jose has a rich history of racing that mirrors what has happened throughout the country. For almost 75 years, the biggest spectator sport in San Jose has been auto racing. The biggest single-day crowd in sports history in San Jose was the first San Jose Grand Prix. On a single day in 1908, half the population of San Jose attended the races at the San Jose Driving Park.

This book traces the history of auto racing in San Jose from the first time Barney Oldfield barnstormed into town to try and set a world record in 1903. That was a time when the streets were dirt and people were getting around by horse and buggy. The area was known as the "Valley of Hearts Delight." Decades later the area became known as the "Garden City" (because of agriculture), and speed enthusiasts went to the high-banked San Jose Speedway on Alum Rock Avenue to get their fix. By the end of the century, as the high-tech industry replaced the crops and orchards in Santa Clara County, the area became known as Silicon Valley. So it was only fitting that with the dawning of a new millennium, the final racing events to take place in San Jose would be the high-tech Champ (Indy) Cars. The San Jose Grand Prix took place just a short walk from where Barney Oldfield wowed the crowds 100 years earlier. In between those two events, San Jose had a glorious yet sometimes bumpy ride. It's all here in this book: the good, the bad and the ugly. This book covers not only the racing and the personalities, but it also gives a complete history of every track that has held an auto race in San Jose and what happened to them and the land afterwards.

You will read about how the various fairgrounds and auto racing intertwined for a century.

There were six tracks (in a 100-year span) that were part of (or adjacent to) The Alameda-Santa Clara Street-Alum Rock Avenue corridor.

San Jose has witnessed just about every marquee name in American auto racing history. Names like Barney Oldfield, Ralph DePalma, A.J. Foyt, Unser, Rick Mears, Joe Leonard, Parnelli Jones, Billy and Bill Vukovich, Sebastien Bourdais and a host of others. They are all here.

Racing is a beautiful sport with rich history and atmosphere that dazzles the senses–color, sights and sounds that are present nowhere else in sports. Unfortunately, it is unlikely that San Jose will ever experience these sensations again.

On the Cover

Howard Kaeding
Tim Green
Ralph DePalma
George Benson
Johnny Key
Burt Foland
Sebastien Bourdais

About the artist

Robert Wise

A native Sacramentan and son of a race car driver, Bob is both an illustrator and historian of vintage automobile racing and vintage motorcycles, as well as being the acting President of the Sacramento West Capital Raceway Alumni Association.

His ongoing passion is working with Prismacolor pencils in recreating finely detailed renditions of actual vintage automobile racing events. History of San Jose Auto Racing is Bob's third book cover illustration.

Abbreviations

AAA: American Automobile Association
AMA: American Motorcycle Association
ARA: American Racing Association
BCRA: Bay Cities Racing Association
BCRRA: Bay Cities Roadster Racing Association
CARA: California Auto Racing Association
CART: Championship Auto Racing Teams
CCRA: Central California Roadster Association
CRA: California Racing Association
CSCRA: California Stock Car Racing Association
GSC: Golden State Challenge
GSRA: Golden State Racing Association
IRL: Indy Racing League
MARA: Midget Auto Racing Association
NARA: National Automotive Racing Association
NARC: Northern Auto Racing Club
NASCAR: National Association Stock Car Auto Racing
NCMA: Northern California Modified Association
NCRRA: Northern California Roadster Racing Association
NHRA: National Hot Rod Association
RURA: Roads Unlimited Racing Association
SCCA: Sports Car Club of America
SCRA: Sprint Car Racing Association
URA: United Racing Association
URI: United Roadster Incorporated
USA: United Sprint Association
USAC: United States Auto Club
USHRA: United States Hot Rod Association
WAR: Western Auto Racing
WoO: World of Outlaws

Chapter 1

In the beginning, there was

Agricultural Park
1859-1906

The huge success of horse racing during the 1800s provided scores of mile and half-mile dirt tracks, complete with grandstands. It seems every town had a fairgrounds oval, and San Jose was no different. This would set the stage for what was to come at the end of the century–the automobile.

In 1859 Henry Naglee sold 76 acres of land, about a mile west of the San Jose city limits, to the Santa Clara Valley Agricultural Society for $6,142. The present location of this land would be at The Alameda and Race Street. The society made improvements, which would include a one-mile horse racing track. Grandstands were added in 1878, making this the ideal site for Santa Clara County's first fairgrounds. Such notable people as President Ulysses S. Grant and Leland Stanford attended horse racing events at the track.

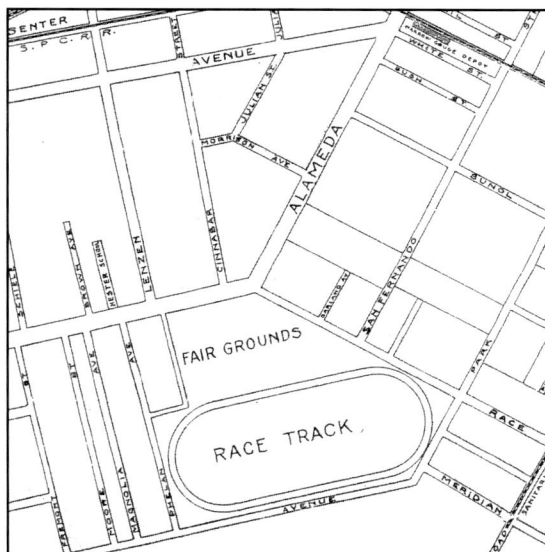

Agricultural Park would serve as the county fairgrounds until 1888 when funds from the state dried up and fair interest waned. It would continue to operate as an agricultural fairgrounds until the end.

For the next decade, the park got along quite well until insurmountable problems took hold. The land was sold to developers in 1901, but the racetrack would continue to hold events for a few more years. In 1906 the rest of the stands and fences were torn down and the property became the Hanchett Park neighborhood.

Before Agricultural Park was developed, San Jose would hold its first-ever, big-time automobile racing event. (Motorcycles had been run there previously.)

On June 20, 1903, Barney Oldfield became the first man in America to drive a gas-powered automobile faster than a mile a minute (60 mph)–a huge achievement in its time. This is how he described his experience to the newspapers: "You have every sensation of being hurled through space. The machine is throbbing under you with its cylinders beating a drummer's tattoo, and the air tears

1904 map, showing the location of Agricultural Park. Race Street received its name because of the proximity to the racetrack.
Martin Luther King Library, San Jose

Agricultural Park was the gathering place of the sports minded. Here one could see horse, bicycle and, in later years, automobile races. This photo was taken in the late 1800's. *Courtesy History San Jose*

past you in a gale. I tell you, gentlemen: no man can drive faster and live!"

Oldfield's press agent elaborated on the dangers of going this fast: "The chest of a driver is forced in, and his pumping plant must be marvelously strong to resist the tremendous pressure in order to inhale sufficient air for the performance of its functions. Average lungs cannot overcome the outward force and the result is like strangulation. Blood rushes to the head, temporary but complete paralysis of mind over body occurs and instantly the driver loses consciousness and control."

These wild and dramatic statements wowed the throngs who would witness his daring feats.

Barney Oldfield was the Babe Ruth of the speed tracks. He was America's flamboyant race car driver. He was a braggart, sentimentalist, gambler, barroom brawler and dirt track daredevil. He barnstormed across America, racing against anything and everything, including airplanes.

With much fanfare, America's legendary speed king arrived in San Jose on November 15, 1903, with the goal of setting a new world closed-course speed record.

The week before Oldfield arrived, the headlines in the *San Jose Mercury* and *Evening News* read "Barney Oldfield will go for world record on Sunday," and added "experts declare Agricultural Park to be the fastest on the coast." The story went on to say the track was in fine condition because rains in the previous few days had hardened the track and dust. Since Barney's last meet held in San Francisco the weekend before, his car–the famous Winton Bullet No.2–had been overhauled. He was confident in breaking his own world record on a circular track. The race was to be sanctioned, meaning it would be an official world record.

There also was an Oldsmobile and a Cadillac race for amateurs scheduled on the program. This involved local citizens racing their streetcars, the winner earning brag-

Oldfield-1903

ging rights for the fastest car in town.

On the day before the race Barney towed the 120 HP 8-cylinder machine through the streets of downtown San Jose, wowing the locals. This was the first time the citizens of San Jose had ever seen a powerful race car.

On race day, 1,500 people assembled at Agricultural Park to watch San Jose's first motor car speed event. This was a big crowd, considering the population of San Jose at this time was 22,000.

The track was in excellent condition and the weather was perfect. Barney Oldfied took to the track with much enthusiasm. He proceeded to pick up speed until he was racing around the track at a mile-a-minute pace and getting faster. The crowd craned their necks and grew enthusiastic as he picked up speed. Just as he was closing in on the world record, the water pump had a major failure. Barney coasted to a stop on the back straightaway. Swarms of people rushed to the car to see what happened. The car was then brought back to the grandstands (there were no pits in 1903) and repairs were attempted. He then went back onto the track, resulting in more damage to the Winton Bullet No. 2 and ending his attempt for a world record in the city of San Jose.

Afterwards, Barney said: "I was more disappointed than the audience, for I always dislike to advertise to do a thing and then not be able to do it." The following day he loaded up and headed down to Los Angles for his next meet.

The two-mile Oldsmobile race was much, much slower. The stock-type cars were only capable of about a mile in three minutes (little faster than modern Olympic track stars run). A Mr. Darby won that race with George Osen a close second. The Cadillac race was a little faster with the two cars finishing the three-mile event in a dead heat, with a time of 6:01. The track would run a few more minor speed events before its demise, late in 1906.

Barney Oldfield posing in the Winton Bullet No.2 in front of an admiring crowd. This photo was taken at a previous meet before his San Jose arrival. *LA84 Foundation*

Barney Oldfield goes for the world record in the Winton Bullet No.2. *LA84 Foundation*

San Jose's local newspaper, the *San Jose Mercury News,* went by many names over the years. Founded in 1851, the paper was named after the local mining industry which produced mercury. Originally the *News* and the *Mercury* were two different papers, but they would merge in 1983 and become the *San Jose Mercury News.* Throughout this book you will see the paper go by many different names as it evolved. Here is the list:

San Jose Daily Mercury
The Evening News
San Jose Mercury Herald
San Jose Mercury
San Jose News
San Jose Mercury News

Chapter 2

Mitchell Automobile Company

Alum Rock Hill Climb
1907-1909

Long before the Pike's Peak Hill Climb became famous, San Jose had its own version of a hill climb.

The Mitchell Motor Car Company was born of a wagon and bicycle enterprise, the Wisconsin Wheel Works. Beginning in 1904, the company produced medium-priced cars which steadily increased in popularity. By 1907 there was a large contingent of Mitchell Car enthusiasts in California.

The company came up with the idea of sponsoring a motoring event for its followers. So on June 7, 1907, the first Alum Rock Hill Climb was staged, exclusively for Mitchell Cars. Two Trophies were up for grabs, a Gold Cup for Touring Cars and a Silver Cup for Runabout (smaller) cars. The cups were valued at over a hundred dollars each, the equivalent about $3,000 now.

MERCURY: SATURDAY MORNING, JUNE 8, 1907

Hill Climbing Contest Grand Success; Crowd From All Over State See Races

Trophy in Touring Car Class Carried Off by Ernest Lion, of San Jose—Dr. R. L. Rigden, of San Francisco, Wins Runabout Cup—Large Crowd of Autoists Will Go to Del Monte Hotel Today.

The staging area was at Alum Rock Avenue and White Road. From there, the cars would get a running start and race up Alum Rock Avenue, past the Linda Vista Golf Course and ending just the other side of Mount Hamilton Road. The distance over the dirt road was one and a quarter miles.

Cars and spectators from all over the state arrived on race day to witness what would be declared a huge success. Seventeen cars participated in the race, with the top three separated by less than a second. Ernest Linn of San Jose won the Gold Cup, while Dr. Rigden of San Francisco took home the Silver Cup.

With the success of the previous year, the July 3, 1908, Hill Climb was even bigger and better yet. The event grew sevenfold, from 17 contestants to nearly 150. Cars and drivers from different parts of the state were represented. A ladies division for Touring Cars, Runabouts, and Roadsters was added to the program for the 1908, race.

A large crowd witnessed what the *San Jose Daily Mercury* described as "one of the most enjoyable and successful events in the history of motoring on the coast." The course was lined with automobiles, most of which were decorated with ribbons and banners. People were in a fes-

1970 map showing where the course would have been run 63 years earlier. In 1907 there were no side streets and the golf course was below McKee Road.

Mitchell advertisement one week after the 1908 race.

5

The staging area (pits) for the Hill Climb. *Courtesy History San Jose*

1907 winners. Touring Car, Ernest P. Lion; Runabout, Dr. R.L. Rigden. *Courtesy History San Jose*

SAN JOSE DAILY MERCURY: WEDNESDAY MORNING, JUNE 5, 1907.

Local Autos, One Piloted by Woman, Will Race Up Alum Rock Hill Friday

Mitchell Cars Will Run Time Test Friday—New Road Planned Into Santa Cruz. Local Men Endorse Proposition—Club Cards to Be Issued Soon for Local Auto People—Santa Clara County Club May Handle Motor League's Interest Here.

J. B. CHASE IN HIS MITCHELL CAR, WHICH WILL BE ONE OF THE MACHINES TO RUN FRIDAY NEXT IN HILL-CLIMBING CONTEST.

tive mood as the cars raced by on the way up the hill. The program lasted nearly four hours. Afterwards, everybody headed downtown for a banquet.

By 1909, the Alum Rock Hill Climb had grown to become an event at which to be seen. William Mitchell himself traveled all the way from Wisconsin to be part of the festivities.

Over 500 cars and 1,600 people lined what was now known as the "Speedway on Alum Rock Hill."

The event had grown to include 16 different classes of cars and drivers; 16 people went home with either a Gold or Silver Cup.

Afterwards about 350 participants and guests attended a banquet at the Hotel Vendome in downtown San Jose put on by the Mitchell Motor Car Company.

After the grand success of the 1909 race it would be assumed 1910 would be bigger yet, but for some unknown reason (cost maybe?) the Mitchell Motor Car Company pulled its sponsorship and there was never another Alum Rock Hill Climb.

A Touring Car gets a running start on his race to the top. The building on the left was called the Three-Mile House.
Courtesy History San Jose

Mitchell Touring Car races up Alum Rock Avenue in 1907. By 1909, people and cars lined the course all the way to the top.
Courtesy History San Jose

Chapter 3

The Great Race

New York to Paris Race

1908

On February 12, 1908, six cars representing four nations (each wanting to prove the superiority of their car) sat on the starting line in New York's Time Square. Their objective was simple–to be the first to arrive in Paris. Their task was one of the most difficult ever undertaken by man and machine.

With a crowd of 250,000 people jammed into Time Square, at 11:15 a.m. the gold-plated pistol was fired into the air signifying the start of the race. The cars with the flags of Germany, France, Italy and the United States flying from them took off on the 22,000-mile journey (13,341 of which were driven and the rest traversed by sea).

Ahead of the competitors were winter conditions, very few paved roads, and in many parts of the world, no roads at all. Often the teams resorted to straddling the locomotive train tracks with their cars riding on balloon tires for hundreds of miles when no roads could be found.

The route took the teams through Chicago, Iowa, Nebraska, Colorado, Wyoming, Utah, Nevada and into California.

The American entry, the Thomas Flyer Special, was the first to reach California. The team entered through Death Valley and made their way to Bakersfield. From there they went up the Central Valley and passed through Fresno on their way to Los Banos where they spent the night. The next morning they traveled through Pacheco Pass and into Gilroy. After passing through Gilroy, the car covered 12 miles in 11 minutes on Monterey Highway. San Joseans had been anticipating the arrival of the Thomas Flyer and were out early, lining up along the Monterey Highway and First Street. At 11:30 a.m. on March 24, amid a cloud of dust, the Thomas Flyer came charging into San Jose to shouts of welcome and cheers from the throngs. The Thomas Flyer paraded through the downtown streets before being led to the city center and the Lamolle house on Santa Clara Street, where they were served a lavish meal among a great celebration. Two hours later, the team climbed back into their car and headed to Oakland where they caught a ferry to San Francisco. A couple of days later they boarded a steamer headed for Alaska.

Ten days later, on April 3, the Italian car, Zust, arrived in San Jose

Cars await the start of the New York to Paris Race on February 12, 1908, in Times Square. The near car is the French "De Dion" which was the third car into San Jose. The car would not finish the race. The middle car is the German "Protos," Which would bypass San Jose and be penalized 30 days for breaking the rules, thus finishing second in the race. *Dennis Mattish Collection*

American Car In Auto Race In San Jose

Thomas Flyer Leaves In Cloud Of Dust

Racers the Guests Of Local Automobile Club At Lamolle House

San Jose Mercury News (Evening Edition) headline on March 24, 1908

where it would spend the night being overhauled in the Rambler Garage. The next morning many members of the local Italian community were on hand to give an enthusiastic send-off to their countrymen.

On April 6, the French Consul of San Francisco met De Dion, the car representing France. The car was taken to the Wallace Brothers Garage for service and viewing. Club La France of San Jose entertained the occupants of the car, and an elaborate banquet was served.

Of the six cars that started the race, only three would reach San Jose.

The German car, Protos, broke down in Pocatello, Idaho. They shipped the car to Seattle by rail where repairs were made. Problem was, they by-passed the designated route to San Francisco.

The Thomas Flyer had a huge lead

ARRIVAL OF THE THOMAS FLYER, MARCH 24, 1908. NEW YORK TO PARIS RACE, AT THE LAMOLLE HOUSE, SAN JOSE. CAL

1908 postcard showing the crowd greeting the Thomas Flyer in front of the Lamolle House on Santa Clara and San Pedro Streets. The building is now (2009) the site of Starbucks. *Dennis Mattish Collection*

Adoring San Joseans admire the Thomas Flyer upon its arrival in San Jose on March 24, 1908. *Edith C. Smith Collection / Sourisseau Academy, San Jose State University*

when it arrived in Alaska but found the trail impassable with deep snow. The route was changed and a new start would take place in Vladivostok, Manchuria. All the advantage that the Thomas had built was gone as the other cars by-passed Alaska and sailed straight to Japan and then Vladivostok.

From Manchuria, the teams headed into the tundra of Siberia, which turned into a quagmire with the spring thaw. At several points, forward movement was often measured in feet rather than miles per hour. Eventually, the roads improved as they approached Europe . The cars went through Moscow and St. Petersburg in Russia, crossed Germany to Berlin, and on into Belgium. From there it was a race into Paris.

The German Protos arrived in Paris three days ahead of the Americans but was penalized a month for various shortcuts (totaling 3,246 miles).

On July 30, 169 days after leaving New York, the Thomas Flyer was driven into Paris by George Schuster, the only American to complete the whole journey. The Italian entry arrived 48 days later, bringing to a close the longest race in history.

It would be weeks before the official winner was declared.

The Final results

American	Thomas Flyer	169 days
German	Protos	195 days
Italian	Zust	217 days

French Car Arrives

The De Dion car in the New York to Paris automobile race arrived in San Jose at 1:30 today. The car was met by a delegation of San Jose and San Francisco enthusiasts and escorted to the Sunset garage on St John street where it was overhauled. The car left for San Francisco by way of Oakland at 2:30 this afternoon.

The car was driven by Saint Cheffray who made a remarkable run from Fresno. The occupants of the car were escorted to the Lamolle House and were given a banquet by the local Club La France.

San Jose Mercury News

Italian Car Is Given a Hearty Welcome

Big Racing Machine Left San Jose At Early Hour This Morning

Accompanied by a number of automobiles, the Italian car, "Zust" in the New York to Paris auto race, sped through the downtown streets at half past seven o'clock this morning, amid the cheers and farewells of a large number of people who had gathered on Santa Clara street in front of the Lamolle House to witness the departure.

IN SAN JOSE OVER NIGHT

San Jose Mercury News

The 1965 movie *The Great Race* was based on the events of the New York to Paris Race.

The Italian car, Zust, spent the night in San Jose being overhauled. It would finish the race in third place. *Edith C. Smith Collection / Sourisseau Academy, San Jose State University*

An artist's drawing from the ASCO collection of American Master Performers shows the Thomas Flyer, with a support vehicle, traveling across America in the dead of winter during the 1908 New York to Paris Race. *Courtesy of the Automatic Switch Co.*

Chapter 4

Record setting

San Jose Driving Park
1909-1915

When Agricultural Park closed in 1906, San Jose was without a racetrack. That changed in 1909.

San Josean Ray Meade saw an opportunity and would invest $30,000 in a new oval. The location was northeast of the Monterey and Umbarger Roads intersection. This was considered a good location because of the proximity of the First Street railroad train. It stopped just across Monterey Road. Also at that location were Oak Hill Cemetery and the upscale, privately-owned Scheutzen Park.

The original plan catered more to horses than race cars; thus the one-mile regulation oval. Stalls for 300 horses were built and a luxury hotel was considered. But the owners soon realized that auto racing would be a bigger asset. When construction was completed, the track was considered a high-banked oval (by 1909 standards). The opening event was scheduled for November 9, 1909, and it was for motor racing.

1909

The excitement the first event created was as big as San Jose had ever seen. After a week of testing, drivers proclaimed the San Jose Driving Park to be the fastest

1931 Aerial photo of the former San Jose Driving Park. *The Fairchild Aerial Photography Collection at Whittier College*

and finest on the coast. Many drivers predicted that new records would be set, and they would not be wrong.

The day before the race, there was a parade of race cars through the streets of San Jose, witnessed by large numbers.

The following morning, 10,000 people (San Jose's population was 25,000) descended on the new track. They arrived by car, taxi, horse and train. People even jammed the roofs of the streetcars. Thousands of people, who were unable to get a ride, walked the six miles from downtown San Jose. They would not be disappointed.

With the blessing of an American Automobile Associa-

tion (AAA) sanction, the event and any record set would be recognized as official. The most notable drivers at the meet were E.B. Ely driving a Gordon Bennett and Harold Hall driving for the Scott Motor Co.

Horses pulling rollers were still working the track into condition as the race cars and motorcycles took to the track for the warm-up session. Yes, both types of vehicles hot-lapped together. Drivers had to swing wide to avoid hitting the horses, but that was only one of the problems. Moments later, as the hot-lap session was intensifying and the dust was kicking up, the track suffered its first casualty. Motorcycle rider Johnny Baumgardner was traveling at top speed down the straightaway and through the dust when he slammed into the back of a slower-moving race car. The impact and subsequent fall and tumble fractured his arm and bruised him severely. Also another rider would be in critical condition before the day was over.

Fences had not yet been built around the track to keep people out of harm's way. Because of the size of the crowd on opening day and lack of crowd control, there were occasions when cars had to take evasive action to keep from hitting people who were wandering onto the track.

There were a number of short-distance races for different classes of vehicles. The main event was a 50-mile Free-For-All event, open to all classes of cars. This race would prove to be the most interesting and entertaining of the day. The 50-lap event started six cars, which kicked up such a dust storm that it shrouded the track in what was described as a giant whirlpool. Drivers could be seen straining their eyes and every now and then wiping their goggles with a cotton rag being held in their hands. The first half of the race was easily controlled by Harold Hall, but on lap 17 the tire blew on his Comet. Hall went into the pits for a tire change, but he would lose eight laps and thus the race. (Pit stops took a long time in 1909.) W.H. Turner driving the Thomas would emerge from the dust as the leader. Because of the short November days, darkness was now setting over the Driving Park, so the AAA officials decided to end the race early. When the cars made it back to the pits, three different drivers filed a protest (without success) against W.H. Turner, claiming he fouled them.

When the day was done, it was a motorcycle that set a new world record on a closed course. The San Jose Driving Park could lay claim as being one of the fastest racetracks in the world.

1910

May 13-15: Halley's Comet was the backdrop for the next big event, which was held in conjunction with the Santa Clara County Rose Carnival.

Every few years, San Jose would stage a rose carnival very similar to the one in Pasadena, California. The city would deck itself out with roses and other flowers. There were parades, a Mardi Gras, concerts and baseball. As part of the festivities, the committee scheduled an aviation and automobile meet at the San Jose Driving Park. The main event was to be Automobile vs. Airship.

On the days leading up to the big event, both cars and aircraft were practicing at speed on the one-mile oval. The lap times between the two were very similar.

— SPECIAL —

Southern Pacific

SERVICE TO

San Jose Driving Park

— AND —

Aviation

— AND —

Automobile Meet

MAY 13. 14. 15

Leave Market Street Depot. 1:00 p. m. and 1:30 p. m.

stopping for passengers at Santa Clara street and Fourth street station.

RETURNING AT CLOSE OF EVENTS
SINGLE TRIP 10 CENTS   ROUND TRIP 15 CENTS

GET TICKETS IN ADVANCE AT DEPOT OR CITY OFFICE AND FOURTH STREET STATION. ON SALE ON GROUNDS FOR SINGLE TRIP RETURNING. PRESENT TICKETS ON ENTERING TRAIN.

SOUTHERN PACIFIC

Southern Pacific Railroad offered train service to San Jose Driving Park during the Rose Festival held in 1910. *Evening News*

On the day of the races, the citizens of San Jose climbed out of bed in the wee hours of the morning to observe a once-in-a-lifetime event, the appearance of Halley's Comet as the Earth passed through its tail. With daylight, the masses headed to the track.

Of the four races that were run each day, the most entertaining were the handicapped 230-451 Cubic Inch Stock Chassis and the Free-For-All (open competition) races. The smaller the engine, the more of a head start a driver was given. All three Free-For-All races were very close, with the Maxwell driven by King and the Matthewson piloted by W.T. Warren sharing the wins. The only major incident to happen during the weekend was on Friday during the Free-For-All races. On mile three, the right front tire on the Winton, driven by McDonald and carrying riding mechanic Keller, exploded. The Winton veered right and went over the embankment, into a ditch and through a 12-foot fence. Both men were thrown from the car and landed over 30 feet away in a grass field. The men were transported to O'Conner Sanitarium with concussions and major bruises.

The main event each day was to be Emile Agraz driving his White Gas race car against the Curtis bi-plane flown by Colonel Frank Johnson. On Friday, as the main event approached and the crowd of 8,000 grew excited with anticipation, the wind started to kick up. The pilots of the day had a saying, "If the wind blows, the aviators do not aviate." And the wind was howling on this day. The crowd grew impatient as the promoter tried to persuade the flyers to race. When it became apparent that there was not going to be a race between the airplane and race cars, the crowd got disgusted and left. The promoters then refused to pay the aviators, which in turn prompted them to park their planes for the rest of the weekend. An ironic twist to this story happened just one month later in Emeryville, Ca. The wind caused two bi-planes to crash in separate incidents while racing around the Emeryville one-mile oval.

1911

During 1911 there was just a scattering of events at the Driving Park. The first two events were combination air shows, horse racing, motorcycle and local car races.

The only AAA-sanctioned race of the year took place on September 3. Five thousand people witnessed San Josean Earl Cooper win three out of four races. The 15-mile Free-For-All main event turned out to be a "battle royal," according to the *San Jose Mercury News*. Cooper, driving his Maxwell, and Frank Free, in a Comet, raced side by side for the last eight miles of the race. Cooper's tire started shedding chunks of rubber with just a couple of

Program from the September 3, 1911, race.

Mercury Herald - 1911

Louis Disbrow, driving the Simplex Zip, broke three of Barney Oldfield's world records on April 14, 1912.

miles to go. With the pair racing toward the finish, Free's car started to miss, and Cooper then pulled ahead for the win in front of an elated crowd.

1912

A record 12 cars were entered for the March 17 race. With heavy rains the week of the event, it was thought that the track would be in prime shape. A big crowd was expected, so the police and Sheriff's office warned that they would shoot anybody trespassing through the nearby recently planted grain fields trying to get to the park.

The day before the race, Australian Rupert Jeffkins set an unofficial track record of 51 seconds for the mile run, driving his Buick. Having driven all over America, he proclaimed the Driving Park to be the fastest in the country.

Once again, local boy Earl Cooper won the 25-mile Free-For-All main event, this time driving a Stutz. Aviator and race car driver Harold Hall came in second driving a Comet.

After the race a fistfight broke out between Emile Agraz and Jeffkins. Agraz, who also promoted the race, accused Jeffkins of bumping him during the race. The fight turned into a melee when crews and onlookers jumped in. The police had to break it up.

April 14: San Jose Driving Park jumped to the front of the pack to become one of the fastest, if not thee fastest, dirt track in the world. No fewer than three of Barney Oldfield's world records would fall.

Rainfall on the morning of the race would prove beneficial to having a hard-packed, somewhat-dust-free track.

All the pre-race publicity was directed toward the 290-hp Jay-Eye-See Fiat being driven by Louis Disbrow. After

Barney Oldfield sits in his famous 300-hp Christie front-drive car while his entourage looks on. Oldfield stated that he was coming to San Jose to reclaim his three records that were broken there in April. Although he didn't reclaim those records, he did break the world speed record for a one-mile closed course on November 12, 1912.
From the collection of onlyclassics.com

16

Australian Rupert Jeffkin set a track record on March 17, 1912, and then was involved in a brawl. *Courtesy of the Collier Collection*

San Jose racing great Earl Cooper driving the Maxwell at San Jose during 1912. *San Jose Mercury Herald*

all, Louis had just previously set a one-mile speed record in Dallas. But it was Disbrow, driving the 100-hp, much lighter Simplex Zip, who would set the records. The 15-, 20-, and 25-mile records that Oldfield had set in Milwaukee back in 1910 were the victims of the assault. With AAA sanction all records were official. Five thousand people paying $1 "cheered and tossed their hats into the air as one by one the records fell" as recounted in the *San Jose Evening News*.

Louis Disbrow had promised San Jose earlier in the week that he would put them on the racing map, and he delivered.

Auto and motorcycle races were scheduled during County Fair week in July. The fair was the first in 18 years and it was located in downtown San Jose. This was to have been an "outlaw" (non-sanctioned) race. Because of the lack of entries, it was decided to call off the auto race. Unfortunately, the motorcycles would race. What took place on that fateful Sunday afternoon was the most deadly crash in the long history of the mile track.

The mishap occurred in turn four when one of the riders lost an exhaust pipe. E.A. House, who was the leader of a closely bunched group of riders, tried to avoid the exhaust pipe. In doing so, he hit the cushion and went down. In an instant, three other riders crashed into him and his machine. When the dust had settled, two riders lay dead on the track, and two others received major injuries and would be maimed for life. The deceased were Reed Orr of Sacramento and W.T. Baker of San Jose.

November 8-12: After seeing three of his world records broken at San Jose in April, Barney Oldfield and his multi-car team blew into town with one goal on his mind: reclaim all his records. A stellar field was on hand for the AAA-sanctioned race, including San Jose sensation Earl Cooper. Once again rain fell leading up to the race, this time postponing it until Tuesday afternoon. This left the track wet (heavy) and fast. Because it was mid-week, and less than ideal weather, only 1,000 people attended. They would not be disappointed, as Oldfield took his famous front-drive Christie and smashed the world record on a dirt one-mile oval.

SAN JOSE DAILY MERCURY: WEDNESDAY MORNING NOVEMBER 13, 1912.

OLDFIELD DOES MILE IN 47 3-5 SECONDS ON A WET TRACK

+ + + + + + + + + +

COOPER SHARES HONORS WITH THE PREMIER RACING PILOT

Snapshots at Yesterday's Race Meet—Top (Left) Start of the Sensational 25-Mile Race; (Right) Oldfield in His 300 H. P. Christie. Below (Left) Earl Cooper, Driving in the 5-Mile Event He Won, and Oldfield Passing the Grandstand in the "Prince Henry" Benz. Earl Cooper's Photo Is in the Center.

17

His 300-hp Christie sprayed a rooster tail of dirt through the air as he turned a 47-second lap, thus reinforcing the Driving Park as the fastest dirt track in the world. But it was Earl Cooper who stole the rest of the show. Cooper would power his Stutz to victories over Oldfield, who was driving a Benz, in the 5- and 25-mile Free-For-All races.

This concluded the most successful year the San Jose Driving Park would have.

1913

After the highly successful 1912 season, one has to wonder why AAA abandoned the Driving Park for the next two years. Without the sanction, the track could not get enough cars for a race of significance. Only novelty events were held.

It was billed as the world's latest sensation; auto polo and motorcycle sulky races were held in Sept. In auto polo, instead of a horse, a man stands on a car's running board with his polo mallet while a driver negotiates the course chasing the ball and trying to score. At the time, this was a sport being played across the country.

Motorcycle sulky racing is very similar to harness racing, but instead of horse, a motorcycle pulls the sulky (one-seat carriage) around the mile track. The times were reported to have been a mile a minute.

On a different note, San Jose's own, Earl Cooper, was crowned AAA National Champion.

1914

World War I had just broken out when the first event of the year was held in April.

Earl Cooper attempted to set speed records in his famous Stutz "White Ghost" race car. He was not successful and even if he had been, without AAA sanction, the records would not have been recognized. There was a match race between Emile Agraz, driving his race car, and a rider on a stripped-down motorcycle. The cycle won. The feature event was to have been a race between Cooper's "White Ghost" and aviator Lloyd Thompson's bi-plane. Once again, just like in 1910, the afternoon winds caused the race to be cancelled.

June 21: This event was billed as the Automobile and

Dust was a problem. *San Jose Mercury Herald*

Motorcycle Speed Carnival and was promoted by 10 local businessmen. Two dozen Stock Cars were entered along with a handful of professionals. The Stock Cars of that era were very slow and proved to be boring for the spectators. A small crowd witnessed mediocre racing on a dangerous track that came apart and created a blinding dust storm. The gate receipts were $238, with 15 percent going to the drivers.

1915

June 27: Except for 1912, when it rained up to the day of the meets, dust storms were becoming a recurring problem at the Driving Park. The year 1915 was no exception.

Because of the injuries that were accruing, this race had, for the first time, a surgeon and an ambulance at the venue. They would be needed.

Attracted by a huge purse, a large field of cars participated in the meet.

For the first time, an Indianapolis-style flying start was attempted. This would prove to be disastrous, as riding mechanic Paul Brasher was mortally wounded when the car he was in collided with another in the first turn and crashed off the track. The driver was okay.

Through the thick cloud of dust, Emile Agraz, would emerge the winner in the Free-For-All main event. But Emile did not enjoy the victory. During warm-ups, race car driver, aviator, and mechanic Harold Hall was critically injured when he was riding a motorcycle alongside the race car that he had just sold to Emile. There was no speedometer on the car, so Hall was testing its speed with his motorcycle when he went into the turn at over 70 mph. Hall went off the track and into a cultivator that the farmers had parked near the track. Harold would remain in a coma for two weeks before he would begin his long road to recovery.

July 4: This race had the blessing of an AAA sanction, the first since 1912.

The *San Jose Mercury News* described the races as "exceedingly tame." Only three of the scheduled five races took place. The *Mercury* did not say why, but I can only assume it was because of track conditions. One incident of note occurred when Clyde Hunt, driving the 1912 Indianapolis winning race car "National," threw a wheel and flipped through the turn. Fortunately Hunt and his riding mechanic were okay.

Because of the track conditions and the dwindling crowds, interest in the Driving Park was at an all-time low. The track would eventually be sold to Kirk MaComber and turned into the Mira Monte stock farm for racehorses.

For the next 25 years the only roar that would be heard on the mile was the thunder of pounding hooves galloping around the oval.

But like the Phoenix, the track would rise from the ashes with a new identity.

San Jose Driving Park Feature Race Winners	
Nov. 28, 1909	W.H. Turner
May 13-16, 1910	W.T. Warren & King
Sept. 3, 1911	Earl Cooper
March 17, 1912	Earl Cooper
April 14, 1912	Louis Disbrow
Nov. 12 1912	Earl Cooper
April 25-26, 1914*	Earl Cooper
June 21, 1914*	Emile Agraz
June 27, 1915*	Emile Agraz
July 4, 1915	Thomas
* = Non-Sanctioned	

By 1913, the track was trying different gimmicks to put people in the stands. *The Evening News*

Chapter 5

The Notorious

San Jose Speedway

1923 - 1939

1923

Santa Clara County had been without fairgrounds since 1888, when the fairgrounds site had been located at Agricultural Park. That would change in 1923 when a new fairgrounds and race track were constructed on the northeast corner of Alum Rock Avenue and King Road. The showcase of the facilities was a high-banked, 5/8-mile, dirt (oiled) track, inside of which there was a half-mile horseracing track, also used for human track meets. Initially, there was seating for 5,000 people.

July 4, 1923, saw the grand opening of the fairgrounds and speed plant, which were designed by architect Jack Wilson, who was also the Santa Clara County Fair Manager. Two days before the race, 5,000 gallons of oil were laid on the surface of the track. (Can you imagine if they tried doing that in the 21st century?)

AAA sanctioned the Big Car race (equivalent of modern-day Indy Cars), the first in San Jose since 1915 at the old San Jose Driving Park.

A standing-room-only crowd of over 6,000 packed into the viewing area. The *San Jose Mercury News* reported: "Seventeen wind-splitting iron steeds roared around the oval in seven fast events. No fatal accident marred the day, although two near fatalities were witnessed." Red Murray of Fresno won the 50-lap main event and went into the record books as the first to claim victory at the San Jose Speedway. He took home the winner's share of the $750 purse.

Following the races, the huge throng (not only in the stands but also on the fairgrounds facility) enjoyed a huge fireworks show.

The program was declared a success, and the next meet was scheduled for County Fair week.

August 11-19 saw the return of the Santa Clara County Fair for the first time in over two decades. San Jose was filled with excitement and anticipation leading up to the event at the new fairgrounds. There were the usual exhibits (displayed in a tent over 300 feet long), contests and amusements, but the centerpiece was the racetrack. The opening act on Saturday was the County Track and Field Championships followed by harness racing. But the feature attraction during fair week was the program of regional AAA-sanctioned races on Sundays, August 12 and 19. Just about all the drivers were from California, and local man Fred Lyon,

Auto Racing was the featured attraction during the 1923 County Fair.
Mercury News

San Jose Speedway as it looked from the air on March 13, 1931. King Road (left of track) was close enough to the track that a car once crashed its way onto the street. *The Fairchild Aerial Photography Collection at Whittier College C-1456-82*

Fred Luelling, from San Luis Obispo, won more main events (3) at San Jose during the first two years than anybody else. This 1924 photo shows Fred sitting in his Fronty-Ford Special next to a freshly oiled track. *Don Bishop Collection*

in his Miller Special, was a pre-race favorite along with Ed Meyer and Jack Hayes driving Gusti's Ford Special. But the big winner of the August 12 race was Fred Luelling driving his Frontenac Ford. Gene Rapp followed him across the line in his baby blue Rapp Special, owned by Gene Wilson, in front of over 5,000 fans.

After the races a story in the *Mercury News* announced: "Participation in local automobile races will hereafter be restricted to the 20 fastest drivers in the state. Santa Clara County Fair Manager Jack Wilson stated that he had just completed affiliation of the local track with the California Dirt Track Racing Association. The 20 drivers were called Class A drivers. Class B drivers could elevate to Class A by beating the times of a Class A driver." It was also reported "the conduct of all races will be in accordance with the regulations of the association which requires its men to appear on the track with clean cars, and attired in white uniforms." The association was organized under the sanction of AAA and comprised of 12 California tracks.

The August 19 race took place on the final day of a record-breaking and very successful fair. For the third time, a capacity crowd gathered to watch the wind burners roar around the track.

In only his third time in a race car, new Bay Area driving sensation Gene Rapp won the 40-lap main event over Fred Lyon, taking home the winner's share of the $400 purse.

After the AAA main event, there was a special challenge race. Since the first race at the new track on July 4, a bitter rivalry had been developing between the drivers from Northern and Southern California, especially since the previous week, when the boys from the South took four out of the top five spots, including first. Watching all the purse money head South didn't sit well with the locals, so the challenge went out. The top three drivers from both the North and South squared off in a 30-lap grudge race. The North vowed vengeance, and they delivered when Jack Hayes sped to victory in a Gusti. The North finished first, third and fourth.

The fourth race of 1923 was scheduled for September 23. Since the last race, more banking had been added to the front straight, making it possible for the cars to carry more speed out of the turn. Also, an oiling system was installed, consisting of a pipeline running entirely around the track. Around 10,000 gallons of heavy oil was sprayed onto the track in the week leading up to the race. This would help keep the dust down and make the track faster. Thirty cars were entered–the most since racing started in San Jose in 1903. The four-race program had a purse of $2,000. There were two heats, a third heat consisting of the top cars from the two heats, and a Free-For-All main

This 1924 ad states that the races are to be dustless and safe. This would be false advertising. *Mercury News*

Horace Wallace of San Luis Obispo was a front-runner at San Jose during the 1924 season. *Don Bishop Collection*

event. Under threatening skies, 5,000 spectators witnessed another entertaining and safe program.

Fred Luelling and Gene Rapp won the heat races while Fred Lyons won the 40-lap main event. The boys from Southern California were back in control. The oiling system (and cloud cover) worked well, as the track remained firm, smooth and relatively dust free.

Everything was going great for the new track–huge crowds and good, safe, competitive races made it the talk of the town. These were the good times, but that would soon change.

The American Legion, celebrating Armistice Day, put on the November 11 event – a charity meet to aid ex-servicemen who were disabled during WWI.

What started out as another promising day at the races turned tragic within moments of the start of heat one. Heading into turn three on the first lap, it was reported that the steering arm on the car driven by Paul Guy Arrighi and Richard Rogers, his riding mechanic, failed. With his wife and son watching from the grandstands, Arrighi's car nosed into the inner guardrail and flipped, ejecting Rogers from the car. Arrighi was pinned underneath the car and would not survive the trip to the hospital. Rogers, although busted up, would recover. After the races, the owner of the car that Arrighi was driving said that it wasn't mechanical failure of the car, but the slippery condition of the track that caused the fatal crash.

Heat two was not much better. Shortly after the start of the second race and in almost the same spot as the previous crash, the cars driven by Gene Rapp and Josh Hess locked wheels. Both cars then careened out of control, hurdled off the top of the track and flipped. Hess and his riding mechanic, Milton Daniels, were thrown from the car. They both received cuts, bruises and broken bones. Rapp, who had just moved to San Jose from San Francisco, was not so fortunate. Just like Arrighi, he was pinned under the car. He was rushed to the hospital with major head injuries and would remain in a coma for days. Adolph Gusti, driving his own car, won the main event, but, in just a short period of time on this day, one promising race driver was dead, another critically injured and two more had serious injuries.

People were starting to mumble: "San Jose Speedway is a dangerous track."

After the tragic events that took place on November 11, the December 2 race was now a benefit race, with 60 percent of the gate receipts going to the widow of Paul Arrighi and to Gene Rapp, who was still confined to San Jose Hospital. Before the race, AAA officials performed a thorough inspection of the track and cars to assure the safety of the event.

On race day, a pitifully small crowd was in attendance. Just before the start of the races, an impressive ceremony was performed, when drivers and officials gathered on the track in front of the stands and paid tribute to Arrighi. Among them was a very frail-looking Gene Rapp. With his head still bandaged, he made the trip from his hospital bed to pay his respects. After the races he returned to the

Adolph Gusti was San Jose's best race car driver during the early history of the track. He won two of the first eight AAA main events before loosing his life in the ninth. He poses with a young fan in the White Roof Special. Photo was taken in downtown San Jose during 1924, shortly before his death. *Don Bishop Collection*

hospital for an extended stay.

The meager crowd was treated to the best racing of the year. Fred Lyon and Adolph Gusti won their heats and then went out and had a spirited battle during the main event. Gusti's car sputtered on the last lap, allowing Lyons to steal the win, averaging 63 mph in his Miller Special.

This brought the curtain down on an eventful first year at the new speedway.

1924

The 1924 season did not begin until June 29. Just like the previous year, all races at the track would be under AAA sanction.

Advertisements leading up to the race stated "the track would be dustless and safe." Thousands of gallons of oil was laid down hoping to keep the dust to a minimum and making for better traction–not worse, as some people thought.

Six thousand racing fans saw Fred Luelling of San Luis Obispo drive his Frontenac Ford Special to victory. The newspapers said Horace Wallace, also of San Luis Obispo, who placed second, was handicapped by being made to eat dust set up by Luelling. It was becoming apparent that dust was a frustrating problem for the speedway. For promoters in the 21st century it remains a problem in daytime races on dirt.

The October 18, 1924, race featured the best drivers in the country. *Mercury News* ad

Clear action photos are rare in the early part of the 1900's because of the slow film and cameras in use at that time. This photo shows Ralph DePalma (inside) and Eddie Hearne (1) battling for the lead of the October 18, 1924, race. DePalma went on to win, his second in a row at the Speedway. *Jack Fox Collection*

Three abreast start during the October 18, 1924, AAA race. Ralph DePalma is on the pole; Eddie Hearne (1) and Tony Marasco (14) complete the front row. *Don Radbruch Collection*

Jack Britschgi sits in his nifty-looking Essex at a downtown San Jose location in 1924. *Don Bishop Collection*

July 27 was the second matinee race of 1924. Five days leading up to the race, the biggest steam roller in the county and three tractors were seen blading (to a depth of six inches), watering and grooming the track. After all that, oil was applied, hoping to make the track more like asphalt than dirt. It was obvious they were doing everything in their power to make a good racing surface. Pre-race hype centered on Al Mulford, from Los Angeles. A board track specialist, he stated that he was going to make both Fred Luelling and Adolph Gusti eat his dust in Sunday's race.

Returning for his first race since the previous year's devastating crash was Gene Rapp.

Time trials were held on Saturday and Adolph Gusti blazed around the track in 29 seconds to set fast time.

Four thousand spectators gathered on Sunday to observe Italian-born Adolph Gusti have a banner day. Having set fast time and winning his preliminary event, Gusti sat on the pole in the feature. In the middle of the front row was Horace Wallace and on the outside was Al Mulford. At the drop of the flag, Mulford shot into the lead, closely followed by Gusti. Gusti applied the pressure on Mulford for the next few laps, trying to pass on the bottom. Coming out of turn two, Mulford looked over his shoulder to see where Gusti was. At this point, Mulford, who had not raced on dirt for a few years, lost control of his Fronty Ford. The car slid up the track and into the fence, bursting into flames on impact, and then catapulting into a series of summersaults. Mulford was thrown from the car and died at the scene. Many observers feel that Mulford, who had been driving on the edge all day, lacked experience on dirt, and this was the cause of the accident. Gusti went on to win the shortened race.

September 1, Labor Day, featured the biggest racing stars that would ever race at the Alum Rock Avenue speed bowl. The headliners were the legendary Ralph DePalma and the 1923 AAA champion

> **During the early part of the 20th century it was noticed that every story leading up to a race published in the *Mercury Herald* was like a promotion. The stories always stated that this was guaranteed to be the best race ever, the track was going to be in the greatest shape ever, records were guaranteed, get your tickets early because it was going to be a sell out and there would be big car counts. A lot of 'Rah Rah' talk. Fellow historians Jim Chini and Tom Motter pointed out that the tracks of the day provided their own pre-race press coverage. The PR person wrote the stories and glossed over the facts just to fill the stands. A reporter attended the actual races.**

Eddie Hearne. Local race fans were well aware of who these gentlemen were, as an estimated 18,000-plus packed the grandstands and filled the spacious infield. (The population of SJ was 47,000 in 1924.)

The record crowd got what they came for, watching Ralph DePalma put on a show. Starting with qualifying, DePalma took to the track and proceeded to smash the track record, driving his Straight-Eight Miller Special to a lap time of 28.3 and a speed of 81mph. He followed this up with a win in his heat and the dash. During the feature, the only person who was able to put pressure on DePalma was a young driver named Elbert "Babe" Stapp. Stapp chased the personable Italian across the finish line, followed by Eddie Hearne, who was a distant third. On this day, the big winner in the hearts of the fans was Babe Stapp.

Unfortunately this was also the day that the locals would lose their best driver. On lap 27 of the 35-lap race, local racing idol Adolph Gusti spun hard into the inside banking. The injured Gusti was transported to San Jose Hospital with a fractured pelvis, fractured shoulder and other contusions and abrasions. Although the injuries were serious, they were not life threatening. A full recovery was expected, but five days after entering the hospital, Gusti developed pneumonia and died two days later. In one short year, he had become San Jose's most prominent racer, and now he was gone.

The October 18 race had the same cast of characters as the September event. The results were the same in that Ralph DePalma won all four events he raced in. Fred Luelling won the other two. National AAA champion Eddie Hearne finished third.

Once again, the meet was marred by a bad accident. During the fourth race, William Forrest, 21 years old from San Francisco, plowed through the back straight guardrail and flipped, pinning him beneath the car. He was rushed to the hospital with three broken ribs, broken collarbone and compound fractures to his legs. The track was getting a reputation, but for all the wrong reasons.

The October 26 event was billed as the Great Motor Circus, with motorcycle, auto and airplane races. The infield was dragged, leveled and turned into a runway for the airplanes, which put on a good show, but for the fourth time in a year, the racetrack made page one headlines. This time motorcycle rider Tess Soares was killed instantly when he crashed hard in his heat race.

In the automobile main event, Harry Hooker was coming out of turn four when he smashed into and took out several sections of the outside fence, scattering wood in all directions. The impact threw Harry out into the middle of the track where the approaching cars had to take evasive action to miss him. To the amazement of the crowd, he stood up, brushed himself off, and walked to the infield. He received a standing ovation. Not to be overlooked in all the carnage was the fact that Fred Luelling won himself another AAA Big Car main

Great MOTOR Circus

Motorcycle Races
Automobile Races
Airplane Races and Stunts

Sunday, Oct. 26 2:30 P.M.
San Jose Speedway

The Record-Breaking Meet of a Record-Breaking Season

Admission $1.00 Including Grand Stand

Mel Kenealy, Babe Stapp, Joe Logan and Fred Lyon drove the three-car De Witt/Joe Brady Specials team during the 1924 season. Ted Wilson took this photo at an undisclosed San Jose location.
Don Bishop Collection

WHAT THE FLAGS MEAN

Spectators may be confused by the assortment of flags used by Starter Jimmy O'Day during the program. For their information the following explanation is published:

Red Flag—Course is clear. Start.

Yellow Flag—Blocked Course. Wreck on track. Stop.

Green Flag—You are entering last lap.

Black and White Checkered—You are finished.

White Flag—Stop at pit on next lap for consultation.

White with Black Center—Competitor is trying to overtake you. Give way to your left.

NOTE:—It is an infraction of the rules for a driver to pass a competitor on the left except in cases of extreme emergency.

Flag rules were much different in the 1920s. Taken from San Jose Speedway program.
Courtesy History San Jose.

event in San Jose. Veteran autopilot Harold Hall (from the San Jose Driving Park days) finished second.

November 27, Thanksgiving Day, was the last race of 1924. Since the previous race, the inside banking had been removed, making for better visibility and one less object to crash into.

Babe Stapp, from Los Angeles, won two out of three races, including the feature. He was fast becoming a fan favorite in San Jose. There was more wheel-to-wheel racing in this one event than the track had seen all year. The second race finished in a dead heat between Fred Lyon and Fred Luelling.

Mercifully, the 1924 season came to an end without any further loss of life.

1925

March 15, 1925, started out with a bang. Sophomore driver Leigh Green must have had dynamite under his hood, as he blasted more than a second off the track record set by Ralph DePalma during 1924. Green negotiated the steeply-banked, heavily oiled track in 27 seconds flat. But he would never make it to the main event, as the crankshaft broke in his Kant Skore Special.

The San Jose Classic, as the main event was now called, was won by Jack Petticord. Finishing second in the eight-car field was Harold Hall.

May 24: The races were overshadowed, yet again, by death.

During qualifying, Jack Kemp, aged 28, from Bell, California, lost control and flipped end-over-end four times, crushing his skull in the process. He was driving the Hooker Special, the same car that Harry Hooker had his spectacular accident in the previous October 26. One month after that accident, Bill Reed was killed in the same car in an

San Jose's leading main event winner, Fred Luelling, escaped death when he crashed through the fence while battling for the lead of heat two on May 24, 1925. He received facial cuts and was now known as Lucky Luelling at San Jose.
Don Radbruch Collection

AUTO RACES
TWO MOTORCYCLE EVENTS ALSO

San Jose Speedway
Sunday, June 14th

EVENTS START PROMPTLY AT 2:30 Parking Free	ALUM ROCK AVE. and KING ROAD, SAN JOSE

General Admission, $1.50; Including Grandstand

28

Manuel Suares, of San Jose, drove the beautiful Guisti Special at San Jose Speedway during 1925. *Don Bishop Collection*

HENRY BEAL DIES ON LOCAL TRACK; IS NUMBER SIX

Pasadena Racing Driver Is Instantly Killed When Car Leaps Bank.

WIFE SEES ACCIDENT

Promoters Say Track Was in No Way Responsible; Car Declared Defective.

In a period of one and a half years, six drivers had met the Grim Reaper on what was becoming known as the suicide bowl. *San Jose Mercury News*

accident at Tanforan Race (horse) Track in San Francisco. It seemed a bad cloud hung over the Hooker Special.

Fred Lyon, Babe Stapp and Leigh Green were the order of finish in the 25-lap main event.

June 14: The day after the race, the first paragraph on page one of the *Mercury Herald* read: "Dirt Track Racing in San Jose added name number six to its toll of victims yesterday. Henry Beal, 30, from Pasadena, was the sixth sacrifice to be offered on the local altar to the God of Speed."

In less than two years, Paul Arrighi, Al Mulford, Adolph Gusti, Jess Soares, Jack Kemp, and Henry Beal had all perished at the speed plant.

Beal was killed during time trials; when rounding turns three and four, the steering broke, causing his No. 2 Fronty Special to thrust through the guard rail on the high bank and plunge to the ground below, with a sickening thud. Beal was thrown out of the car, and then the car rolled over his hapless body. It was reported virtually every bone in his body was broken in the crash. To add to the drama, Beal's wife, who had witnessed the crash from the grandstands, ran to the scene and fainted.

As in previous cases, track owners Jack Wilson and Bart Lorigan were quick to defend the speedway, stating: "The track was no way responsible. Mechanical failure was the sole reason for the accident." That didn't stop the press from calling for a halt to racing at the track (see sidebar).

After witnessing his friend die in qualifying, Leigh Green pulled out of the races and announced his retirement. Babe Stapp, who had just won heat one in his own car, stepped into the Kant Skore Special that Green had been driving (and which held the track record of 27 seconds) and finished second in heat two. Stapp jumped back into his own car for the feature and had things his way, leading from start to finish, in a race that was shortened from 25 to 15 laps.

After the latest death, AAA had seen enough and abandoned San Jose for the second time (the first being 1912 at the San Jose Driving Park). They would not be back for five years. The speedway also shut down and would not reopen for more than a year – and then as an 'outlaw' track.

The person who used this June 14th, 1925, ticket had the misfortune of seeing the track's sixth fatality.

EDITOR'S ANALYSIS

WHEN ARE WE GOING TO STOP THIS?

To some persons dirt track racing may be a sport. To those San Joseans who have watched six men go to death on the local speedway it is more apt to be placed in the class of suicide. No matter who or what is to blame for these deaths, whether it be a faulty track, poor supervision, or mechanical inferiority, it is time to put an end to the gruesome tragedies which have occurred at nearly every local racing event, and it is time for San Jose to bar any sport which takes so heavy a toll of human life. San Jose wants its sports—its golf courses, its tennis clubs, its school teams and its playgrounds. But it wants none of the reputaton that goes with the community that permits undue recklessness. Most sports have an element of danger, but there is a line between that which is daring and that which is foolhardy. Let us draw it.

San Jose Mercury News editorial calling for the madness to be stopped.

SPEEDWAY CELEBRATION PROVES TO BE FAILURE

1926

July 4 : After all the negative publicity in the newspapers and public opinion, the speedway re-emerged as an outlaw track.

With its new identity, the first show scheduled was a combination air show followed by auto, horse and motorcycle racing.

Gone were the many big names that raced there previously; the most noted racer for this meet was Fred Lyon.

The headlines in the sport section the day after the race screamed, "Speedway celebration proves to be failure." A crowd of 5,000 became disgruntled when the program turned into a fiasco.

The day started out well, as the air show proved entertaining, but it was all downhill after that. The first problem occurred when there was no timer for qualifying. Then when the heat races started, the organizers realized there were no scorers. To make matters worse, the motorcycle racers had a sit-down strike on the front straightaway that lasted for over an hour. They were mad about the meager purse they were racing for and eventually packed up and went home without racing, much to the dismay of the fans who had come to see the cycle riders. At this point, promoter Jack Wilson decided to parade the horses in front of the grandstands before their race. When the crowd saw Wilson they rained down a loud chorus of boos. The horse races turned out to be no more than an exhibition instead of a real race. By now the crowd was screaming for their money back and yelling "robber!"

The final event was the feature race for cars. Manuel Suares was chasing Freeman Howard for the lead in the

Headlines (above and below) from the two 1926 races. *Mercury Herald*

AUTO RACES REAL SUCCESS

By STAN WALDORF
The crowd went home satisfied yesterday.

15-lap main when a rock went through his goggles, cutting his eye. Suares dropped out and Howard went on to victory.

As people were exiting, many were yelling that they would never return.

The first race without AAA was a failure.

September 5: After the debacle in July, the track needed something positive to happen and this race was a step in the right direction. Besides racing, the program also had the novelty event, auto polo – a sport which had been introduced to San Jose in 1913 at the San Jose Driving Park. Between each race, one-quarter of the polo match was played, keeping the crowd entertained and amused at all times. The auto races on this day were very good too, with no crashes, no mechanical problems and the racing was close and competitive. Mike Moosie was the star of the day. He drove the Culp Special to a clean sweep of all his events, including the feature.

Although they would continue to play auto polo for the rest of the year, this event concluded the short, two-race season for the oval.

1927

June 27: Twenty-four cars were pre-entered for the season opener. It was announced that any car that could not turn a 32-second lap or better would not be eligible to race.

Coming out of retirement for the opener was track record holder Leigh Green. As usual, the program consisted of qualifying, two elimination heats, a consolation

Oops! During 1926, the speedway management had a dam built on Silver Creek, which ran just outside turn two, because–they said–the water was needed for the speedway. That winter, during a big rainstorm, the creek backed up because of the dam and flooded its banks. Water rushed through the nearby neighborhoods, flooding many homes. Because the track was on county property, and the flood happened in the city, the problem ended up before the City Council and the County Board of Supervisors. The dam was removed.

RECORD CROWD EXPECTED TO WITNESS 250-MILE CLASSIC

and a feature race.

After a short and safe 1926 season, the new season started on a bad note. During warm-ups, Johnny Johns threw a tire and crashed through the fence. He was only shaken, but otherwise okay.

But things would really take a turn for the worse in the first elimination heat race. One of the most sensational crashes ever seen at the speed bowl took place when Art Bremer lost control heading down the front stretch. He over-corrected and went into the inside bank where he shot high into the air. As the car came back down to earth, it took a direct hit on the 20-foot-high judges' stand, throwing all the occupants to the ground and reducing the structure to rubble. Meanwhile, the car continued on it destructive path–hitting a mechanic and breaking his leg before finally crashing into the race car owned by Harry Jacques. Jacques' car had enough damage that it was not able to compete later in the day. One person in the stand had a painful knee injury while another received a broken bone when they hit the ground. It could have been worse.

Another spectacular accident happened on lap nine of the main event. Fred Lyon, who had won a number of main events at San Jose, started to make the turn into the homestretch but was unable to straighten the car. It then tore through the retaining rail and proceeded toward and then into the grandstands, knocking out two supports under the stands. Although the grandstands shook like an earthquake, none of the 6,000 occupants were injured.

Meanwhile, out on the track, they waved the flag to stop the race. Bill Spence threw on his brakes to stop his Hooker Special. Barney Kloepfer, who was following Spence, rode up over his wheel and then cart-wheeled wildly into the infield, scattering people once again. When the dust had settled, Lyons was rushed to the hospital with a serious head injury. The main event was called at this point and no winner or money was awarded. A meeting was then held and it was decided to hold a 10-lap race for the purse money, open to all cars that were still in driving condition after the carnage that took place that afternoon. Bill Spence, who had earlier in the day equaled the track quali-

Program for the 250-mile National Championship race. *Courtesy of History San Jose*

fying record of 27 seconds, won the race.

Once again, the track was in the news, and it wasn't good news. In the days after the race, stories and photos were run on the front page showing and describing the carnage. Fred Lyon was still in the hospital in critical condition. But the show must go on.

July 4: One week later, the annual Fourth of July race was held.

After a police investigation, Fred Lyon was cleared of all blame for the crash that damaged the grandstands and put spectators in danger. It was determined that a faulty spindle snapped, sending the car out of control.

The pit area was moved farther into the infield and away from the track. A new judges' stand was constructed, and that was also moved farther away from the track.

The race was billed as the Fred Lyon Charity Race. The track's hottest driver, Bill Spence, piloting the Hooker Special, won his second feature in a row – and by such a wide margin that the race was described as dull. There were no accidents.

September 11: The day following the race, the first sentence of the *Mercury Herald* sports page stated "Thrills minus accidents were dished out to the racing fans at the San Jose Speedway yesterday when Barney Kloepfer of Los Angeles won the 25-lap sweepstake race after a great duel with Jack Buxton of Hollywood."

October 16 saw the fourth and final race of 1927. An unusual side attraction as part of the program was bull fighting. No bulls were harmed–the matador had just a cape and no sword.

With all the top drivers sidelined because of mechanical problems, Barney Kloepfer, in the Barney Special, took control of the main event at the start and was never challenged. San Jose newcomer Ernest Triplett worked his way up from the back of the pack to claim second.

The bullfights turned out to be a flop. The mixture of steers, bulls and cows were uninterested in the matador and either wandered off or stood around appearing bored. Some boos could be heard from the crowd.

1928

March 18: Advertised as the longest race in dirt-track history, the 250-Mile Classic kicked off the season. Advanced billing stated the race would start 30 cars and run 400 laps around the oval. Los Angeles-based Consolidated Amusement Company leased the track from Jack Wilson and promoted the event, which was sanctioned by the National Automotive Racing Association, making it the first sanctioned race since AAA left in 1925. Tickets were priced at $4.40 for box seats and $3.30 for grandstands, a very high price in 1928. It didn't matter; all those seats sold out a day before the event.

The city decked itself out in flags and banners, including the three-mile route from the city center to the racetrack. A parade of race cars, which started in San Francisco, wound its way down the peninsula to San Jose.

The grandstands, fences and concessions were whitewashed and banners hung at the racetrack. The race was filmed and would be shown at the California Theater for the next five days. They were really rolling out the red carpet for this race, which was also broadcast live on radio station KFWI. All the top drivers in the west were to be there, including Ascot champion Francis Quinn and the four-wheel-drive car driven by Chuck Gelston, said to be the fastest in the world.

Excitement was building at a fever pitch for the big event. But once again, some of the people would be disappointed.

A big crowd of 10,000 packed into the racetrack expecting to see a 250-mile race with 30 cars, but neither happened. The race was scheduled to start at 2:30 p.m. But several of the drivers refused to race unless they were paid in advance. The crowd grew restless as the bickering went on. The promoter finally paid the drivers, but by now it was 4 p.m. To make matters worse, there were only 12 cars eligible to run the marathon race. With only a certain amount of daylight left, they reduced the race to 250 laps (156 miles). Considering the high price of tickets and parking, people felt cheated.

The racing itself was reported as entertaining. For the first time at the speedway, pit stops were required to go the distance. Barney Kloepfer, who won the last race back in October, powered the Kloepfer Special to victory by a margin of six laps. At mid-race, Sam Palmer brought the Hooker Special in for a pit stop. The car caught fire while receiving gas. Palmer was seriously burned before being pulled out. The fire was quickly extinguished with no harm to the car. Ernest Triplett took the wheel off the Hooker and sped back out onto the track, 11 laps down. He drove the car from the back of the field all the way to second place, avoiding spectators who were running across the track trying to make an early exit for home, when the checkered flag flew. Jack Buxton finished third. Six cars out of the 12 finished the 250 laps.

That night the top drivers made an appearance at the California Theater.

Because race fans were short-changed, track owner and promoter Jack Wilson declared he would never lease out the track again.

A. A. A. Sanction Issued for Auto Races on Sunday

With AAA sanction, a track usually got the best drivers, the biggest crowds and a well-run program. *Mercury News*

May 20: Racing was back to the normal 20-lap distance, now called sprint races. Since the track opened in 1923, Southern California drivers had won most of the races. Jack Buxton, who was from Los Angeles but now resided in San Jose, was showing his alliance for the North. Not since Ralph DePalma had somebody had a day like Buxton did on this day. Barney Kloepfer, who had won the last two races, had to follow in the dust cloud being kicked up from the wheels of Buxton's Bobby Special all day. By the end of the day Buxton's hands were bruised and blistered from the beating they had taken. Finishing third, and making his first appearance since receiving head injuries the pre-

Mel Kenealy from Hollywood sits in a Miller in front of a downtown dealership. Mel won three main events during the 1929-1930 period. *Don Bishop Collection*

1930 photo showing the cars taking the flag on the not-so-straight, front straightaway. The cars were always turning on the big 5/8-mile oval. The horse stables sit outside turn four. *Don Bishop Collection*

1930 view of the infield pits. *Don Bishop Collection*

Turn-one action on the high-banked oval during 1930. The Enos Dairy Farm sits in the background. *Don Bishop Collection*

vious year, was Fred Lyon. Four thousand spectators were satisfied that they paid a nominal fee to see a show that was superior to the 250-lap race two months earlier.

June 10: The speedway hosted dog (whippet) racing. The main event pitted two whippets against two racehorses in a 200-yard sprint. No results are available.

June 28: A rivalry had developed between San Jose's two fastest racers, Barney Kloepfer and Jack Buxton. On this day, Kloepfer tied the track record of 27 seconds in qualifying and Buxton won the main event.

July 4: Jack Buxton was now the undisputed king of San Jose, as he won his third San Jose main event in a row after a great duel with Kloepfer. He also shattered the track record in qualifying, turning a lap of 26.2 seconds–a world record for a 5/8-mile dirt track.

September 16: The Pacific Coast Championship brought a strong field of cars. After lowering his track record to 26.1 during qualifying, Jack Buxton sat on the pole for the feature race. But his hopes for a fourth win in a row were dashed in the first turn of the race. Ernie Triplett, who was sitting on the outside of the front row, sharply cut down on Buxton and they locked wheels, damaging both cars and knocking them out of the race. This opened the door for Stubby Stubblefield to pick up his first win. Buxton, with the backing of many, protested the race, but he was denied.

October 21: The pre-race hype had Jack Buxton stating he had a grudge to settle with Ernie Triplett. In the previous race, Triplett had recklessly chopped down on Buxton, costing him a chance at a clean sweep for the day. The *Mercury* wrote "Ernie Triplett is undoubtedly the most reckless pilot to ever race on the San Jose track." But he was also fast. He opened the program with a victory in the first heat and Buxton won the second heat. Buxton won

the main event, leading from start to finish. The action took place behind him. While trying to overtake Barney Kloepfer for the second spot, Triplett collided with him, knocking Kloepfer out of the race. He then caught Buxton but couldn't get by him before the race ended. Buxton was crowned the California Dirt Track Champion.

So the year ended on a positive note, which would help set up the coming season.

1929

February 17: The big news for the speedway was the return of AAA.

The *Mercury Herald* reported: "Local automobile racing fans seem to believe that on Sunday the sport will again be lifted to the high plane on which it flourished before outlaw drivers and promoters ignored the AAA and conducted no descript speed programs at the speedway."

AAA reinstated all outlaw dirt track drivers on the Pacific Coast. Captain Eddie Rickenbacker, a WWI flying ace and now chairman of the AAA contest board, supervised the meet, while legendary Barney Oldfield was the referee. The pre-race drivers' meeting was held at the Montgomery hotel.

All the big names were there, including 1928 Indianapolis runner-up Lou Moore. He would drive the Miller Special, which George Souders had piloted to victory in that Indy 500.

Much of the pre-race build-up centered on a special match race between Lou Moore and Babe Stapp. Both drivers would be driving Indianapolis Speedway cars fitted with super-chargers, a device never seen before at the San Jose track. Moore was in a Miller and Stapp in a Deusenberg.

"Johnny Sawyer, dark horse driver, cleans up in San Jose

35

Arvol Brunmier (48) and Mel Kenealy (9) occupy the front row during the October 19, 1930, AAA race. A packed house saw Francis Quinn set a 100-lap track record in winning the feature. *Ted Wilson Photo*

Jimmy Sharp from Los Angeles sits in the Gabhart special on May 11, 1930. He was the most successful driver during the 1930 season at San Jose Speedway, winning the first four races. A year later he would become Oakland speedway's first fatality. *Dennis Mattish collection*

Walt May, shown in the Padre Special during 1930, was a San Jose main event winner before being thrown out of his car and killed at the track on June 21, 1931. *Edith C. Smith Collection / Sourisseau Academy, San Jose State University*

Babe Stapp Steals Show At Speedway

Quinn Wins Time Trials and Spends Day Trying to Catch Babe

By "BUDDY" LEITCH

Mercury News

meet yesterday afternoon" said the headline the day after the race. Sawyer, from Los Angeles, won all four events he was in. His closest challengers were 1928 champion Jack Buxton, and Ernie Triplett.

Moore nosed out Stapp in a crowd-pleasing, five-lap match race between the super-charged cars.

With AAA controlling all facets of the program, the show was over in less than two hours.

June 23: Los Angeles driver Mel Kenealy was the star driver at this meet, witnessed by a large crowd. 'Speed' Hinkley finished second. Once again, thanks to AAA, the show was run in a prompt and efficient manner. Also on the card for the first time in speedway history were Stock Cars.

July 28: After six lead changes by five different drivers, Walter May emerged victorious in the 25-lap Classic. It was a painful victory for May who fractured two ribs when he hit a bump in the track, which threw him into the steering wheel. In between races, local auto dealers paraded their brand new 1929 cars in front of the grandstand.

September 15: Mel Kenealy, of Glendale, won the 25-lap sweepstake event. Kenealy's victory followed the crash in which Gordon Webster was seriously injured while attempting to pass Ernie Triplett. Webster, who had just won the consolation race, locked wheels with Triplett and flipped high over the guardrail. This was his first and last attempt at racing. After the races, 20 old cars were piled in front of the stands, doused with gas, and set on fire.

October 27: The largest crowd of the year enjoyed for the first time a public address system. Two legends, Earl Cooper and Barney Oldfield, were spotted bench racing. Speed Hinkley won the 100-lap main event over the fastest field of cars ever to assemble at San Jose. Francis Quinn led the first 54 laps before a flat tire set him back. Johnny Kreiger set a new one-lap track record of 26 seconds flat during qualifying but struggled to a seventh-place finish in the feature.

1934 Indianapolis 500 winner Bill Cummings sits in the Sparks Special prior to the December 28, 1930, race.
Edith C. Smith Collection / Sourisseau Academy, San Jose State University

Dignitaries, announcers and AAA officials occupy the scoring tower during a 1930 race. *Don Bishop Collection*

1930

May 11: Many improvements were made to the speedway before the opener. Besides new paint on everything, which gave a pleasant contrast to the green grass around the facility, a new pavilion and scoreboard were added to the infield to accommodate the media and officials.

Around 10,000 people crammed into the speed plant to witness the 30-car show. AAA was on board for another year. The boys from Ascot Speedway in Los Angeles showed their dominance once again. This time they took the top eight spots in the 100-lap feature event. Jimmy Sharp was the winner.

June 1: Six thousand spectators witnessed close racing in all events, including a three-lap race for the three fastest qualifiers, with the winner receiving a silver trophy worth $100. This new event (to San Jose) was called a Trophy Dash.

Jimmy Sharp, driving the Bohart Special, won his

"Stubby" Stubblefield of Los Angeles won four times at San Jose. *Edith C. Smith Collection / Sourisseau Academy, San Jose State University*

Speed Hinkley, from Pasadena, sits in the Kingsley Special, which he piloted in 1931. He won the June 21, 1931, main event (his second at the speedway) but then was injured in a spectacular accident on October 4. *Don Bishop Collection*

Chet Gardner of Los Angeles won the June 7, 1931, race driving a Miller. *Dennis Mattish Collection*

Local Races to Be Broadcast by NBC Announcer

Mercury News

second main event in a row. Francis Quinn, his rival from Los Angeles, finished a close second, followed by Mel McKee.

July 13: Jimmy Sharp hit a grand slam, winning all four events he was in. Once again Francis Quinn was runner-up.

August 17: It was "Jimmy Sharp Day" again. He had a clean sweep of all four events - his fourth win in a row at San Jose and his seventh win in a row in the AAA Pacific Coast Championship races. As usual, Francis Quinn finished second, having tied the track record during qualifying.

One accident marred the meet - Cliff Wilson of Hanford blew a tire during qualifying. The car turned end-over-end twice and then rolled over sideways three times. Wilson was thrown clear of the wreckage on the first flip. He lost some skin on his shoulder, but was otherwise okay, even addressing the crowd afterwards.

September 21: The hottest driver of the year, Jimmy Sharp, was not able to defend his win streak. The week before, Sharp was injured in a wreck during a race in Fresno. He was not only through for the year, but it cost him the championship.

That opened the door for the other drivers, and Mel Kenealy took advantage, winning all four events he was in, including the 30-lap feature. Johnny Kreiger was second.

October 19: "Setting a new record for 100 laps, Francis Quinn of Glendale, yesterday won the feature event in the San Jose speedways racing program before a crowd of 7,500 fans" read the *Mercury Herald*. Finishing second was Mel Kenealy. Arvol Brunmier, who earlier in the day set a new track record of 25.7 seconds, came home third in another well-run AAA show.

November 30: Babe Stapp returned to San Jose, where he cut his teeth, and stole the show, even beating nationally know driver Wilbur Shaw before a good-sized crowd.

One of the reasons for big crowds this year was because the races from Ascot Speedway in Los Angeles were broadcast on radio station KFRC every Saturday night in the Bay area, which went a long way to popularizing the sport in the Bay Area in those days before television.

December 14: A special match race, consisting of five five-lap races, was staged between Babe Stapp and Mel Kenealy. Stapp, who had reportedly been racing in Europe and the East Coast during the season, led every lap of the five races.

Big Cars pull out onto the grid for the feature event on April 5, 1931. "Stubby" Stubblefield (5) won the race while Francis Quinn (99) encountered mechanical problems. *Edith C. Smith Collection / Sourisseau Academy, San Jose State University*

Ernie Triplett, Los Angeles's Golden Boy, won back-to-back races at San Jose in 1931 on his way to winning the AAA Pacific Coast Championship. *Dennis Mattish Collection*

Babe Stapp, who lived in San Jose off and on over the years, sits in the Bobby Special during 1931. *Don Bishop Collection*

The three fastest qualifiers, Lloyd Axel (68), "Stubby" Stubblefield (5) and Mel Kenealy (18), participated in a new event called a trophy dash on July 12, 1931. Stubby won. *Edith C. Smith Collection / Sourisseau Academy, San Jose State*

December 28: An all-star lineup participated in this season-ending winter race.

A good many stars from the National AAA series were entered, the most prominent being Bill Cummings and Wilbur Shaw.

"Quinn wins 100-lap Speedway Classic to become 1930 Coast Champ," said the headlines the next day. But it wasn't easy. Some 8,000 fans were in attendance on this cold December day to watch a very good race. Quinn held off the challenges of Bill Cummings for most of the race, only to see him get by with just a handful of laps to go, but a lap later and running high on the track, Cummings brushed the hub rail and blew a tire. It was then clear sailing to the checkered flag and the Pacific Coast Championship for Quinn. To add to his perfect day, Quinn also set a new track record with a lap of 25.3 during qualifying.

This brought the curtain down on the safest and most successful year in the track's history.

1931

March 15: Ninety-five hundred spectators showed up to watch the knights of the roaring road on opening day - not bad, considering this was during the great depression.

Ernie Triplett turned a time of 25.2 seconds at over 89 mph during qualifying to set a new track record.

Before the main event, AAA decided to reduce the scheduled 80-lap main to 50 laps because of unsafe track conditions, but the announcement prompted boos from the crowd, which led to AAA meeting again and putting the race back to 80 laps. Ernie Triplett led the first 44 laps before a flat tire forced him to the pits. Stubby Stubblefield then took command and went on to win the 80 lapper. Chet Gardner finished second and Mel Kenealy third. Los Angeles area drivers continued to own the North.

April 5: Stubblefield took home the lion's share of the purse with his victory in the 50-lap feature. During one of the races, the car driven by Chuck Gelston threw a connecting rod and caught fire. The car was then engulfed in flames, shooting 25 feet into the air. The car, which was valued at $2,500, was a total loss.

June 1: Chester Gardner, veteran Indianapolis pilot, beat 30 Pacific Coast dirt track wizards before another standing-room-only crowd of 7,500. His four-cylinder Miller led Carl Ryder and Mel Kenealy across the line.

June 21: Speed Hinkley led Chet Gardner to the checkered flag in the 60-lap feature. The first serious accident in two years took place during qualifying. Walter May suffered a concussion, several broken ribs and a fractured shoulder when the front end of his car collapsed in turn three. The car went into a series of flips, ejecting May onto the track. He died two days later. Robert Scovell

Francis Quinn of Los Angeles proudly sits in the Dayton Thoroughbred Special during 1931. He had two feature wins and the one-lap track record during 1930.
Edith C. Smith Collection / Sourisseau Academy, San Jose State University

Arvol Brunmier, the "Flying Frenchman" from Pasadena, sits in the Sparks Special during September, 1931. On October 4, he set a new track record during qualifying and won the main event.
Edith C. Smith Collection / Sourisseau Academy, San Jose State University

Al Gordon set fast time on October 16, 1932, driving the Quinn Special.
Dennis Mattish Collection

Lester Spangler of Los Angeles poses for the camera in his Fronty Special. Lester won two of the three AAA races held at the speedway in 1932. *Dennis Mattish Collection*

Babe Stapp drove the Gilmore Speedway Special to a thrilling victory over Lester Spangler on September 25, 1932. The pair raced wheel to wheel the last five laps as the crowd went wild. *Don Radbruch Collection*

Clay Bushman, local driver, had modest success in the few years he raced at the speed bowl. He sits in his own car ,Bushman Special, in this 1933 photo. *Jack Fox Collection*

was lucky to avoid being thrown out when his car suffered a similar fate later in qualifying. Thankfully Scovell escaped with only scrapes.

July 12: Stubby Stubblefield and Mel Kenealy battled through 40 dust-ridden laps on a soft and treacherous track. Stubblefield emerged victorious. Officials decided to put crushed rock in the turns to help improve track conditions, but this led to many drivers suffering cuts and bruises as they were splattered with rocks throughout the program. Drivers didn't have much protection then. Al Gordon crashed his car through the fence and ended up on King Road–a first.

August 16: Barney Oldfield and Eddie Hearne were in town to officiate this race for AAA. Also back from a stint on the Eastern circuit was hometown favorite Babe Stapp and his rival, Ernie Triplett. A capacity crowd saw Triplett and Speed Hinkley have a seesaw battle for the lead of the feature. Triplett won by a nose in one of the closest finishes ever at the speedway. Stapp pulled into the pits when sickness overcame him.

September 13: New to the speedway was a steel guardrail all the way around the track. This would keep cars from going through the fence and over the bank.

His days as a reckless driver at San Jose now a distant memory, Ernie Triplett had become one of the country's premier drivers. He won the main event going away by a half lap. Following in the dust were Francis Quinn and Chet Gardner.

October 4: The announcement that this race would be broadcast by NBC was big news for the track.

Five thousand fans cheered as youthful Arvol Brunmier was the star of the day. He set a new track record during time trials, won the dash, his heat and dusted off Babe Stapp in the main. During the main, Speed Hinkley blew a tire and flipped in front of the stands. As his Miller Special rolled over and over, the dust rose in clouds and hid him from view of cars behind him. It was a miracle nobody hit him. He regained consciousness in the hospital a few hours later. Besides the concussion, he had a painful back injury.

November 29: The fans got their money's worth, as a stellar field of wind burners was entered, and they didn't disappoint. After setting fast time, winning the dash and his heat, Brian Saulpaugh, driving the Gilmore Special, sat on the pole. Right behind him was Indy's 'Wild Bill' Cummings. At the drop of the green, Saulpaugh shot into the lead with Cummings in hot pursuit. They would swap the lead two times, but on lap 15, the ring gear on the Sparks Special broke, forcing Cummings out of the race. Meanwhile, Babe Stapp, who started fifth, was working his way forward. With just a couple of laps to go, Stapp caught up to Saulbaugh. On the last lap, all the water ran out of Saulbaugh's car, the result of a couple of screws falling out of the water

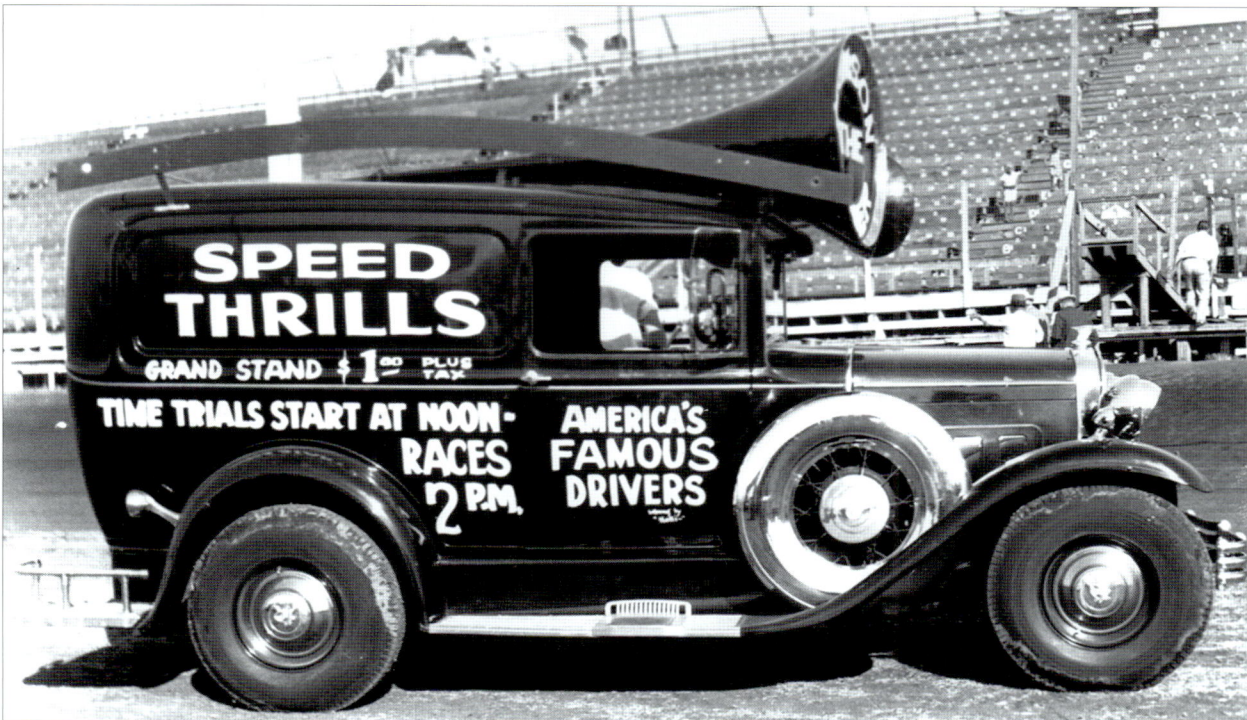

Promotional vehicle. That's one big speaker on the roof. *Don Bishop Collection*

The masthead reads:

Bergen The **Herald**

NATIONAL

AUTO 7 **RACING**

SUPER **SPEED**

AMERICAN SPEEDWAYS' NEWS PICTURE NEWSPAPER
RACING EDITION

$1.00 PER YEAR by mail

VOL. XIII, NO. 48 Entered as Second Class Matter Post Office East Paterson, N. J. EAST PATERSON, N. J., NOV. 8, 1934 Published Every Thursday Telephone SHer 2-9070 PRICE FIVE CENTS

ART ARMSTRONG WINS SEMI-STOCK CAR RACE AT SAN JOSE

Story on Page 3

San Jose made headlines in *The Bergen Herald National Auto Racing News* in 1934. *The Bergen Herald* would later become *National Speed Sport News*, The dean of all motor sports publications.

The new sport of Roadster racing, or Semi-Stock Cars as they were called in the early years, was just starting to get a foothold in San Jose when this photo was taken in 1934. Buck Whitmer (3) leads Johnny Fanucchi (10) through the turn. *Don Bishop Collection*

Ed Weinholz raced this Roadster at San Jose Speedway during the 1934 season. He was seriously injured in the car when he rolled over five times on October 28. *Don Bishop Collection*

jacket. As Saulbaugh slowed to a crawl, fan favorite Stapp sped by for the victory.

Although Ernie Triplett was in the hospital receiving skin grafts for burns suffered at Ascot Speedway, he had enough points to be crowned 1931 AAA Pacific Coast champion.

1932

April 22: For unknown reasons, the first two races of the year were outlaw races – frowned upon by AAA. For these events, promoter Jack Wilson barred Miller Specials from participating in an effort to even the field.

Because of the non-sanction and the absence of the big-name drivers, only a few fans showed up. Earl Mancell, from Los Angeles, won the main. Motorcycle great Al

Chasteen drove to a second-place finish.

July 17: The Pacific Coast Auto Racing Association was in charge of the second outlaw event. 'Babe' Stanyer of Alhambra won and Al Chasteen was second before a meager crowd.

August 28: AAA was back and so were the crowds and drivers. Seven thousand people packed into the speed plant to see Lester Spangler of Los Angeles set a new track record for 100 laps on his way to victory.

September 25: AAA was now split into two divisions. The premier division was for the faster Miller cars, called the A Division. The B Division was for all other cars. Babe Stapp passed Ernie Triplett, and then held off the challenges of Lester Spangles to win the 60-lap A Division main event. Up and coming driver Ted Horn won the 15-lap B Division main. Some 5,000 folks were on hand.

SAN JOSE NEWS
EVENING
Leased Wires From the Associated Press and the United Press Associations

Vol. 102, No. 67, 52nd Year   SAN JOSE, CALIFORNIA, MONDAY, OCTOBER 8, 1934   FOURTEEN PAGES   Price 3 Cents

THE WEATHER
SANTA CLARA VALLEY: Fair tonight and Tuesday. Warmer Tuesday. Gentle to moderate northerly winds.
TEMPERATURE—At noon today, 77; highest yesterday, 75; lowest this morning, 53.

SAN JOSE AUTO RACER KILLED

Howard Ordrop, 23-year-old San Jose resident, lost his life in this Roadster not long after this photo was taken on October 7, 1934. *Don Bishop Collection*

October 16: Lester Spangler took the lead on lap 12 and never looked back on his way to victory in the 100-lap main. Half a lap back was Ernie Triplett and then Lloyd Axel. Triplett won his second AAA Pacific Coast crown in a row. Ted Horn won his second B Division main in a row at SJ.

1933

June 4: AAA was back for another year and so were the big names, Rex Mays being the latest great to take to the high banks.

A couple of very unusual incidents took place during this program. In the 10-lap main event for B Division cars, Ray Patton of San Francisco spun into the guardrail, tearing down a section. As his car was crashing, his leg flew out onto the track, to the horror and screams of the crowd. As the crowd sat stunned and the cars circled under the yellow, somebody ran out and picked up Ray's leg. It was then announced to the crowd that Patton, a relatively unknown driver at San Jose, had an artificial limb.

In the next race, the 40-lap A Division main, 'Frenchy' La Hogue lost control of his car and went through the very same opening in the fence that Patton had just created. Having done no damage to his car, La Hogue put the pedal to the metal and raced around the outside of the track and behind the grandstand, missing anybody who might have been in his way. He re-entered the track in turn one and went on to finish in third place. Swede Smith won the race in front of Frank Suess and La Hogue.

July 15: Herb Balmer of LA was able to pass high, low or anywhere he wanted, on his way to winning the main. Swede Smith and Ted Horn followed him across the line.

September 10: For many years, Al Chasteen dominated the motorcycle races, which had been run on the big track, usually in conjunction with the cars. A couple of years before, he had started racing on four wheels and now he had claimed his first AAA win. George Webber and Ralph Greg followed him across the line in front of just 600 spectators.

October 8: Les Dreisbach of Oakland took home the first-place trophy for winning the 30-lap main. None of the Los Angeles area drivers participated in the last two races, and AAA must have agreed with them, because they would never race on the much-maligned track again.

45

These three photos, *Courtesy of the Tom Motter Collection*, show the Speedway during the mid 1930s. The pictures also bear witness to one of the problems that plagued the Speedway over the years, dust. Two drivers wearing cowboy hats can be seen in the middle photo.

FANS LEAVE TRACK IN DISGUST

Rajo Jack, Negro Ace, Declared Official Winner

By BILL FEIST

1935: *San Jose News (*See story on pages 49-50.)

Bayless Leverett, of San Diego, was one of the best of the new group of Outlaw drivers to race at San Jose after AAA left. He won two feature events during 1935. *Don Radbruch Collection*

Rajo Jack, popular Southern California driver, poses with Mable Agabashian in 1935. Jack won two San Jose main events but was not allowed to kiss the trophy girls because he was black. *Don Radbruch Collection*

1934

In July, plans were in the development stage to build a 1/5-mile Midget track behind the grandstands, with new back-to-back stands providing seating for 3,000 spectators. The plan was to move the racing from the Alviso Speedway dog track closer to the city. In part because of a workers' strike, it was never constructed.

August 5: Gone were AAA, the Big Cars and their drivers.

Considered one of the most dangerous tracks in the West, San Jose would not reopen till late in the year, under new management. A whole new cast of characters and cars would greet the opening-day crowd. A new, much slower class of race car called Modified Stock Cars (or Roadsters) were the featured division.

A young driver named Freddie Agabashian introduced himself to local race fans by winning the main event in the season opener. Fat Mario and Dave Oliver finished behind him.

Just as a leopard can't change its spots, the speedway couldn't seem to shake its image. Four drivers went to the hospital with minor injuries. One of them, Tony Dutra, took a rock square in the face.

Many of the drivers who participated in the opener would have illustrious careers in auto racing.

Future Midget driving great Freddie Agabashian drove his first race at San Jose Speedway in 1934, driving a Roadster. This photo shows him in the infield for the 1937 California Championship Big Car race where he challenged Rajo Jack for the lead of the 100-lap race until he blew his engine on lap 60. *Don Bishop Collection*

1937: Tony Dutra of San Jose drove Midgets, Big Cars and Roadsters. *Don Bishop Collection*

August 19: Dave Oliver won the 30-lap main event, followed by Buck Witmer and Tony Dutra. Fred Agabashian fractured his jaw in a qualifying flip. It would take months to heal.

October 7: The Grim Reaper struck again. Before the start of the main event, Howard Ordrop of SJ was joking with the ambulance driver. He told him "If you take me out of here in one of those things (ambulance), you'll never bring me back." Moments later, he was mortally wounded. Ordrop was leading the main event on lap five when the steering knuckle (which had been welded after breaking

in qualifying) broke again, sending him into the railing at a high rate of speed. As he tore through the fence and down the embankment, his body was tossed out of the car. Once restarted, Buck Whitmer took command of the race and won.

October 28: A county fair crowd of 1,500 witnessed three drivers escape death. Curt Krummes received a broken leg, shoulder and back when he flipped end-over-end two times. Ed Weinholz received major injuries when he flipped five times. Beal Simmons plowed through the guardrail, down the embankment, through a ditch and

This photo, taken from the stands, came from the album of Miss Rose Mace, a San Jose resident.

stopped near the horse stables. He climbed out without a scratch. Art Armstrong emerged from the carnage the victor.

November 11: Trying to attract a bigger crowd, admission price was lowered to 40 cents. All proceeds were to help pay for all the medical expenses that had been accruing during the year. Dave Oliver returned after three months to win the Semi-Stock Car main event. The only incident of the day took place during that main event. John Timmons spun into the infield mud and flipped. He was thrown out of the car, and then walked away without a scratch.

Crowds were down drastically from the previous years but this was also the start of an era in San Jose–the Roadster era.

1935

February 17: Under another change of management, the track had an early season opener. Tommy Quinn, the new manager, booked two classes of cars. Back were the single seat Class B Big Cars – the same as those raced with AAA but now under the sanction of the California Auto Racing Association (CARA). Also on the card were the Modified Stock Cars (Roadsters). Four thousand race fans, the biggest crowd in two years, welcomed back the Big Cars, although there were only six.

But on this day, the Roadsters were the featured attraction. Al Chasteen outlasted the field in the 50-lap main event. Fat Mario was second. During the main, "Wild" Bill Walbridge was hit from the side. The collision sent him toward the infield where he took out 50 feet of fencing before smashing into a racecar in the pits and flipping. He was unhurt.

March 17: Although they were independents (outlaws), the Big Cars were back, under the CARA sanction. The cast was different from AAA, but no less talented. Among the drivers were Bayless Leverett and Rajo Jack (the first African-American driver to race San Jose).

Over 3,000 fans shivered through the program as a cold north wind hit the unprotected grandstands. The *Mercury Herald* stated, "The entire program was run off

Auto Races Once Again

The San Jose Speedway is to be reopened next Sunday.

According to the promoters and publicity sharks, all the boys will be there, all the cars will be fast, and the track will be in fine shape.

If San Joseans have heard that line of lingo once, they've heard it a thousand times. . . . Don't get me wrong. . . . I'm not saying Sunday's show will not be satisfactory. . . . Neither am I saying that it will be a pippin. . . . The success of the show depends upon the size and quality of the field.

What the promoters have in mind I can't say. . . . But I can say that the race game here will never be brought back from its grave with shows four or five months apart. . . . The promoters should decide for once and for all if they are to "do or do not."

1937 Letter published in the *San Jose Mercury News* showing displeasure with all the promised hype that never materialized.

in a slipshod and aggravating manner. Bickering, delays and indecisions marked the meet." This all came about from the 100-lap main event. Rajo Jack, driving the Sparks Special, and Bayless Leverett in a "Fronty" traded the lead numerous times during the first 88 laps. Then motor problems knocked Leverett out of the race. Art Armstrong, who had been following the pair, then passed Jack with just a

49

Tom Motter Collection

George Rakatani was one of the few Japanese Americans racing in the country before WWII. He is pictured at San Jose behind the wheel of his Modified Stock Car (Roadster) in the late 1930s. *Don Radbruch collection.*

couple of laps to go. He took the checkered flag first, for what appeared to be a victory. Jack approached officials and protested the race, saying he had lapped Armstrong. After arguing for three hours, the win was given to the popular Rajo, much to the irritation of Armstrong. By then, everybody had left the track. They didn't find out who won until they saw the headlines the next morning that read, "Fans leave track in disgust, Rajo Jack, Negro ace, declared official winner." Below that headline, it read, "the dangerous bowl produced three spectacular crack-ups, with all pilots escaping serious injury only through good fortune."

May 12: A small crowd saw San Diego's Bayless Leverett beat Freddie Agabashian and Duane Carter to the checkered flag in the 75-lap race. There were a lot of quality drivers from the West at this race.

June 2: Jack Dinsmore won the 40-lap feature over Rajo Jack before another small crowd.

June 16: Another death marred the races at the speedway. Eugene McCarthy crashed his Modified Stock Car through the rail and then flipped. He was crushed in the process. Gene Figone won the 50-lap race on this all-Roadster show.

August 11: "Confusion Reigns at track" read the headlines the following day. It would appear that the track had lost favor with the local paper. There was a lot less press coverage than in the past, and a lot of that coverage was critical, but probably truthful.

The CARA sanction program started out with Charles Gate getting some of his teeth knocked out in a qualifying flip. Because of this and the fact that they ran warm-ups long, the races started three hours late. Nerves were already on edge when they pushed off for the main. After many parade laps before the start, trying to line up the cars in their proper position, the flagman grew impatient. Out of frustration he threw the green anyway. This riled up some of the drivers and a couple of them pulled into the pits. Art Armstrong, who sat on the pole, was one of them, and he and his crew were steamed. The race continued, and on lap 25, Art Scovill's car caught fire. He pulled into the infield where the one fire extinguisher was. The paper said that the extinguisher was the size of a "Wienerwurst" which quickly emptied. The car then burned to a crisp. Two people fighting the fire also got burned. The ambulance could not get to the infield to care for the injured because the race was still running and the organizers refused to throw the caution flag.

Through the chaos, Bayless Leverett would emerge with his second main-event win in a row.

After the races, the payoff was at the West Santa Clara Street Hotel. With many of the drivers, car owners and crews there, some still hot under the collar, words got heated. An all-out brawl then broke out, with fists, chairs, lamps, and other items flying. The police arrived (all two of them) and the fighting spilled out onto the street before order was restored.

Although there was supposed to be more

racing at the track, this turned out to be the season finale. A short time later the track manager resigned.

1936

March 15: For the third year in a row, the speed bowl opened under new management. This time the promoter was William Wallace.

Because of the chronic dust problem that had plagued the track, Wallace said thousands of gallons of oil would be dumped on it.

American Racing Association was the sanctioning body for the Semi-Stock Cars that would run at SJ this year. Some 3,500 fans saw Ernie Criss win the 100-lap Roadster race by five laps. The *Mercury* reported that this race was run perfectly.

April 19: Art Armstrong won the 40-lap ARA Roadster race. On lap 37, his left rear wheel came off and flew into the stands. Luckily, no one was hurt. At the time, Armstrong had a three-lap lead, so he stayed on the track and limped to the checkered, just ahead of a fast closing Gene Figone and Beal Simmons.

May 10: An entry of 29 cars signed in for the ARA race and 3,000 fans were in the stands for the third well-run show in a row. Art Armstrong won the 12-car main event, with Jack McNamara a close second, followed by Duane Carter of Fresno. Jack Menser hit a big rut in the track, injuring his back. When he stopped, the pain was so bad that he passed out.

1937

May 23: The Big Cars, or Sprint Cars as they would later be called, were back. Bud Rose of Los Angeles stole the show, winning every event entered, in front of 3,000 fans. Walt Davis and Freddie Agabashian followed him across the line.

June 13: Rose repeated his previous month's performance, leading flag to flag in front of Agabashian and Tony Dutra.

September 6: Rajo Jack won the 100-lap main event over Lloyd Logan and Ed Normi. A small rain-threatened crowd attended.

November 7: Pacific Coast Championship Auto Race, the biggest independent race in the West, was held in front of a fair sized crowd. Duane Carter took home the winner's share of the purse money. Wally Shrock and Ernie Criss finished second and third respectively.

Agabashian was crowned the Champion.

1938

June 12: The latest change in management saw Charles Curryer take charge. He was one of the best in the business, with successful promotions at such tracks as Ascot Speedway and Oakland Speedway. A field of 28 Big Cars signed in, many of them top quality. *Mercury News* reporter Buddy Leitch wrote, "Hal Robson, a major-league race pilot, found the bush-league San Jose Speedway track to his liking yesterday afternoon and roared to victory in the 75-lap main event on the program sponsored by the Veterans of Foreign Wars Convention Committee." Bud Rose and Rajo Jack followed behind, eating his oily dust in the

SUNDAY Aug. 6th—2 p. m. ROADSTER RACES
San Jose Speedway
80 LAPS OF THRILLS SPEED
40c   Any Seat in the Grandstand   40c

This was the final race ever run at the Alum Rock Avenue speed plant.

Class A race. During the 25-lap B Class main, Fred Fram and Herk Edwards tangled and went through one of the many openings in the wobbly old fence on the back straight. Fram's car hit one of the fence posts, which was occupied by a 16-year-old boy. The boy was taken to the hospital, unconscious and with internal injuries and a crushed arm. Fram was also transported to the hospital, with a fractured skull and internal injuries. Edwards was okay. During the same race, Joe Wilber lost a wheel, which left the track and crashed through one of the horse stables. Buck Whitmer emerged the winner. The first four positions transferred to the A Class main. Curryer ran a short and snappy show for the near-capacity crowd.

July 10: The same cast of characters came back for this meet. The dust didn't bother race winner Tex Peterson, who was out front all day, making the second and third-place finishers–Bud Rose and Rajo Jack–eat it. A capacity crowd watched another snappy program.

July 31: Charles Curryer was to promote a 150-lap Big Car race on this date, but he cancelled and the San Francisco Roadster Club scheduled a Roadster race instead. Bob Jensen won the 10-lap main event in the most unusual finish in track history. As Jensen was approaching the checkered flag, he went into a spin on the rough track. As the car was bouncing along, it ejected Jensen out the side and then the car ran over him, at the same time crossing the finish line for the win. He was taken to San Jose Hospital with moderate injuries and released later that day, with his trophy.

It was a strange end to a short two-month race season for the track.

1939

May 28: The "Suicide Bowl" as the *Mercury News* was calling the track, was now promoted by Charles Phil Camp. A good-sized crowd of 4,500 attended, but only 12 cars participated.

Fat Mario took the lead of the 100-lap race at the start with Tony Dutra in pursuit. As both drivers were battling for position and lapping the field, Dutra banged wheels with one of the back markers. Immediately the San Josean lost control. The car rolled over twice and then shot high into the air, ejecting Dutra. In mid-air, the pilot's body and machine collided and Dutra was thrown unconscious to the track. Amazingly, he suffered only cuts and bruises and no broken bones. He was released from the hospital that night. After a long delay, the race was restarted, and Mario would lead the rest of the race and claim first prize. George Dent was second and Andrew Ponzini third.

July 9: No longer called Semi-Stock Cars, the Roadsters were coming into their own. *Mercury News* sports reporter Bill Feist, who was just beginning a 30-year career covering local racing, wrote: "Big time auto racing promoters, who move into San Jose's city limits amid column after column of ballyhoo and promises that outstanding attractions will appear and then disappoint the fans, might take a page from the Roadster races at San Jose Speedway yesterday."

A crowd of 2,500 saw Bob Murden beat Mauri King and Johnny Soares to the checkered flag in the 40-lap, 12-car main event. The three cars dueled in close quarters for much of the race, to the delight of the crowd.

August 6: It seemed like any other day at the races for the 17-year-old track, with 2,000 people there to watch the roaring Roadsters put on another good display of racing. Mauri King and Bob Murden continued their battle for the top spot in the main; this time King was victorious. Buck Bowers was third.

As the crowd filed out of the grandstands, somebody apparently threw their cigarette under the seats into the litter below. Forty-five minutes later, track watchman Thomas Scherreback noticed flames under the stands. He called the fire department. First on the scene was the volunteer fire department, but they could do nothing because of strong winds and lack of water. By the time the San Jose Fire Department arrived, the grandstands were completely engulfed. Because it was out of their jurisdic-

---

HOME EDITION

SAN JOSE EVENING NEWS

Leased Wires From the Associated Press and United Press Associations

Vol. 115, No. 13, 57th Year   SAN JOSE, CALIFORNIA, MONDAY, AUGUST 7, 1939

FIRE RAZES SAN JOSE SPEEDWAY

Pictures Show Flames Sweeping Local Speedway

Cause of Fire Which Destroys Grandstand Unknown

Cause of a spectacular fire which razed the 5000-seat grandstand at San Jose Speedway in East San Jose last evening was sought by officers and owners of the property today.

Breaking out at the west end of the huge structure a half-hour after 1500 persons had vacated the stands at conclusion of an auto racing event, the flames were discovered by Thomas Scherrebeck, watchman, who resides nearby, and spread rapidly. Chief James Hedberg and a crew from the Hedberg volunteer fire department responded to an alarm, but found their efforts to quench the fire unsuccessful due to a brisk wind and lack of water supply.

CIGARET BLAMED

San Jose city firemen were called to the scene, standing by across the city limit line at Santa Clara Street

(Continued on Page Three, Column One)

Snapped a few moments after fire broke out in the west end of the grandstand at San Jose Speedway, this picture was taken early last evening and shows fierceness with which the flames were burning when the blaze was discovered.—Photo by Herb Sample.

Speed with which the $10,000 fire which destroyed the grandstand at San Jose Speedway spread last evening is graphically shown in this picture, taken a few minutes after the blaze was discovered. Flames are shown racing eastward along the structure, after razing the west end of the stands. The small boys shown in the foreground are shielding their faces from the intense heat.—Photo by Herb Sample.

San Jose Speedway Destroyed By Fire

West's First Dirt Track Makes Huge Bonfire After Sunday Races; Loss $10,000.

The 1000 spectators who thrilled to pulse-quickening auto races in the San Jose speedway at Alum Rock avenue and King road yesterday afternoon missed the most spectacular event of the day.

Shortly after 5, only a half hour after they had emptied the grandstand, the structure was discovered on fire, presumably started by a cigarette one of them had dropped, and quickly burned to the ground.

Swept by a brisk wind, the wooden stand built to seat 5000 at a cost of $10,000 in 1927, was burning beyond control when the Hedberg fire department arrived.

HUNDREDS WATCH.

Hundreds of motorists jammed adjacent highways as spectators watched the ravenous flames race through the structure which crashed to the ground in huge gusts of sparks and smoke

The Hedberg department pre-

tion, they refused to fight it, saying the track was in the county and they were employed by the city. They backed off and stood guard over the nearby homes that were in the city, protecting them from flying embers. Hundreds of motorist jammed nearby roads to watch the spectacle as the stands came crashing down. By the time the fire burned itself out, the structure, built in 1922 at a cost of $10,000, was completely gone. The only things left standing were the stables and the livestock in them. The rodeo, which was to take place the following week, was canceled. (The biggest rodeo in state history–up to that point in time–took place there in 1927). This was the fifth and final fire to hit the stands. The others had been quickly extinguished.

Initially Bart Lorigan, owner of the speedway, talked of building new stands, but this never happened. Lorigan, who was a real estate developer, decided to turn the historic site into a housing development.

On February 20, 1940, tractors and scrapers started leveling the old banked track, and in a matter of months, new homes were being constructed.

It is estimated that 750,000 gallons of oil was poured onto that site during the history of the track. Few of the residents, who now live in that neighborhood, probably have any idea of what was dumped into the ground beneath their homes. Nor do they know about the ghosts of the many drivers who perished there.

San Jose's deadliest track was gone.

**San Jose Speedway
One-lap track record
5/8-mile**

Big Car track record.
1923
No time trials recorded

1924
Adolph Gusti	29.0
Ralph De Palma	28.3

1925
Leigh Green	27.0

1928
Jack Buxton	26.2
Jack Buxton	26.1

1929
Johnny Kreiger	26.0

1930
Arvol Brunmier	25.7
Francis Quinn	25.3

1931
Ernie Triplett	25.2

Roadster track record.
1934
Art Armstrong	27.1
Fat Mario	26.6

Author's Note. The track surface was so bad in the later years, there was never another track record set after 1934.

San Jose Speedway
Main Event Winners
1923-1939

July 4, 1923	Red Murray
Aug. 12, 1923	Fred Luelling
Aug. 19, 1923	Gene Rapp
Sept. 23, 1923	Fred Lyons
Nov. 11, 1923	Adolph Gusti
Dec. 2, 1923	Fred Lyons
June 29, 1924	Fred Luelling
July 27, 1924	Adolph Gusti
Sept. 1, 1924	Ralph De Palma
Oct. 18, 1924	Ralph De Palma
Oct. 26, 1924	Fred Luelling
Nov. 27, 1924	Babe Stapp
March 15, 1925	Jack Petticord
May 24, 1925	Fred Lyon
June 14, 1925	Babe Stapp
July 4, 1926	Freeman Howard
Sept. 5, 1926	Mike Moosie
June 27, 1927	Bill Spence
July 4, 1927	Bill Spence
Sept. 11, 1927	Barney Kloepfer
Oct. 16, 1927	Barney Kloepfer
March 18, 1928	Barney Kloepfer
May 20, 1928	Jack Buxton
June 24, 1928	Jack Buxton
July 4, 1928	Jack Buxton
Sept. 16, 1928	Stubby Stubblefield
Oct. 21, 1928	Jack Buxton
Feb. 17, 1929	Johnny Sawyer
June 23, 1929	Mel Keneally
July 28, 1929	Walter May
Sept. 15, 1929	Mel Keneally
Oct. 27, 1929	Speed Hinkley
May 11, 1930	Jimmy Sharp
June 8, 1930	Jimmy Sharp
July 13, 1930	Jimmy Sharp
Aug. 17, 1930	Jimmy Sharp
Sept. 21, 1930	Mel Kenealy
Oct. 19, 1930	Francis Quinn
Nov. 30, 1930	Babe Stapp
Dec 28, 1930	Francis Quinn
March 15, 1931	Stubby Stubblefield
April 5, 1931	Stubby Stubblefield
June 7, 1931	Chet Gardner
June 21, 1931	Speed Hinkley
July 12, 1931	Stubby Stubblefield
Aug. 16 1931	Ernie Triplett
Sept. 13, 1931	Ernie Triplett
Oct 4, 1931	Arvol Brunmier
Nov. 29, 1931	Babe Stapp
April 24, 1932	Earl Mancell
July 17,1932	"Babe" Stanyer
Aug. 28. 1932	Les Spangler
Sept. 25, 1932	Babe Stapp
Oct. 16, 1932	Les Spangler
June 4, 1933	Swede Smith
July 16, 1933	Herb Balmer
Sept. 10, 1933	Al Chasteen
Oct. 8, 1933	Les Dresback
Aug. 5, 1934*	Fred Agabashian
Aug. 19, 1934*	Dave Oliver
Oct. 7, 1934*	Buck Whitmer
Oct. 28, 1934*	Art Armstrong
Nov. 11, 1934*	Dave Oliver
Feb. 17, 1935*	Al Chasteen
March 17, 1935	Rajo Jack
May, 12, 1935	Bayless Leverett
June 2, 1935	Jack Dinsmore
June 16, 1935*	Gene Figoni
Aug. 11, 1935	Bayless Leverett
March 15, 1936*	Ernie Criss
April 19, 1936*	Art Armstrong
May, 10, 1936*	Art Armstrong
May 23, 1937	Bud Rose
June 13, 1937	Bud Rose
Sept. 6, 1937	Rajo Jack
Nov. 7, 1937	Duane Carter
June 12, 1938	Hal Robson
July 10, 1938	Tex Peterson
July 31, 1938*	Bob Jensen
Sept. 11, 1938*	Gene Figone
May 28, 1939	Fat Mario
July 9, 1939*	Bob Murden
Aug. 6, 1939*	Mauri King

All races are Big Car except where noted with *
* = Roadster Race
Red means non AAA sanction

Chapter 6

East Side Speedway
1934

Early November, 1934, J.R. Wilson (builder of the original San Jose Speedway) met with the Wise Riding Academy with a plan to transform their horse track into a speedway for cars. The track was located at the corner of Alum Rock and Capitol Avenues, just a mile up the road from San Jose Speedway. It was a flat dirt track with a paper clip shape, meaning long straights with tight corners. It was advertised as a half-mile, but that seemed to be stretching it a bit. Once Wilson received the okay, he widened the track to 60 feet and constructed grandstands that measured 240 feet long by 40 feet high. The first race was scheduled for December 2, 1934.

Flat track, Modified Stock Car (Roadster) racing was very popular in the Eastern United States, and this was their debut event in San Jose. Modified Stock Cars were much heavier than what people were used to seeing down the road at San Jose Speedway, but they were guaranteed to provide a lot of action.

Drivers entered who had seen action at San Jose Speedway were Tony Dutra, motorcycle great Al Chasteen, Dave Oliver, Gene Figone and Art Armstrong.

On race day, 2,500 fans packed into the new grandstands to witness this new type of auto racing. What they saw was an exciting program. It started in morning warm-ups, when V. Dent flipped his car over, receiving minor injuries. The main event had Dave Oliver and Buck Whitmer racing wheel to wheel, lap after lap before Oliver claimed the win. The *Mercury News* reported that the cars were skidding through the turns, which probably meant they were power sliding. On the last lap of the main, Gene Figone tore out over 50 feet of fencing, bringing the spectators to their feet.

The crowd went home satisfied by what they had witnessed. It was predicted that huge crowds would come out to future events.

The next race was scheduled for December 16, but heavy rains during the month caused its cancellation as well as the December 30 race.

The *Bergen Herald National Auto Racing News* reported in January, 1935, that there were problems developing

TOMORROW

AUTO RACES

On the New Flat Track

Plenty of Thrills On the Turns

ADMISSION 50¢

CHILDREN 25¢

Grandstand and Parking Free

RACES START 2 P. M.

ALUM ROCK AVE. Near Capitol Ave.

Enter At the Riding School

NEW FLAT AUTO TRACK OPENS HERE ON SUNDAY

A new sport thrill for San Jose fans will be introduced at the new East Side Speedway, Alum Rock Avenue, near Capitol Avenue, tomorrow afternoon. Six races and time trials over a new half-mile, flat dirt track will be the feature.

between the Wise Riding Academy, who owned the land, and the J.R. Wilson led racing group. Things got so bad between the two sides that there were threats of tearing down the new grandstands and buildings and selling it for lumber. When the two sides couldn't settle their differences that is exactly what happened. There was never another auto race held at the short-lived East Side Speedway.

During May, 1941, the Riding Academy staged a "Circus of Death" thrill show put on by Ace Lillard and his daredevil auto pilots. Sixteen hundred bleacher seats were installed and a good-sized crowd occupied those seats.

With World War II only a matter of months away, there would be no more auto-related events on the premises.

The land that the Wise Riding Academy occupied was later developed into a cannery after WWII. At that time, agriculture was the main industry in San Jose. The cannery was torn down in the 1970s and a shopping center now occupies the land.

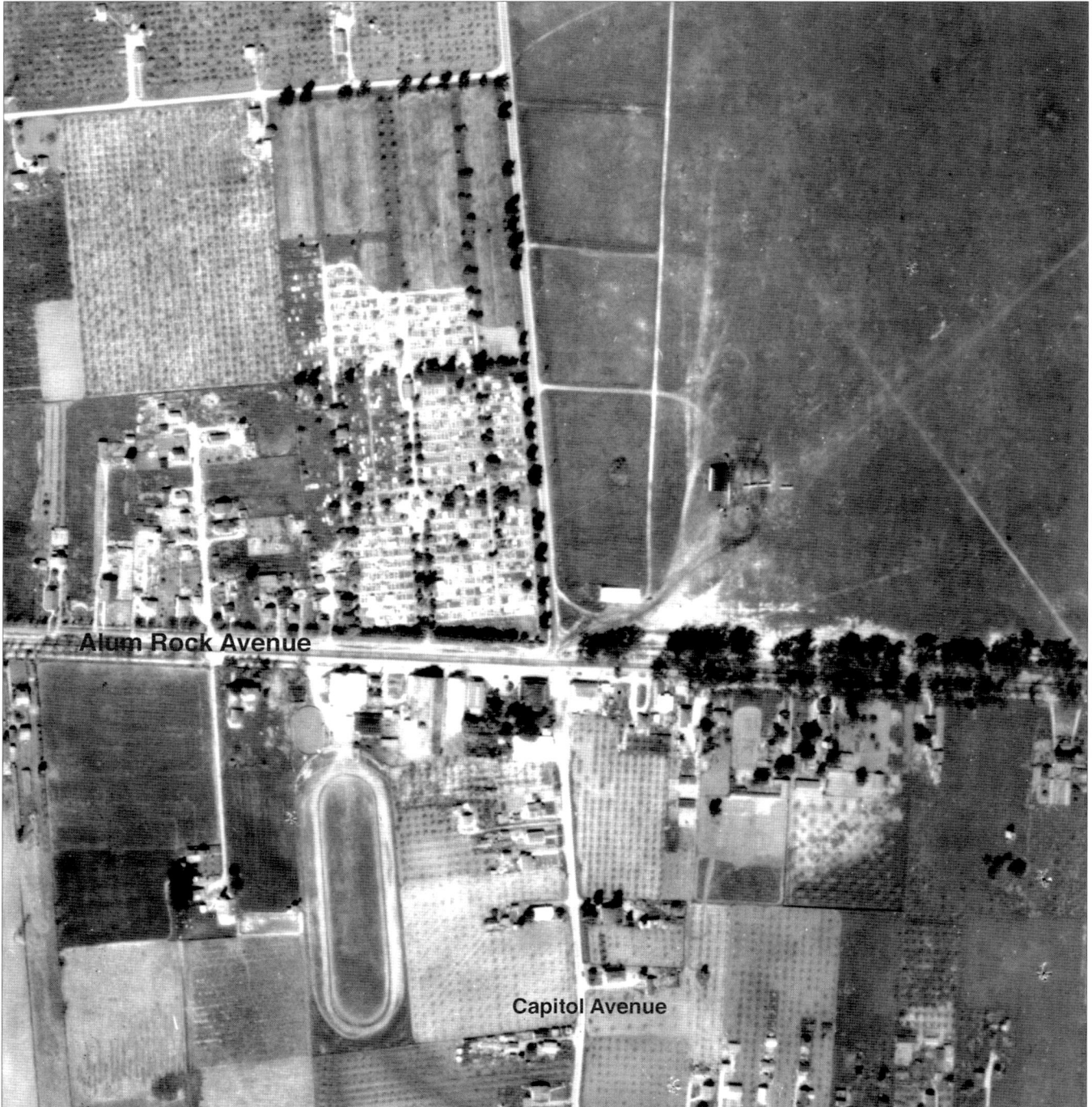

Eastside Speedway was the name given by the *Mercury News* to identify the track for its news stories. The track was a training ground for the horses of the Wise Riding Academy. As this photo shows, the track had long straights and very tight turns, probably because of the shape of their lot. The first San Jose Airport was located across Alum Rock and Capitol Avenue. The Airport had already been shut down for a year when this photo was taken in 1931.
The Fairchild Aerial Photography Collection at Whittier College C-1456-82

Tony Dutra slides his Modified Stock Car through the turn as the East San Jose hills act as a backdrop. It appears Tony came straight from church for this Sunday afternoon race because he still has his suit and tie on.
Don Bishop Collection

San Jose's First Airport
1924-1929

About 200 yards northeast of East Side Speedway was San Jose's first airport (see photo). Built around 1924, there was little air traffic at first. But with the growing popularity of airmail delivery, it was determined that San Jose needed to upgrade its airfield. With the trolley service running from downtown San Jose up Alum Rock Avenue and adjacent to the airport, it made for an ideal location for a municipal airport. With the backing of the U.S. Postal Service, the U.S. Army flyers and leading citizen groups, a hangar was built and lights installed on the runway.

Airmail service commenced in early 1928. About the same time, a shuttle service between Oakland and Salinas, with a stop in San Jose, started.

Almost immediately, the neighbors downwind from the runway started to complain about the huge dust clouds that kicked up when twin-engine airplanes landed. The District Attorney filed suit against the airport on behalf of the citizens. An injunction was obtained and the airport was given 14 months to solve the problem. In the meantime, Curtiss Flying Services was in negotiations with the airport about setting up an aviation plant and services.

Early November, 1929, 14 months after the injunction was brought on the airport, the dust was still flying, so the courts shut the airfield down. It was believed that with arbitration, the airport would remain open. Harriet Howell, owner of the land that the airport was leasing, had no desire to fight with her neighbors and their lawsuits. She stated: "They had an injunction to prevent dust, and the only way stop it is not fly." That spelled the end for the airfield and its short five-year history.

The land that the airport sat on is now occupied by James Lick High School and residential homes.

Immediately after the Alum Rock site was shut down, construction started on a replacement airport on King Road near Story Road, complete with oiled runways.

The first planes took off in late November, 1929, just a couple of weeks after the closure of the Alum Rock Avenue San Jose Airport.

Many years later the King Road Airport would be transformed into a Drag strip, with a historic name (see page 69).

Chapter 7

The Infamous Dog Track

New Alviso Speedway
1934 - 1935

During July, 1932, rumors were circulating about a planned dog-racing track in Alviso. In August those rumors came true when permits were issued to the Alviso Greyhound Breeders Association.

The track sat on 30 acres of land co-owned by 90-year-old widow Pauline Young and F. A. Niggerman, (Young later became sole owner) half a mile north of Highway 237 on Taylor Street.

With permits in hand, construction on a 5,000-seat grandstand started immediately. Two months later, with 30 percent completed, construction was halted on the $100,000 project. The owners stated that because of public opinion and the many lawsuits currently against California dog tracks, they wanted to take a wait-and-see approach. More likely, it was because they ran out of money.

January, 1933: Contractors and workers were still waiting to get paid for labor and material from October. Some of the workers went in and removed the electric track, which propelled the rabbit. Things looked hopeless for the track.

Two months later a lawsuit was filed on behalf of the workers. This was followed by a lien being placed on the property.

Things started to look up in April when all legal issues were resolved and all parties paid. Construction resumed in May. In a good public relations move, all unemployed

The New Alviso Speedway had one of the nicest grandstands in San Jose auto racing history. This photo was taken when the track was new. *Courtesy Alviso Library*

59

Auto Races To Be Held Soon At Dog Track

Dominic Distarce, president of the Midget Racing Car Association, announced today that contracts had been closed with the San Jose Recreaton Association which will insure midget car races here late this month.

Evening News

THRILLS NITE AUTO RACES

WORLDS FASTEST SHORT TRACK RACING CARS

Tonight

Gen. Admission 50¢ Children 25¢

NEW ALVISO SPEEDWAY!

legal residents of Alviso were employed by the track. This was at the time of the Great Depression.

Dog racing began in June, but it was short lived. During a July meet, Dog #1 won a race by two lengths. The victory was handed to Dog #4 who finished sixth, eight lengths behind. When the officials wouldn't change the outcome, a riot broke out. The sheriffs arrived and broke up the fight. They also confiscated all the proceeds, so nobody got paid.

The next day, the Alviso Kennel Club shut its doors indefinitely.

To add to the track's problem's, workers and track crew still had not been paid for work completed. Material to finish construction also hadn't been paid for. Another lawsuit was filed. When the president, vice-president and secretary of the track did not show for court, a warrant was issued for their arrest. A day later, they were all in jail. Meanwhile, another lien was put on the track.

With lawsuits still swirling around, the track resumed racing in September. But then it was raided and shut down again for some type of illegal gambling. Racing resumed, but then in October, a huge storm blew half the roof off

Leo Faulkner from Beverly Hills won five main events at New Alviso Speedway during 1934, including the first. He is at the wheel of his Saxon, which would later be painted in Gilmore Special colors. This photo was taken at Letcher's Garage at First and St. James Streets in downtown San Jose. *Dennis Mattish Collection*

6500 Watch
Midget Cars
Open Season

NEWS SPORTS

SAN JOSE EVENING

THE EVENING NEWS, SAN JOSE, CALIFORNIA, SATURDAY, APRIL 28, 1934

STAFF WRITERS

"BUDDY" LEITCH, Sports Editor
CONTRIBUTORS

LEN KULLMANN   ELITA HUGGINS
RUSS NEWLAND   FRANK LOWREY
ALLAN J. GOULD   COACH DUD DE GROOT   HENRY McLEMORE

Midget Car Opener Big Success; Weekly Races Planned for Alviso

the stands. Right after the roof blew off, foreclosure of liens was asked on the track.

By December, there were eight different lawsuits involving 149 people brought against the racetrack.

1934

In January of 1934, a new group of people, called the San Jose Recreation Association, was brought in to manage the beleaguered track. There were still problems, so dog racing was stopped permanently. All together, there were a total of 20 dog racing programs run in the history of the track.

In April, the new management team got together with Dominic Distarce, President of the Midget Auto Racing Association (MARA). Contracts were drawn up and signed and a race scheduled.

The dog track, which was one-quarter-mile long, was reconstructed. A slight bank was added, and new lights were moved to the outside of the track.

The track was now called "New Alviso Speedway."

The April 27 opener was the first race ever run under the lights in the San Jose area. (Alviso was annexed into San Jose years later.) The Midget races were part of the Pacific Coast Championship Series, similar to the Big Car Series racing over at the 5/8-mile San Jose Speedway. Noted race drivers and celebrities were in attendance; the biggest was child film star Jackie Coogan who presented the trophy. The starters were Rex Mays and "Babe" Stapp.

The day after the race, The *Mercury Herald* read "With 6500 cheering fans urging them on, 22 midget cars made their successful debut at the New Alviso Speedway last night in a series of thrilling races in which Leo Faulkner carried off the Hun's portion of the honors by winning a well-driven 35-lap main event." The largest crowd in the history of the dog track went home satisfied. Because of the suc-

Bill Betteridge (center) makes an appearance at an athletic field promoting Midget racing. The popular Southern California driver won five main events during 1934 at Alviso, most of them in this beauty. *Courtesy of the Collier Collection*

Harry Alley turned the fastest lap during warm-ups for the track's inaugural event. He was then involved in a crash. Harry was a regular during the two years of auto racing at the track. *Jim Montgomery Collection*

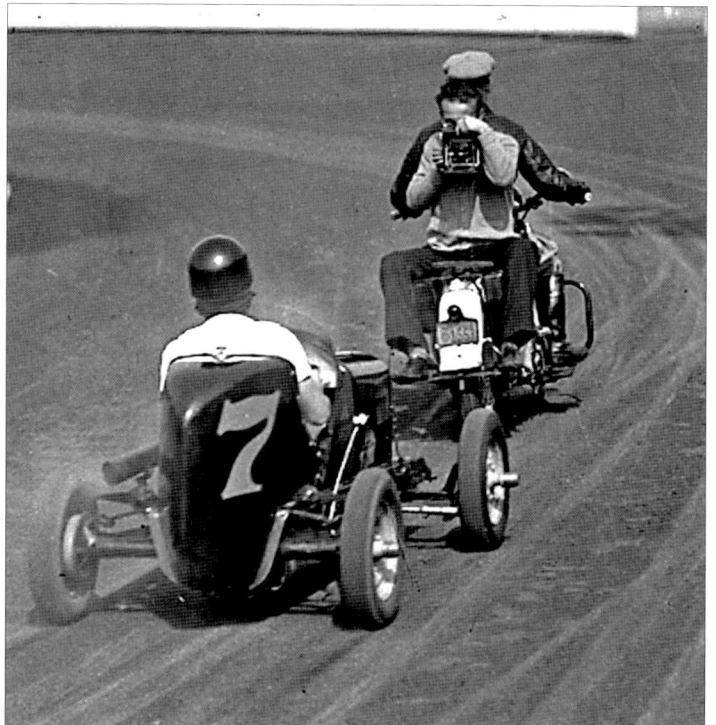

Bill Betteridge showcases his fine-looking Outboard-Powered Midget for the cameraman. *Courtesy of the Collier Collection*

cess of this event, races were run on a weekly basis.

There were 13 weekly races run during 1934.

Southern California drivers completely dominated the contest, winning every race during the season. Bill Betteridge and Leo Faulkner were the class of the field, winning five main events each.

Car counts averaged about 12 per show but started dwindling by July.

Meanwhile, AAA was threatening to suspend any drivers from their organization who raced Midgets at Alviso or anywhere else.

Because of the races at Gilmore Stadium in Los Angeles, and the refusal on the part of several big name drivers to make the trip North, promoter Truman Letcher cancelled the August 3 race and the rest of the season.

Because there were over a dozen cars under construction in the Bay area, plans were already in the works for 1935.

After the Midget season was cut short, the American Motorcycle Association (AMA) signed a contract to run Flat-Track Speedway Motorcycle races for the rest of the year at the track. The slight banking was removed from the track. The opening event packed the stands and the rest of their season was successful.

1935

On July 26 the Mighty Midgets were back for the grand reopening of the New Alviso Speedway. Local garage owner Truman Letcher was the manager of the series. Unlike 1934, just about all of the drivers were from Northern California this year.

The Letcher Garage three-car team poses behind the grandstands. Jack Davis (75) Louie Foy (53) and Freddie Agabashian (74) sit smartly dressed in the beautifully built cars. Owner Truman Letcher was a legend in early San Jose auto racing history.
Dennis Mattish Collection

HEAVY TRAFFIC AS MIDGETS BEND AROUND BEND

The midget cars roar again tonight at Alviso and traffic jams, such as pictured here, will come thick and fast. Snapped here in an afternoon exhibition workout are Lynn Deister, Russ Hays and Les Dreisbach.

Taken from the sports page of the *San Jose Evening News* before the final race at New Alviso Speedway. Although this was an exhibition run, it still seemed odd that Lynn Deister was not wearing any kind of headgear.

Les Dreisbach, from Oakland, negotiated the long straights and short turns better than his competitors in winning the opening main event witnessed by a near-capacity crowd.

Dreisbach proceeded to win the first four races in convincing style. In fact, he won all races entered except for one heat race.

Before the August 23 race, the track was reduced from a quarter-mile to one-fifth of a mile and the turns widened to 70 feet. The reason was to accommodate the gear ratios on the little cars and provide more action and passing in the turns for the fans. With Les Dreisbach having motor problems all night, he was unable to up his wins to five in a row.

"Skeets" Jones, "Dutch" Van Tassell, Al Stein and Dave Oliver had a four-way battle for the lead of the main event. They would finish in that order.

Despite the large crowds the track was getting, about 4,000 per event, only 11 cars showed up for the last race. Promoter Truman Letcher announced that rather than disappoint racing fans in the future, he would close the track. Just like that, it was over for what was really an excellent facility.

These were the only two years in the history of the track that there were no raids, shutdowns or problems.

Pauline Young, the 92-year-old owner of the land that the speedway (dog track) occupied, was stuck paying all claims against it from contractors, workers and for the material used to build the track. Young, who in the begin-

Popular San Jose driver Louie Foy sits in the Letcher Saxon in St. James Park, across the street from Letcher's Garage. Although Foy never won a main event at Alviso, he finished second in the inaugural race and was consistently running up front. *Dennis Mattish Collection*

Carl Rosenthal in the Aarup Special at Letcher's Garage during 1934. *Jim Montgomery Collection*

ning was sweet-talked with visions of grandeur about dog racing, didn't have the money to pay. A lien was placed on the track and it was sold at auction by the sheriff's department. Young lost everything in the ill-fated adventure.

1936-1939

A group of Chinese became the new owners in 1936. They invested $10,000 in fixing up the space under the grandstands as an elaborate gambling room. Over the next couple of years there were numerous raids carried out by the sheriff's department on the casino. In early 1939 the final raid took place, and the gambling room was shut down.

O.L. Anderson, a contractor, purchased the track. Demolition was done in June, 1939, and the company was able to salvage 500,000 board feet of usable lumber.

The biggest losers that June were the 10,000 swallows who lived in the roof of the stands and the two-dozen goats that lived at the notorious track.

George Mayne Elementary School now occupies the land.

One Lap Track Record	
1934	**Quarter-mile**
Leo Faulkner	20.40
Bill Bettridge	20.10
Bill Bettridge	19.30
Bill Bettridge	19.01
Al Sherman	18.80
1935	**Fifth-mile**
"Skeet's" Jones	18.40

*See appendix for complete list of winners.

Razing of Notorious Dog Track Is Begun

Workmen began razing Alviso's notorious greyhound racetrack this morning after the site was purchased from its Chinese owners by a San Jose wrecking contractor. The entrance to the gambling room run by the Chinese in the past may be seen to the left of the truck.—Lomar photo.

San Jose evening News

Chapter 8

Asahi Baseball Park

San Jose Motordrome
1941

During the 1890s, the first generation of Japanese, known has the Issei, began immigrating to the United States.

The Issei loved baseball and would establish a Japanese baseball team in San Jose called the "Asahi" (meaning "morning sun") in 1913. The team disbanded in 1917 but was reestablished a couple of years later.

As baseball grew in popularity in America and the Japanese leagues, it soon became apparent the Asahi team needed a new ballpark. In 1925, the Japanese community bought some land at Seventh and Younger, just north of Hedding Street. The purpose was to build a full size ball park, with covered grandstands, restrooms and concessions.

Construction was completed in eight months, and opening day was July 4, 1926. A capacity crowd packed the grandstands and witnessed an aerial show before the Asahi lost to the Stockton Yamatos. There would be many championships won and many memorable moments at the stadium over the next decade and a half.

Because of the expense of maintenance and the availability of other fields, Asahi Field started to deteriorate around 1939. By 1941, the field was overrun with weeds and the bathrooms were bad. There would be no more baseball games played there.

In order to make a little money, the owners of the land decided to rent the property out. The ballpark was converted to a 1/5-mile flat dirt track and renamed the San Jose Motordrome.

Before the track was carved out, there was an auto thrill show put on by Ace Lillard called the "Circus of Death." Fifteen hundred spectators packed the grandstands only to be disappointed when half the stunts were cancelled because the tall grass (lack of traction for stopping the cars) made for unsafe conditions for the spectators. During the feature attraction, Ace Lillard's wife, Babe, suf-

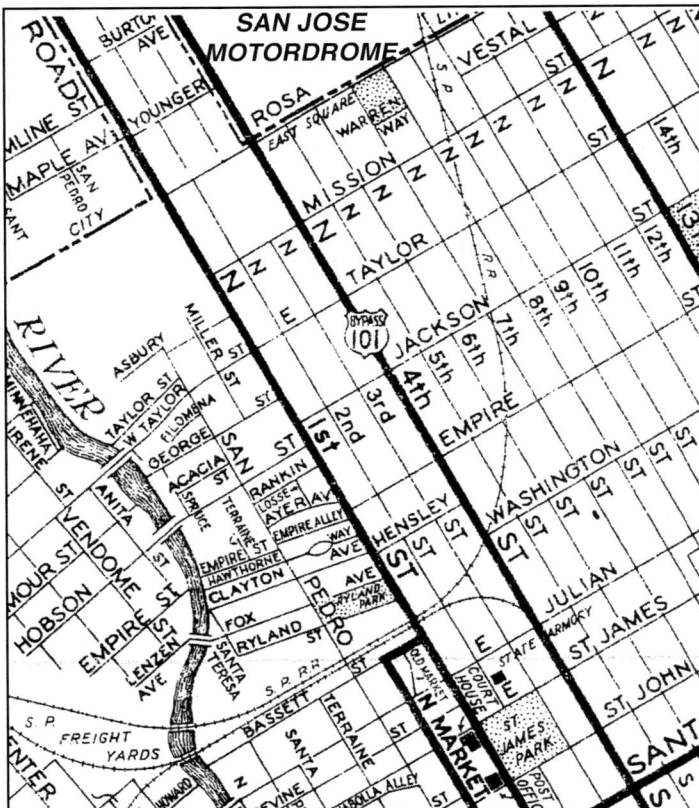

1936 map showing the location of Asahi Park at the corner of Rosa and 4th Street. That location was at the boundary of the city limits and this map.

fered burns to the hands and face when she drove her car into the flaming wall.

September 28, 1941, saw the Mighty Midgets performing for the first time in San Jose since they were in action at Alviso six years earlier. A good field of 20 cars and drivers was entered in the non-sanctioned event, many of whom had seen action at the high-banked San Jose Speedway driving Big Cars and Roadsters. Ted Ayers, leading contender for the championship, had his Midget on display in the lobby of the California Theater on First Street during the week leading up to the race. Gene Figone won the 25-lap main event in front of 1,000 fans. Jimmy Joy, Ayres and Tony Dutra followed him across the line.

Certain that San Jose auto race fans would support Midget events, BCRA business manager Floyd Busby scheduled another event for October 19.

Points leader Ted Ayers and San Jose ace Tony Dutra were the favorites heading into the program. Buck Whitmer, who had been racing nationally, returned home to San Jose to lead a large contingent of cars to victory in the 25-lap main event. Ayers suffered minor injuries when he flipped in a preliminary event. A large crowd braved a cold north wind to see the event. Another show was in the planning stages for the future.

The world of auto racing changed forever on December 7, 1941. Early in 1942, the United States Government ordered all auto racing to cease for the duration of the war. The lives of Santa Clara Valley's Japanese Americans changed dramatically as well, as they suddenly found themselves caught between two worlds at war. The local Japanese had only a short time to make provisions for the care or sale of their property before their forced departure

Midget race fans pack the ballpark grandstands on September 28, 1941. The newly carved out 1/5-mile track is visible. *Dennis Mattish Collection*

The Mighty Midgets get ready to push off for their event on the very flat track. *Dennis Mattish Collection*

Ed Normi poses in his immaculate-looking Midget.
Dennis Mattish Collection

Gene Figone drove the George Bignotti-owned V8 to victory on September 28, 1941. *Dennis Mattish Collection*

Gene Figone (54) takes the outside to get by Ed Normi (16) on his way to victory in the main event. *Dennis Mattish Collection*

Buck Whitmer (15) struggles with his Midget while battling for position. *Don Radbruch Collection*

Jimmy Joy drove to a second place in the inaugural event at San Jose Motordrome. *Dennis Mattish Collection*

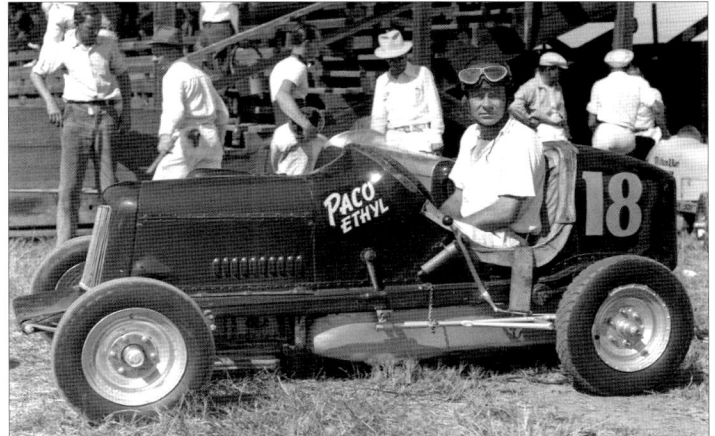

Jimmy Robertson gets ready to take to the track during the September race. *Jim Montgomery Collection*

San Joseans came to a full realization that their country is at war as troops were rushed here from army posts, carrying full war equipment. Some of the troops are shown above marching into the old Japanese ball diamond north of the city, where they will be under canvas temporarily, at least. — Lomar Engraving Service photo.

On December 9, 1941, two days after Japan's bombing of Pearl Harbor, American troops set up camp inside the Japanese ballpark. In this photo from the front page of the *San Jose News*, soldiers can be seen standing on the recently used track.

from the valley. The Japanese owners of Asahi Field, home of the San Jose Motordrome, made hasty provisions for the sale of the property before being evacuated to internment camps in March of 1942. After two Midget races and a thrill show, the short life of the Motordrome had come to an end. It would be five long years before San Jose would witness another auto race.

The property became slated for development and some years later, houses stood where the crowds had once gathered.

Program
SAN JOSE MOTORDROME

NORTH 4th ST. NEAR BAYSHORE
SUNDAY AFTERNOON

Distributed free of charge by A. P. Busby and

State Finance Company

TRACK OFFICIALS

Floyd Busby	Manager and director
Allan P. Busby	Pit Manager
Joe Piva	Starter
Manuel Piva	Assitant starter
Bert Whitaker	Chief steward
George Haney	Scorer
Jack Carmody	Announcer
Jimmy Joy } Tony Dutro}	Car owners and Drivers Representatives

Tom Motter Collection

68

Chapter 9

King Road Airport

Little Bonneville Drag Strip
1954 - 1958

When airmail service was halted at San Jose Airport on Alum Rock Avenue (see Chapter 6), the West American Aviation Corporation rushed in and constructed a new airport on a former dairy farm on the southeast corner of Story and King Roads. It took just a matter of weeks to

DRAG RACES
SAN JOSE AIRPORT, KING ROAD
TOMORROW, Sunday (AND EVERY SUNDAY)
TIME TRIALS 9 A.M. ELIMINATIONS AT 1 P.M.
19 DIFFERENT CLASSIFICATIONS
HUGE TROPHIES TO BE AWARDED
GENERAL ADMISSION $1.00
SANTA CLARA COUNTY TIMING ASSOCIATION

The first race was held in April, 1954. *Mercury News*

build the $250,000 airport. San Jose was one of 130 cities nationwide offering airmail service, and the first delivery at the new airport was made on November 19, 1929. In short order, a hangar, runway lights, offices, classrooms and a restaurant were added. For the next 10 years, the airport was a center for activity with many airlines using it, including Pacific Air Transport, a forerunner of United Airlines. Although it was a municipal airport, there was no financial support from the city. The citizens of San Jose voted down two bond issues. Stating they had no choice, the airport went private and started charging for its use.

One of its customers was the U.S. Army. With World War II just a couple of years away, the military was getting ready by performing war games on the 120-acre site.

In 1937, groundbreaking for Reid Hillview Airport took place just a mile away from the King Road Airport.

Three years later in 1940, the citizens of San Jose passed a bond measure to build a new municipal airport by Cole-

1948 aerial photo of San Jose Airport on King Road. This was San Jose's second major airport. In 1954, the runway was converted to a drag strip on Sunday afternoons. Drag racing lasted at the facilitiy until November, 1958.
The Fairchild Aerial Photography Collection at Whittier College C-1456-82

man Avenue. The King Road site was being used less. By the end of the decade, the owners decided to lease the airport to San Jose State College.

When war broke out, the U.S. Army Air Force took control of the airport and used it for defense. Barracks and training facilities were built. The Civil Air Patrol also used it as a base for patrolling coastal waters for enemy submarines. When the war ended, the Army abandoned the airport and a new group (Pacific Airmotive Corporation) took control and renamed it Pacific Airmotive Airport. That name did not stick, but the Herman Barnick-led group would own the airport till the end.

1954

The young sport of drag racing was gaining in popularity when promoter Brent Anderson approached the Barnick-led group about using the airport as a drag strip on Sundays. Deals were made and races scheduled, the first being in April. Over 2,000 people turned out that spring afternoon to watch Eugene LeBlanc, driving the Red Jones Special, win the event with an unofficial speed of

134 mph. (Author's note: Because these speeds were much higher than the track would see in the next two years, it is believed either the distance of the track or the timing was off on this day.) It was decided to pave the runway after the first race, resulting in just a handful of races for the year.

1955

The new year brought a new name to the airstrip, "Little Bonneville Drag Strip." Racing was held on a bi-weekly schedule under the watchful eye of the Santa Clara Timing Association.

Fifteen hundred drag fans turned out to watch 180 machines perform at the March opener. Ed Lamano clocked in at 104 mph to claim top speed. Local garage man Les Joseph picked up the next win before the track was shut down for repairs. The track also closed for three weeks in August to allow the racers to make the trip to the Bonneville Salt Flats in Utah to participate in the land speed records. When racing resumed at the end of August, 185 cars raced in over 700 timed runs in one day.

Flagman in action with different types of Drag Cars (or Hot Rods as they were also known) at Little Bonneville Drag Strip. *Al Soto Collection*

The first San Jose Championship Drag Meet was held on October 9. Over 400 cars from all over the West took part in the huge event. An appreciative crowd of 2,500 witnessed non-stop Drag racing from 8 a.m. till dark.

Because the track had been accident-free since its start, the National Hot Rod Association granted Little Bonneville an extension to race until weather conditions prevented safe operation. A very successful year continued until late November.

1956

The drag strip was awarded the sanction approval of the California Highway Patrol, Santa Clara County Sheriffs and the San Jose Police Department. It was well known that the drag strip gave the street racers a place to race safely.

The season kicked off on April 15 with Hank Silva setting a new track record with a speed of 123 mph. In September, Louis Soto bumped the record up to 125 mph. Four hundred cars participated in the second annual San Jose Championships on September 23. Delwyn Thorkelson powered his Oldsmobile Dragster to a speed of 120 mph to claim the top eliminator trophy. Over 2,500 were in attendance.

1957

In June, Jay Cheatham became the first driver to win four trophies at one meet in San Jose. No prize money was ever awarded at any of the meets.

It was at this time that Half Moon Bay Drag Strip opened and started alternating weekends with San Jose.

Jack Graham powered his Aston-Martin to a top

DRAG RACING
CHAMPIONSHIPS
Little Bonneville Drag Strip
SUNDAY, JUNE 15

Gates Open 7:A.M.
Time Trials Start 8:00 A.M.
Qualifications until 12:30

SAN JOSE
AIRPORT—
KING ROAD

Jay Cheatham from Sunnyvale took this Cadillac-powered Ford Coupe to Pomona in 1955 and set a national record in the B Altered Class. Shown here in the San Jose pits where he won many races in the car. *Courtesy of John Moore and Nitrogeezers.com*

Al Soto, driving The Soto Bros. Hot Rod, smokes the tires during a meet in 1955. *Al Soto Collection*

71

Dragsters at San Jose in 1955. *Al Soto Collection*

speed of 107 mph to win a Sports Car-only drag racing meet during the summer.

Cheatham dominated the last two months of the season, including the third annual San Jose Championship where he blasted the track record. The track enjoyed a banner year in both car counts and attendance.

1958

This marked year five for the track. The pit area was enlarged and other improvements were made before the May 4 opener. There were now 40 classes of cars consisting of Fuel, Gas and Blowers. Jay Cheatham broke his track record with a speed of 137 mph. More than two thousand fans saw 17 class records broken during the inaugural race. A month later, Elmer Snyder challenged Cheatham's record with a speed of 136 mph.

In July a new surface was put on the track. The first meet on it, Cheatham went out and set a track record of 141.5 mph.

At the next meet, Sharon Warner became the first and only woman driver to win a class trophy in drag racing at Little Bonneville Drag Strip.

By the end of the year Cheatham had moved the track record up to 147 mph. Tragically, he would die during a March 1959 drag meet held in Bakersfield, California.

In October, developer A.L. Branden of Branden Enterprises purchased the airport. This doomed the racetrack. His plan was to build 10,000 homes that sold for about $10,000 each. The development was called Tropicana

Future oval track great Burt Foland prior to his Open Gas run during May, 1955. He set top speed for the meet. *Al Soto*

By 1958, Jay Cheatham was setting World records.

Village. He wanted to do it fast, and he wanted the airport vacated as soon as possible. So the next race, which was held on November 2, was the final race in the track's successful five-year history.

The final ceremony was held on January 1, 1959. One final airmail delivery was made with special commemorative covers to mark the event. Planes flew in formation and made one final touchdown.

By May, new houses occupied the land. What was once beautiful farmland would eventually become the most crime-ridden area of San Jose.

Team and club racing were big throughout the five-year history of the track. Trophies were awarded to the clubs with the highest number of competing drivers.

Here are the more notable clubs:

San Jose Igniters

San Jose Rod & Wheelers from Willow Glen
(32 cars @ one meet)

Gear Jammers of Santa Clara
(30 cars @ one meet)

San Jose Guzzlers

San Jose Esquires

Pacers of San Francisco

Road Knights of Morgan Hill

Hayward Rod Benders

Burt Foland and car owner Al Soto with their Top Eliminator trophies. *Al Soto Collection*

In the early years of drag racing, a person waved a checkered flag at the end of the quarter-mile. *Al Soto Collection*

November 2, 1958, was the final drag meet to be held at Little Bonneville. *Mercury News*

73

Little Bonneville Track Speed Records

1954	MPH
Les Joseph	115

1955	
Johnny Perata	116.23

1956	
Hank Silva	123
Louis Soto	125

1957	
Jay Cheatham	134.12

1958	
Jay Cheatham	137
Jay Cheatham	139.5
Jay Cheatham	141.5
Jay Cheatham	147

Chapter 10

WAR

Alviso Speedway
1955 - 1965

Aerial photo taken in 1958 showing the track in the marshland.
Dennis Mattish Collection

The history of the second Alviso Speedway (no relation to the dog track) starts with the Western Auto Racing Association, or WAR, as it was known.

During the early 1950s, television was just beginning to become popular and people were staying home to watch it on weekends. The results were dwindling crowds at the local speedways. San Jose Speedway was no exception.

In early 1954 NASCAR came West under the guidance of promoter Bob Barkhimer. Some of the drivers did not like paying dues to (or being told what to do by) an organization that was 2,500 miles away. Late in the 1954 season, with crowds dwindling, Barkhiemer went to Stockton Speedway to invite the Jalopy drivers to run San Jose as part of a two-division show with the popular Hardtops, hoping to perk up attendance. He did this without consulting the Hardtop drivers. The following week when the Hardtop drivers checked into the pits, they found their favorite pit spaces occupied by Jalopies. Tension grew as the drivers discussed the situation, and then they really got mad when they realized they were going to have to share the purse money with the Jalopies. Popular Hardtop driver Ray Raineri, who became the spokesman for the drivers, stormed into Barkhimer's office and told him: "If the Jalopies run, the Hardtops won't." Barky then shot back with a threat of any driver who walked out would be suspended by NASCAR. Many drivers pulled out, and they were suspended. This cost Raineri the San Jose track title and Dean Holden the Belmont championship. Many drivers were irate.

Meetings were held by the disgruntled drivers at Siemens Garage in San Jose and WAR was founded. Bill Tester was elected the first president. As word spread of the split, drivers in the Central Valley at Stockton Speedway joined the action.

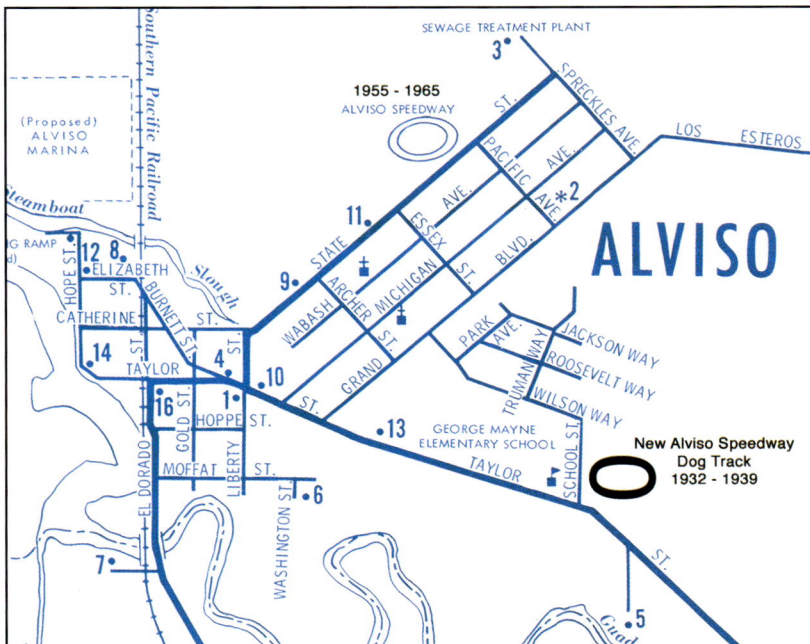

1950s Alviso map shows the locations of the two Alviso tracks.

Johnny Smith won the first main event held at Alviso in 1955. *Dennis Arnold Photo*

WAR began its series at tracks in Salinas, Santa Rosa, Stockton and Madera. Just Like NASCAR, it had track champions and a state champion.

The season began with Salinas as WAR's home track. As the season wore on, the crowds became smaller to the point only a few hundred people were in the stands. Oddly, the stands burned to the ground in November. Some speculated that it had something to do with the feud, but that was never proven.

WAR was without a home track, so the members decided to build their own speedway in the sleepy little town of Alviso, located at the southern tip of the San Francisco Bay. The quarter-mile dirt oval was located on State Street, out in the marshlands, next to a levy and below sea level. The location was both beneficial and not. The benefit was when the tide came in, you had one of the heaviest (stickiest) tracks around. The downsides were the frequent floods that inundated the track and the costly repairs to fix it.

From July to September, 1955, members of WAR donated their money and spent their evenings and weekends building the track. Originally seating was for 1,200

WAR!
GRAND OPENING
ALVISO
SPEEDWAY

HARDTOP AUTO RACING

Free Admission

SUNDAY, SEPT. 4, 2 p.m.

See all your old favorite drivers in action again Ray Raineri, Bob Barg, Earl Smith, Johnny Smith, Al Johnson, Larry Luongo, etc.

See and Hear Big Jim DeNoon's Western Band . . .

1955 Alviso Speedway program featuring Bill Tester's Ford Flathead on the cover. Tester was the President of Western Auto Racing from 1955 to 1957. *Jim Montgomery Collection*

people and parking for 3,000 cars.

The opening event on September 4 was a shake-down event and free to the public. Over 3,500 people turned out to watch the exhibition, which was won by Johnny Smith.

After the success of the first event, seating was expanded to 3,000 for the second race, when Rod Zanoline emerged victorious in front of 1,500 people. Others picking up wins during the year were Marshall Sargent, George Rogge (on a night when the crash wall was reduced to kindling wood in five places) and Ray Raineri. Going into the last points race, there was a four-way battle for the championship between Don Lloyd, Zanoline, Rogge and Sargent. Rogge won the hotly contested feature, but second-place finisher, Sargent, won the track championship. Sargent was also voted most popular driver for the year. Don Lloyd won the state championship.

The post-race season began with an added attraction, called a grudge race. Bill Hallet and Dave Rogers battled in an anything-goes race with winner take all of $400 put up by the feuding car owners. Rogers won the slam-bang affair.

During the season-ending main event, Marshall Sargent executed a double flip before landing on top of Dick Green's car, which then launched Marshall over the wall and into the pits where he landed on top of a Hardtop. He was okay, but Green was injured.

The track averaged 1,500 spectators during the short season.

1956

Two thousand fans watched 51 Hardtops perform in the season opener on March 25. Ernie Safley of Salinas walked off with the main event win. Earl Smith won the Best-Looking Hardtop award. Two weeks later, Earl destroyed the car when he took out 150 feet of crash wall and flipped three times.

Twelve hundred were in attendance on Easter Sunday to witness Jim Lawson win.

The racing then switched from Sunday afternoons to Friday night, but sparse crowds turned out to see Rogge and Dean Holden win on successive Fridays.

Because of flood damage and the pothole-filled, unpaved roads leading to the track, attendance was down. Trying to entice people to come out to the track,

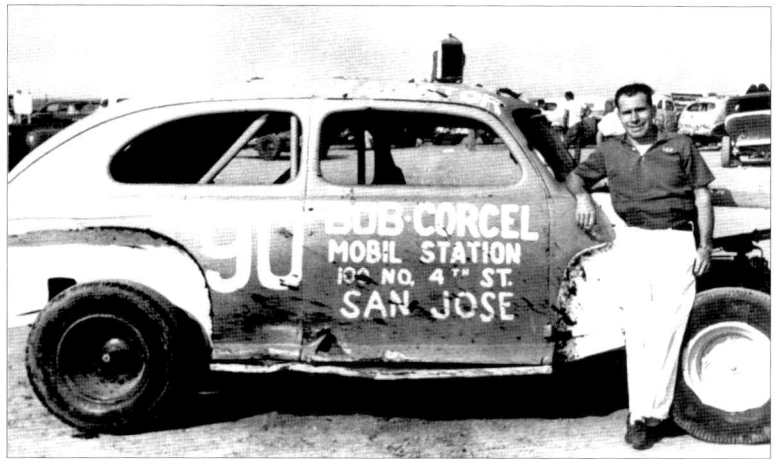

George Rogge of Palo Alto (shown in 1956) was one of the star drivers at Alviso during 1955 – 1958, winning 12 main events and the 1956 track championship. *Dennis Mattish Collection*

Rod Zanoline won seven main events during the 1955 season. *Dennis Arnold Photo*

Wild Hardtop main event action in turn four during one of the 1956 day shows. *Jim Montgomery Photo*

Champions LEFT to RIGHT   **WESTERN AUTO RACING CHAMPIONS**

- George Rogge   - "Boots" Cantrell   - Don Loyd   - Dave Rogers   - Bill Hayley   - Tony Amaral   - Harry Siemens
- Jim Lawson   - Marshall Sargeant   - Ernie Safley   - Don Herd   - Dick Siemens   - Don Perez   - Paul Orr

The top drivers during 1956 at the Western Auto Racing Banquet. *Jim Montgomery Collection*

the next race was free to the public. Holden won that race, but since the first two races, attendance figures were not released for the rest of the year.

Marge Freitas was the first woman to flip in a Powder Puff Derby, a race for women, usually driving their husband's cars.

Escalating the feud with NASCAR and San Jose Speedway, WAR president Bill Tester announced that Alviso Speedway would switch to Saturday night racing, the same night San Jose (a few miles down the road) was running. A week later, Tester offered a challenge to Bob Barkhimer, a match race between Raineri and San Jose's best driver, one race at each track. Barkhimer's response was the race would have to take place at San Jose, under NASCAR rules. Tester declined. The following day, WAR ran an ad in the *San Jose Mercury news* blasting Barkhimer.

In late July, Raineri won his fourth main event in six races, spinning Rogge out of the lead in the process. This set up a grudge race between the two the following week. This excited the throngs, and a standing-room-only crowd showed up to watch. Raineri won the grudge but Rogge won the main that night. The following week was the first Johnny Key Benefit 100-lap race, in honor of the driver who died in a Midget accident in 1954. The proceeds were donated to Johnny's widow and two children, who were there to present the trophy to race winner Raineri. Key's brother, Owen, was a WAR official.

The California Racing Association (CRA) paid a visit to the Speedway in August. Jim Hurtubise led the first 20 laps of the Sprint Car race before being overtaken by Art Bisch. Five laps later, Roger McClusky took command and

went on to win the exciting 30-lap race. Hurtubise and McClusky would go on to fame in the Indy Car Roadsters. Wayne Wieler set fast time at 15.32, not much faster than the Hardtop track record.

George Rogge captured both the Alviso and the state championships on the final night of the points season.

During one of the post-season races, Frank Luongo took out 40 feet of crash wall, flipped and burst into flames. Fellow driver Paul Orr pulled the dazed driver out of the inferno. Frank was stunned but okay.

1957

For the first time in recent memory, the area where the track was situated was not under water at the end of the year. The mild winter brought an unusually early opening-day race, called the Icebreaker, held on New Year's Day. Stockton-Lodi champion Buck Wenzel won the event and took the early-season points lead. He also won the traditional March 25 opener. Norm Garland and Billy Everett won the other two Sunday afternoon races before switching to Saturday nights in April. That plan fell through when all the April races were rained and flooded out. Once racing resumed in May, over 350 feet of crash wall was destroyed in short order, along with a few Hardtops.

Because of disagreements and the infighting on the board of directors of the Western Racing Association, President Bill Tester resigned.

A 100-mile WAR race was scheduled for the one mile Santa Clara County Fairgrounds oval. The deal fell through days before the scheduled June 23 event, so a 200-lap race was run at Alviso. Points leader Wenzel won after a

78

Dean Holden set two qualifying records and won ten main events during 1955-1957. *Dennis Arnold Photo*

Ray Raineri was the most accomplished driver to defect from NASCAR to WAR in 1955. He won eight main events before returning to San Jose Speedway in 1957. *Dennis Arnold Photo*

Stockton's Joe Giusti won eight feature events during the 1955-1957 period. *Dennis Arnold Photo*

race-long duel with George Rogge. A week later, Stan Luhdorff flipped over the wall and somehow kept his Hardtop going. He then drove back out onto the track and continued the race.

During the summer, Dean Holden reeled off four main events in a row, becoming the first person to do so. One of the races he won had a Le Mans-style start. This is common in Europe. The drivers stand at the starting line with their cars on the infield. When the green flag is dropped, they run to their cars, jump in, buckle up, and then take off.

Wenzel, who led the points chase since January 1, was crowned the state and track champion.

WAR and NASCAR signed an agreement to run a two-race series pitting drivers from each group against each other. The first race was held at San Jose Speedway, and NASCAR drivers, taking the top eight positions in the main, dominated it. The winner was Dave Leroy. The following week (November 3) the race was held at Alviso.

Red Millican, a NASCAR driver from Fresno, won the feature. Leroy, who had won the week before, set a new qualifying record. It was now apparent which organization had the fastest cars and drivers.

1958

There was a time when WAR had seven tracks under its sanction. When the 1958 season started, Alviso was the only one left.

Heavy rain and winter floods had deposited several inches of mud on the property. It took until May before the grounds dried out and repairs made, including a new lighting system.

Don Perez won the first race. The following week Bill Hayley slid across the finish line sideways, just inches in front of Paul Orr and Bill Everett, and won the race. Words were exchanged between Hayley and Jack Epperson, so

Alviso Speedway

New Year's Day Classic

Jan. 1st, 1957

★ Full Program of Racing
★ First Points for 1957
★ Champion Drivers
★ Faster Cars, Fastest Track
★ Time trials 12:15 p.m.

WESTERN AUTO RACING INC.

Remember New Year's day! Enjoy the races

The only race to ever take place on New Year's Day in San Jose.

WAR
Versus
NASCAR
The auto race YOU have asked for

WAR and NASCAR will run the second of their match races this weekend, pitting members of each group plus open competition to other groups. NASCAR had their day last Sunday—now WAR drivers will meet all comers this Sunday, Nov. 3, on their home track.

The program will consist of FOUR MAIN EVENTS, plus a trophy dash and a consolation event. Come and see the WAR drivers on their home track.

THRILLS — CHILLS — & SPILLS

Admission: Adults $1.75   Kids under 12 50¢

ALVISO SPEEDWAY

NOV. 3 — 1:45 P.M. (Rain Date: Following Sunday)

The feuding associations got together for two races in 1957. *Mercury News*

"Big Chief" Norm Garland with one of seven main-event trophy's he won in 1959 on his way to winning the track championship. Garland, a full-blooded Native American , won a total of 28 main events at Alviso during the eight years he raced there. *James D. Geiger Photo*

a grudge race was set up between the feuding drivers to take place at the next meet. Epperson won the coin toss and got the important inside position(it's easier to stuff your opponent into the wall from the inside) and won the race.

In the next race, Don Klock hit the crash wall hard, sending lumber flying everywhere. He then bounced back out onto the track where he was t-boned. His leg was fractured , which was one of the few injuries suffered at the track.

Trying to draw more spectators, the adult admission price was reduced to 50 cents for the next race. Racing on the same night as San Jose Speedway was taking it toll.

The hottest driver in the second half of the season was Paul Orr, who won five main events in a six-week period, including the 75-lap Johnny Key race. It wasn't enough to catch points leader Ernie Safley, who won the track championship by two points over Don Lloyd. Only 16 points separated the top four drivers in the closest point finish in Alviso history.

1959
Once again, the annual flooding in Alviso caused the track to get off to a late start, this time on June 13. "Big Chief" Norm Garland won that day and then proceeded to be the hottest driver of the year, winning four main events in a row at one point.

In September, the floodgates near the speedway broke, flooding the track and parking lot. Two more races were lost while the place dried out. The first race back was the Johnny Key race, which Garland won. He would win a total of seven main events on his way to capturing the track championship. Bob Basye finished second in points. Away from the track, Paul Orr was seriously injured in a highway accident, thus eliminating him from the points chase.

Don Calopy (20) and Jerry Epperson (30) mix it up during the 1959 season. *James Geiger Photo*

80

Mattish Automotive Service (my father's company) had a stable of three Hardtops during 1959. Sonny Calopy (left) drove this attractive looking car. *James D. Geiger Photo*

Whitey White (7-11) won the Best-Looking-Car contest in 1959 in this candy apple red beauty. Whitey not only had the best-looking cars, but he also won four main events at Alviso. This was one of the cars in the Mattish Automotive stable. (Author's note: I still have fond memories of cleaning the mud off this car the day after the races!) *James D. Geiger Photo*

Paul Orr (center), shown in 1960, won more main events (49) than any other driver in Alviso Speedway history. *Dennis Mattish Collection*

Long before John Viel was winning Super Modified championships, he was winning NASCAR $99 Claiming Races at Alviso.
Bob Mize photo courtesy of Don Mize.

1960

Now called Modified Hardtops, the limitations of past years were thrown out and unlimited engine sizes were permitted on all flathead engines.

Paul Orr was the top performer for the year, winning four main events in a row, seven altogether. It would have been eight if not for bad luck. He was leading the main with just a couple of laps to go when a loose wheel rolled in front of his car. The wheel launched him into a series of flips, cracking two ribs and injuring his shoulder. Despite Orr's domination, Don Lloyd won the championship on consistency. Although he won only one main event, he had 18 top-five finishes.

1961

Stan Luhdorff picked up the first win of his career on opening day, which helped him finish second in the final standings. Boots Cantrell picked up three wins on his way to winning the track championship. Don Lloyd won five main events but finished fourth in the final points.

1962

This year, the annual flood in the marshlands did not dry out until late May. Don Lloyd won the June 3 opener.

The mid-June headline in the *Mercury* sports section read "Racing Associations end long dispute." The first paragraph read, "Peace has settled over Santa Clara Valley's auto racing world. After seven years of disagreement, the National Association of Stock Car Auto Racing and the Western Auto Racing have reached an armistice under which they will work together at the Alviso Speedway." The agreement was for races to be held on Friday nights. Also the NASCAR $99 Claiming Stock Cars which had been running at the San Jose Speedway on Sunday afternoons would shift operations to Alviso on Friday evenings. The Modified Hardtops

Don Lloyd (50) made it through this incident on his way to winning the 1960 track championship. Lloyd also won the 1964 championship and a total of 29 main events at the Bayside track. *James D. Geiger Photo*

82

would still run under WAR sanction and the Claimers under NASCAR. Any Modifieds racing at SJ who were not in the top 25 could run at Alviso without penalty. Starting with the first race, press coverage for the track doubled, with the Claimers getting equal print. With the addition of the Claimers, 90 cars packed the pits - 35 WAR Hardtops and 55 NASCAR Claimers.

Ron McMillan took the early points lead in the Claimers when he won the first two main events. But it was Jim Clennan who came on strong with seven feature wins on his way to claiming the track title. Future Super Modified stars Ed Hopper and John Viel each picked up a main event win in the Claimers.

On Labor Day over 1,800 people turned out to witness the first Midget race on the quarter-mile dirt track. Bob DeJong shattered the track record in qualifying and Mike McGreevy won the BCRA main event. The Midgets were invited back for an October 5 appearance, and Charlie Lawler won that race.

Paul Orr won eight main events but still could not win the Modified track championship, that honor falling to Jack Epperson. With NASCAR and WAR ending their feud, the Johnny Key Memorial race would run solely at San Jose Speedway from this year forward, thus ending the six-year

run at Alviso.

Damage caused by heavy rain and flooding shut the track down in mid-October.

1963

With Flood and storm damage repaired, the season kicked off on June 7. The biggest season-opening crowd in several years watched Paul Orr beat Jack Epperson to the checkered flag in the Modifieds. Orr won the first six main events, a record. Epperson, who finished second in all but one of those races, won the seventh race. He then

Alviso Speedway was one of the local lumberyard's best customers. Incidents like this [Al Toland (444) is crashing] sent lumber flying on numerous occasions at the track. Boots Cantrell (2) was one of Alviso's top drivers with 19 main event wins in eight years. *Dennis Mattish Collection*

went on a hot streak, winning eight main events by September. Going into the final race of the year, only a few points separated Orr and Epperson. There was much anticipation leading up to that race when the skies opened and flooded the track. Epperson was crowned champion.

The Claiming Cars, now called NASCAR Limited Sportsman, also went down to the wire with Butch Bishop winning the title by one point over Joe Roletto.

1964

In the past there had been a number of melees among the drivers and crews, so extra security was added during the year.

One of the most thrilling point battles took place in the Modifieds this season. Paul Orr had a fast start, picking up most of his seven main event wins in the first half of the

season. He carried his point lead into late August when Don Lloyd took command after winning six main events in a short period. Lloyd just barely held on to win the championship when Jack Epperson scored four of his five wins in the last month. During one of the Modified races, Dick Langsdale was badly shaken when his car hit the crash wall and flipped end-over-end into the pits, missing cars, equipment and fleeing pitmen before he hit the manager's booth. Not to be outdone, Joe Esperanca escaped injury when his Sportsman flipped six times.

Although Lyle Lister won half (11) of the Sportsman main events, mechanical misfortune throughout the season would cost him the title. Tom Duensing won the championship with four wins and a lot of top-five finishes. Ron Yetter won the final Sportsman race ever run at Alviso.

Since the Sportsmans joined the card at Alviso, the track had been enjoying some of its most successful years.

Dick Slate (right) made a run at the 1964 NASCAR Claimer title, but fell short. *Dick Slate Collection*

Scene of carnage after a 1962 pileup.
Bob Mize photo from the collection of Don Mize.

Don Calopy after one of his four main event wins. Calopy won the final track championship in 1965. *Bob Mize photo.*

Wings started showing up on top of the Modifieds during 1964. Jack Epperson (1A), "the Racing Auctioneer," was one of three drivers to run all 11 years at Alviso. He was one of the most decorated drivers with 23 feature wins and the 1962 & 1963 Alviso Championships. The long career of Ed Hopper's (55) started at Alviso in 1962 driving Claimers. *Bob Mize Photo*

The fourth Epperson to race at Alviso, Don won ten main events, including seven in a two-month period during 1965. *Bob Mize photo courtesy of Don Mize.*

Rare color photo from Alviso Speedway shows Don Epperson (32) and Don Lloyd (1) during a 1965 day race. Keith Douglas is on the outside of Lloyd. *Bob Mize photo from the collection of Don Mize.*

Sparse crowds like this one from the final year were part of the reason the track ceased operation after the 1965 season. *Bob Mize photo from the collection of Don Mize.*

1965

In the off-season, NASCAR announced that it was moving its Sportsman division from Alviso Speedway to Champion Speedway, near Candlestick Park in San Francisco. This move cut the crowds and the back gate in half, a major blow to the track's finances.

Another late-season opener saw Jack Epperson beat Don Calopy to the checkered flag on June 4. Paul Orr won an accident-marred main event that was shortened by four laps due to lack of cooperation on the part of several drivers. On August 6, Bill Bowerman set a new track record with a time of 14.29. This beat the Midget record of 14.41 and would be the final record ever set on the oval. Picking up wins in the closing months of the season were Bob Merrill, Bill Hill, Nick Ringo and Junior Coppla. Don Epperson won seven main events. His brother Jack was injured when his throttle got stuck, sending him full speed into the crash wall. The points chase turned into a two-man battle between Don Lloyd and Don Calopy with just two shows to go. Calopy won the first race and then finished third in the final show, to seal the championship. Don Epperson won the final race, with his brother Jack finishing second.

By the time the awards banquet rolled around that winter, the racetrack was already under several feet of water. Members of the Western Auto Racing Association were getting tired of performing the costly repairs every spring. (Moral of the story: don't build a race track in a marsh.) Combining that with the meager crowds the track

Nick Ringo was one of the hottest drivers during the 1965 season. At one point, Nick won three main events in a row. In a few years he would win the NASCAR State Championship. *Bob Mize photo from the collection of Don Mize.*

was getting after the NASCAR Sportsman left and the fact that they were losing money, it all spelled doom.

At the banquet, it was announced that Alviso Speedway and the Western Auto Racing Association were through.

Nowadays the land sits next to a wildlife refuge, the streets in Alviso have been paved and flood control is much better.

Alviso Speedway Champions
Hardtop/Modified
1955 – 1965

1955	Marshall Sargent
1956	George Rogge
1957	Buck Wenzel
1958	Ernie Safley
1959	Norm Garland
1960	Don Lloyd
1961	Boots Cantrell
1962	Jack Epperson
1963	Jack Epperson
1964	Don Lloyd
1965	Don Calopy

Claimer/Sportsman
1962 - 1964

1962	Jim Clennan
1963	Butch Bishop
1964	Tom Duensing

Alviso Speedway
One-Lap Track Records
1955-1965

1955	**Time**
Hardtop	
Bobby Barge	16.38
Bob Strain	16.15
Bob Strain	15.99
1956	
Hardtop	
Dean Holden	15.73
Sprint Car	
Wayne Wieler	15.32
1962	
Hardtop	
Stan Luhdorff	15.61
Paul Orr	15.38
Paul Orr	15.32
Midget	
Bob DeJong	14.41
1963	
Hardtop	
Jack Epperson	15.29
Richard Luhdorff	15.08
Don Epperson	14.94
Jack Epperson	14.75
1964	
Hardtop	
Jack Epperson	14.70
Jack Epperson	14.51
NASCAR Sportsman (Claimer)	
John Viel	20.64
1965	
Hardtop	
Nick Ringo	14.43
Bill Bowerman	14.29

Chapter 11

Tully Road Action Track

San Jose Speedway
1946 - 1977

Within months of the end of World War II, Ross Page and C.H. Mosiman put together a plan to build a racetrack on Tully Road. The location was on the western side of Reid Hillview Airport and across the street from Hillview Golf Course.

1946
Construction started in early 1946 and was completed in April at a cost of $75,000. The track was a flat quarter-mile dirt oval, built specifically for Midget Cars.

A month before the first event, Page and Mosiman signed up the United Racing Association (URA) as its sanction for the track. The URA, which was based in Southern California, had two circuits for Midgets. The red circuit was for cars that had Drake and Ford engines. The blue circuit consisted of Midgets with the more powerful Offenhauser engines. San Jose raced the blue circuit, which also had the best drivers.

San Jose Speedway Stadium, as it was known then, held its first race on May 19, 1946. Problems arose right from

1948 aerial photo showing the half-mile and quarter-mile dirt tracks. *The Fairchild Aerial Photography Collection at Whittier College C-1456-82*

1947

the start when 5,500 auto racing fans converged on the speedway at about the same time. With only one narrow entrance to get into the parking lot, there was a massive traffic jam. Once they were parked, they were faced with only one ticket booth to serve them, which created another long line to get in.

Things didn't get any better once the racing started. The dirt surface came apart early in the program and became very dusty and treacherous. The show went on, but the races were run at a snail's pace. The main event was cut from 30 to 20 laps and was run under very poor visibility.

Three-time BCRA Champion Freddie Agabashian was the first big star of the track. Shown here in 1947 driving the Jack London car. *Courtesy of Tom Henry.*

Emerging from the dust cloud as the first feature winner was Swede Lindskog. Sadly, just a couple of weeks later, Swede would die in a Midget race at Gilmore Stadium in Southern California. As the dirt-covered spectators exited, they were faced with another massive traffic jam to get out of the parking lot, taking over an hour to reach the main road.

Embarrassed by what transpired that day and taking full responsibility, Mosiman vowed that the track would be paved, more ticket booths added and another entrance to the track would be built before the next race.

Improvements were made and the next race was held in mid-June. It went well for the drivers and 4,885 fans. All the problems that took place during the opener had been taken care of. The pavement was much faster, but even more importantly, it was dust free. The track record was lowered from 19.00 seconds on the dirt surface to 17.52 on the pavement. Winning the feature race was Ed Haddad.

Indianapolis 500 driver Sam Hanks raced in the third event, finishing third behind winner Lyle Dickey. After the race, promoter Mosiman divorced himself from the URA, which had failed to live up to its agreement to supply 20 to 25 Midgets per show.

The Bay Cities Racing Association, based in the Bay Area, took over as the sanctioning body. July 4 was the first race, and it ended in controversy. Ed Normi took the

Jack London behind the wheel of his own mount in 1947. Jack had a Hall of Fame career as a car owner, and in 1950 he became business manager for BCRA, a position he held for 30 years. *Dennis Mattish Collection*

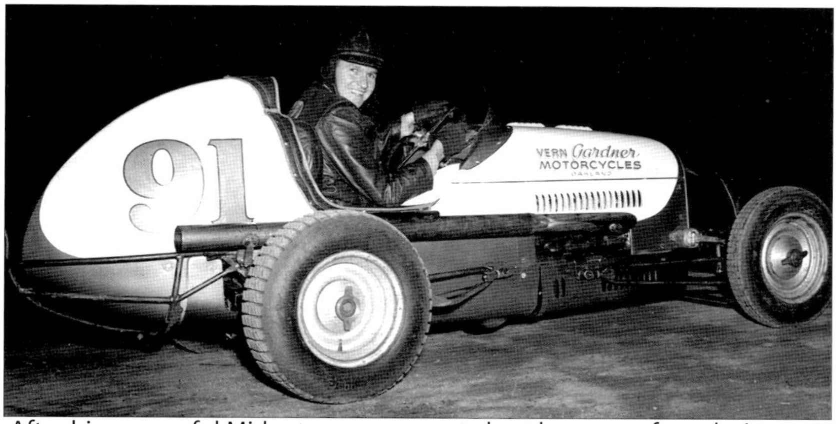
91
VERN Gardner
MOTORCYCLES

After his successful Midget career was cut short because of paralyzing injuries, Bert Moreland had an equally successful career as a promoter at Watsonville Speedway. *Dennis Mattish Collection*

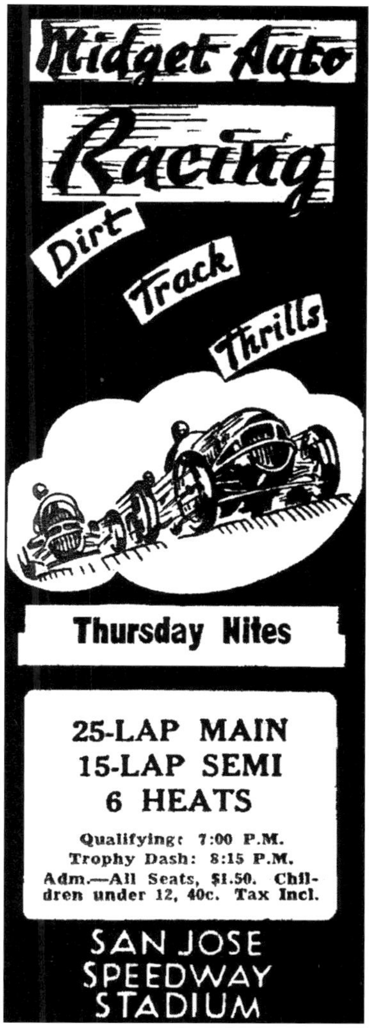
Midget Auto
Racing
Dirt
Track
Thrills
Thursday Nites
25-LAP MAIN
15-LAP SEMI
6 HEATS
Qualifying: 7:00 P.M.
Trophy Dash: 8:15 P.M.
Adm.—All Seats, $1.50. Children under 12, 40c. Tax Incl.
SAN JOSE
SPEEDWAY
STADIUM

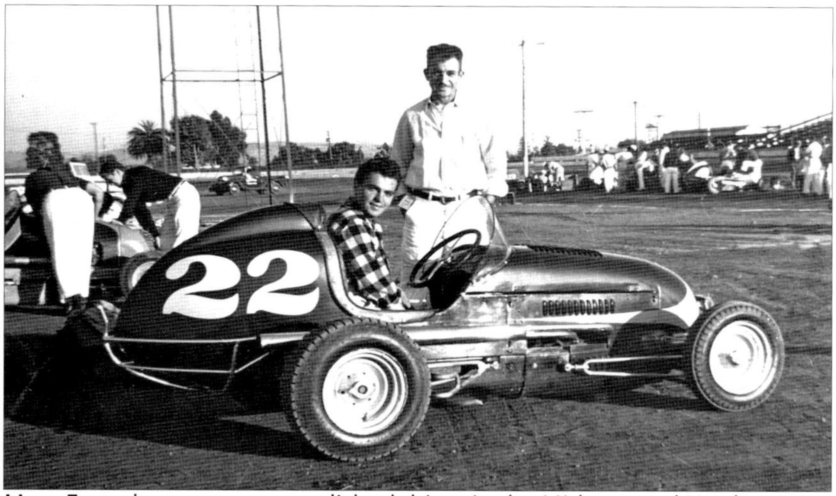
22

Merv Furtado was an accomplished driver in the Midgets and Hardtops. He later became a successful car owner. *Jim Abreu Photo*

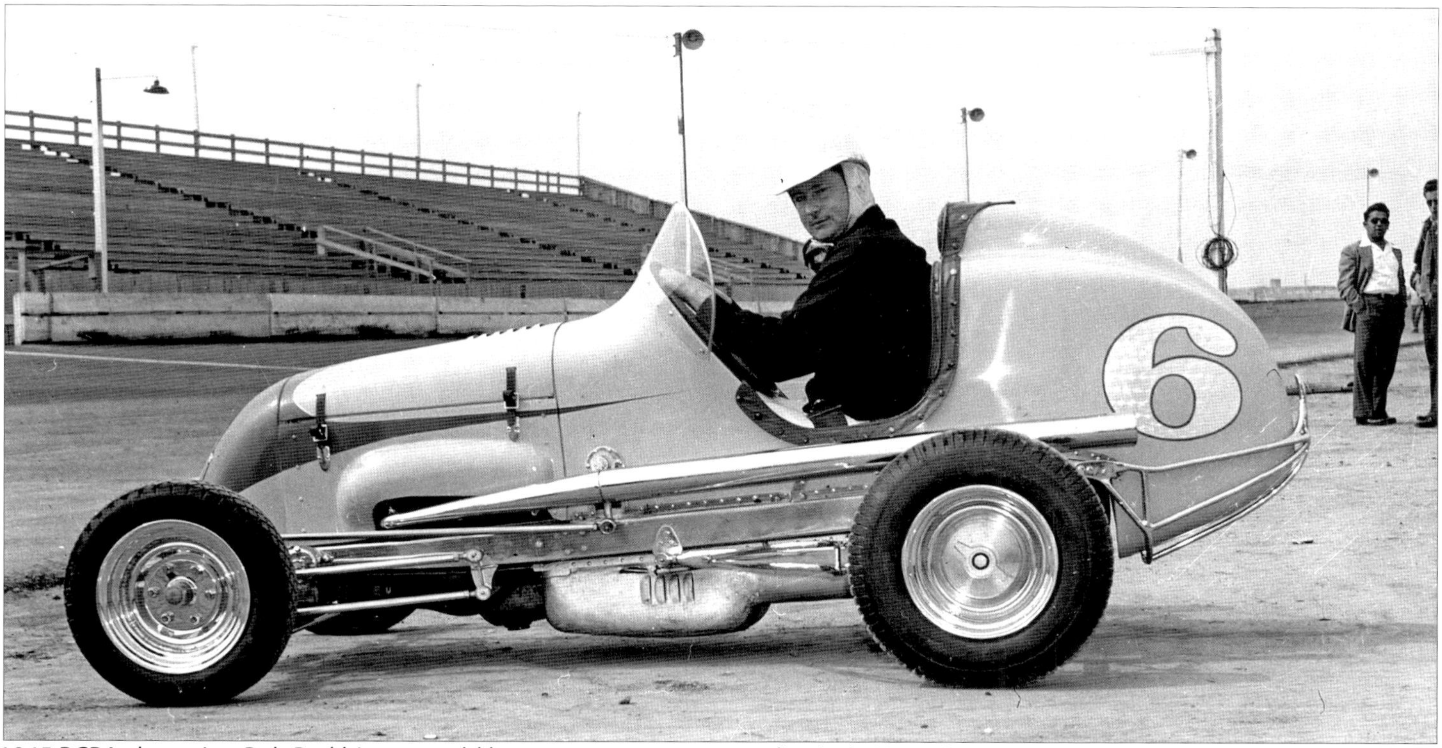
6

1945 BCRA champion Bob Barkhimer would become promoter extraodinaire in West Coast auto racing. *Dennis Mattish Collection*

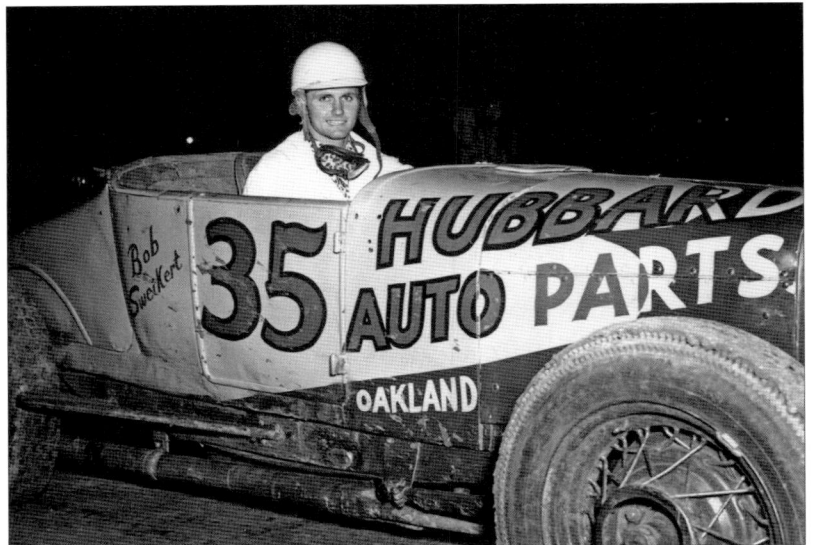

Bob Sweikart raced Roadsters at San Jose in 1948. He also set the Midget qualifying record in 1949. From there he went on to win the 1955 Indianapolis 500. *Dennis Mattish Collection*

Ed Elisian, shown in 1948, won over five main events on both the dirt and paved San Jose track. *Dennis Mattish Collection*

Roadsters on the quarter-mile dirt track in 1948. *Dennis Arnold Photo*

lead of the 25-lap main event on lap three with Freddie Agabashian in hot pursuit. Agabashian was setting Normi up for the pass for the lead when, for some unexplained reason, the checkered flag was waved on lap 21. Aggie was not happy.

The next couple of weeks were spent installing lights around the track and getting ready for the regular Thursday night shows that would be part of the BCRA schedule.

Thirty-two hundred were on hand to see the first night show held in the area since the old days at the Alviso Speedway dog track (chapter 7). For the second race in a row, Normi beat Agabashian to the checkered.

Buck Whitmer and Johnny Soares picked up wins, but after that it turned into a two-man show for track superiority between arch-rivals Jerry Piper and Agabashian. By the end of the season in October, Agabashian had won six features and Piper had won five. Aggie was crowned the BCRA champion.

The season ended in November with a Roadster race. Originally one race was scheduled, but when 5,500 spectators showed up, Page and Mosiman added another race for November 17. Al Slinker won the main event and set the one-lap track record with a time of 19.90, over two seconds slower than the Midgets, but it was the sheer excitement, thrills and accidents that attracted the customers.

San Jose's first post-war racing season was a huge success, with weekly attendance averaging 5,000.

1947

Year two at the Stadium had Larry Sunseri joining Ross Page as co-promoter.

The Mighty Midgets of the Bay Cities Racing Association raced every Thursday night as part of the BCRA circuit.

The Roadsters were the featured class for the season opener on March 30. Sam Hawks was the dominant driver, winning all four races he was in, including the 25-lap main event. This was the only appearance at the stadium by the Roadsters during the year.

Three weeks later the 26-week San Jose season started for the Midgets. Freddie Agabashian turned in a stellar performance, setting a track record in qualifying and winning the main event. The following week, former BCRA champion Bob Barkhimer picked up his second San Jose win.

Marvin Burke won his first San Jose BCRA Midget main event in July. During the same show, stuntman Jimmy Washburn attempted to jump from a ramp over the prostrate form of his wife. Things went bad when the wheels of his motorcycle slammed into his wife's face, breaking her nose.

The points season ended in late October with Agabashian winning his sixth feature and the BCRA Championship.

Billed as the California Championship 150, the November 9 race was the biggest yet at the young track. Sixty pilots were on hand to try and qualify for the 16-car main event. A standing-room-only crowd

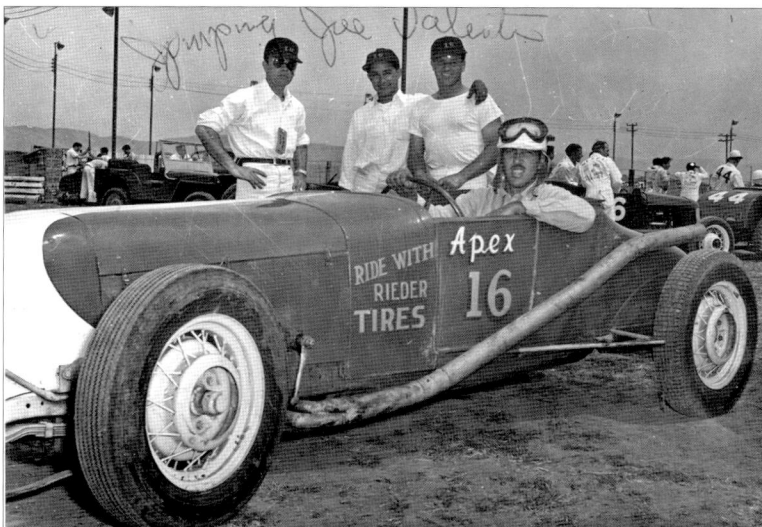

"Jumping" Joe Valente was the 1948 & 1949 Northern California Roadster Racing Association Champion. Joe was also known for his crazy antics and enchanting personality. *Dennis Mattish Collection*

Bob Machin was a consistent winner at San Jose in both Roadsters and Midgets. *Dennis Mattish Collection*

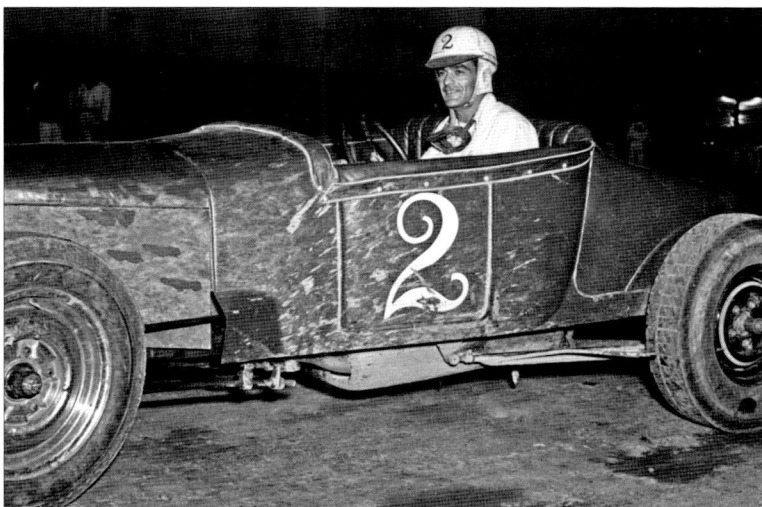

George Pacheco, Pictured in 1948, had at least six main event wins at San Jose in the Roadsters. *Dennis Mattish Collection*

of 10,000 witnessed Agabashian lead 93 laps before a flat tire sent him to the pits. His bitter rival, Jerry Piper, then sped to victory and the $2,000 first prize.

1948

During the winter months, the speedway had another complete makeover. The asphalt was removed from the quarter-mile, and a half-mile dirt oval was added, complete with lights. The *Mercury News* read, "Promoters Larry Sunseri and Ross Page spent all winter tearing out the asphalt surface which covered the quarter-mile race strip at the Tully Road speed plant, and it looks as if their efforts were successful. At least some 4,000-odd fans roared their approval last week." Norm Holtkamp won the main.

Only two races were held on the refurbished track before they enlarged it to a 1/3-mile and added new clay. The new clay worked, as Johnny Soares set a new track record (one of five set that night) in winning the first main event on the reconfigured track. Only a limited number of Midget races were run this year as dwindling crowds warranted changes.

Back by popular demand after a year's absence were the Roadsters. Cars and drivers from both the Northern California Roadster Racing Association (NCRRA) and the Central California Roadster Association (CCRA) participated in the weekly shows, the first taking place on June 18. Oscar Betts had a fast start, winning two of the first three features to start the season. The first significant injury at the track happened when the Roadster driven by Mel Alexander blew up while at speed, giving him severe burns to the face. Bob Gonzales won the final race of the year on a night when Joe Valente was crowned NCRRA champion and Paul Kamm won the CCRA crown.

Big Car (Indianapolis-type) racing returned to San Jose during July after a 10-year lapse. The big half-mile dirt track, which rimmed the Midget oval, was used for the first time. The American Racing Association (ARA) was the sanctioning body and Charles Curryer was their managing director. A capacity crowd of 5,400 saw Lennie Low win the 25-lap feature race during an incident-free show. They returned in August for a day race. The program was marred by high winds and heavy dust. Al Benoit took the lead on the final turn to win the slow race.

Big Car on the half-mile. *Dennis Arnold Photo*

The first Late Model Stock Car race took place on October 9 and was held on the half-mile oval over a distance of 150 laps. Charles Curryer, promoter of the race and recognized as the dean of auto racing in California, stated that to his knowledge "this will be the first Stock Car race ever held in the northern part of the state on a half-mile dirt track." The race had an unusual format. The 16-car field consisted of eight different models, two each. Each car could only start with five gallons of gas, thus requiring a pit stop during the race.

Bud Rose, the pre-race favorite, held the lead for the first 71 laps but blew a tire on the 72nd and gave way to the pressing Troy Ruttman. Ruttman then piloted a Hudson 8 to victory.

Throughout the year, the drivers had been complaining about the track, saying it was "unsuitable for competition." That would be taken care of during the off-season.

1949

Big changes took place in the front office at the end of the previous season. The Speedway changed hands with Joe Mastrini and Ray Leon buying majority interest (they paid Mosiman $100,000) and Larry Sunseri holding 25 percent. Larry's brother, Joe, ran the concessions. Bob Barkhimer, who was still driving Midgets, was hired to manage the track.

For the fourth time in four years, the track had a makeover, but this time it was permanent. San Jose Speedway Stadium hit a home run when they built the 1/3-mile, high-banked, paved oval. The turns had a dish shape with three distinct grooves, making it one of the raciest tracks in the country. The parking lot, concessions and grandstands all had major improvements. A state-of-the-art lighting system was installed on 20 50-foot poles. The cost for the reconstruction was $52,000.

The week before the reopening of the track, there was a free open house so that spectators could see the improvements and watch the cars warm up on the new track. As the Roadsters were racing around the track, the Ynez Hernandez family of four was walking through the parking lot, just outside the turn. Suddenly a Roadster hurtled out of control and over the uncompleted crash wall. It then shot down the embankment and into the parking lot, mowing down the Hernandez family and a fifth person, Harold Wingert. All four members of the family were severely injured, including numerous compound fractures, concussions and spinal injuries. Wingert also received body fractures. All told, more than $200,000 in lawsuits was brought against the track. On that note, the big reopening was the following week.

The grand marshal for the reopening gala was none other than racing legend Ralph DePalma. For the first time at the speedway, two featured classes of cars were on the same program. Roadsters and Big Cars shared the bill on the April 24 opener.

An estimated 5,800 saw Bob Mclean beat Buck Whitmer to the checkered flag in the Big Car race. Sam Hawks, who finished third, won the Roadster main event. After the races, the drivers were unanimous about their praise for the track, stating it was "one of the best on the coast."

Roadsters line up for their feature event during 1949. *Jim Abreu Photo*

Roaring Roadsters charge out of turn four during 1949. These fine looking machines are driven by Lloyd Ragon (6), Sam Hawks (61) (next to Ragon), Jerry Hill (9), Chet Richards (60x), Joe Valente (7), Paul Kamm (19), Don Miller (53), Ernie Reyes (42) and Bob Gonzales (60). *Reginald McGovern Photo*

The Roadsters then went onto a weekly Friday night schedule.

At the next Roadster race, Ben Alexander was critically injured when it appeared the throttle stuck on his car as he crashed at high speed into the wall. His car caught fire as it continued to accelerate around the track with the unconscious driver behind the wheel. The car finally stopped when it slammed into the wall again.

Dave Carter won the following week but was suspended for two weeks because of rough driving.

During the summer, Ed Huntington won four main events in a row to become the man to beat in the Roadsters, but it was Gene Tessien who emerged the champion.

The Midgets were signed up to run on Sundays, and their first race on the new track was in May. Fifteen hundred spectators saw Chuck Stevenson win that race. The Midget drivers also gave an enthusiastic appraisal of the new-and-improved San Jose Speedway.

At the next Midget race, Jerry Piper lapped the field to win the 40-lap main event before a sparse July crowd of about 900. Speedway officials announced that this would be the last Midget-racing card to be presented at San Jose Speedway for some time.

Gene Tessien won the 1949 NCRRA Championship.
Dennis Arnold Photo

Don Radbruch, pictured in 1949, raced all types of cars in his career. His second career was as an author, writing three books, two on the history of Roadster Racing (see Bibliography).
Jim Abreu Photo

Because of declining attendance in both the Midget and Roadster shows, Barkhimer was looking for a solution to attract the crowds and make the speedway profitable again. He noticed that the Stock Cars were becoming popular in the Eastern half of the country, so he went out and bought twelve old junkers and hired some drivers. Those junkers were called Hardtops. Barkhimer then formed the California Stock Car Racing Association (CSCRA), which sanctioned the races. Jerry Piper was appointed the president.

Without much fanfare, the Hardtops made their Saturday night debut in July. Dave Carter won the first race in front of a crowd of 1,600. He would control the rest of the season, winning four out of the last five races for a total of six in the year. Carter was crowned the first CSCRA Champion.

The Hardtops enjoyed modest success during its short first season, averaging about 1,500 fans per race, but that would change. The Midgets and Roadsters also averaged about 1,500 spectators for their shows. This was a far cry from the 5,000 just three years earlier.

1950

A duel Hardtop/Roadster show kicked off the season on April 2. An overflow crowd saw Chuck Tatum win the Hardtop main and Bob Gonzales take the Roadster feature.

"Hardtop racing, a form of reckless driving over a regulated course" is how the *Mercury News* described Hardtop racing. Many of the Roadster drivers were either racing in both divisions or switching over to the Hardtops. Joe Valente was one of those drivers enjoying success in the Hardtops, winning back-to-back main events early in the year.

In what was believed to be the first event of its kind in the United States, a 24-hour Stock Car endurance race was held on June 24-25, 1949. The ARA-sanctioned race was run in two 12-hour segments with a 12-hour intermission in between. Twenty-one cars started and eleven finished. John Darendinger completed 3,300 laps and won the race by 29 laps over his closest opponent. As these photos show, a pitifully small crowd was in attendance. In his book, *Tales of the Oval,* Bob Barkhimer talks about this event being one of the biggest mistakes he ever made as a promoter. *Jim Abreu Photos*

Johnny Key piloting his Roadster around San Jose in 1949.
Dennis Mattish Collection

Elmer George posing in his fine-looking Roadster with tuck "n" roll Upholstery. *Jim Abreu Photo*

Dave Carter won this Roadster race and then a couple of months later won the first Hardtop race at San Jose in 1949. He also became the first Hardtop Champion. *Jim Abreu Photo*

Picking up his first two wins was a dashing young man named Clyde Palmer. The following week Russ Margolati, brother of Mac, was mortally injured when he ran to the edge of the track to try and slow the cars down after a pile up. Coming out of the turn, Johnny Freitas lost control of his car and hit Russ. Russ was transported to the hospital where he would die from his injuries. Al Foster claimed the last race of the year, joining Johnny Key and "Jumping" Joe Valente as the only three-time winners of the year.

The Roadsters held their Friday night opener in April. George Pacheco won that event, which was held in front of 1,800 spectators. On July 21, Sam Hawks beat Elmer George to the stripe to win the final Roadster race of the year. With attendance averaging just over 1,000, the promoters decided to cut their season short after just six races.

San Jose Speedway hosted the $10,000 California Gold Cup Air Races on June 25. The program was co-ordinated with Reid Hillview Airport, located next door to the track.

On July 4, a 250-lap Late Model Stock Car Championship race was held. Danny Weinberg won the American Racing Association-sanctioned race in front of 4,178 fans.

Offenhauser-powerd Midget race cars, under the sanction of the American Automobile Association (AAA), made their only appearance at San Jose Speedway in August. George Amick passed Roger Ward on the last lap to claim the win in the 50-lap feature. Only 1,456 were in attendance for the Sunday night race.

With the Midgets and Roadsters only attracting between 1,000 to 1,500 per show and the Hardtops 3,000, it was apparent what the most popular form of racing was. Barkhimer's gamble paid off.

1951

The first race was a dual United Roadster Inc. (URI) and CSCRA Hardtop show, with 4,900 seeing Sam Hawks win the Roadster race and Norm Garland the Hardtop feature. Gene Tessien won the only other Roadster race that year, held on May 29.

Al Gaetano was the hot Hardtop driver during the year, winning six times. Joe Soares, his closest competitor, had three wins.

In August, two spectators went to the hospital after Carmel Fernandez crashed into the front straightaway wall, showering the stands with flying lumber. Two months later, Joe Valente hit the same wall, sending more wood into the stands and two people to the hospital.

There was a seven-race open competition series run at different tracks, pitting CSCRA against the BCRA Hardtop division. Merv Furtado and Al Toland won the San Jose main events.

By the end of the year, the Hardtops were averaging 60 cars per show and the attendance was about 3,500. The speedway had found its niche.

1952

The longest Hardtop race ever staged on the West Coast took place on May 30. Titled the "Little Indianapolis," the race started 33 cars and ran for 500 laps. An amazing 150 cars pre-entered in a bid to win the $1,000 first prize.

Johnny Key took the lead on lap 41, made his pit stop on lap 342, and then proceded to win the race by 18 laps over second place finisher Rod Zanoline. Thirteen cars finished the race, which ran for 3 hours and ten and a half minutes.

A few races later, Chuck Tatum had an improbable win. On lap five, the hood flew up into the windshield and stayed there. He was able to peek through a small opening by his windshield post and at the same time hold the field behind him at bay for the last 20 laps on his way to victory.

Forty-four hundred spectators saw the 50-lap Mid-Summer Championship Race held in August. Ray Raineri and Johnny Key staged a brilliant duel over the final nine laps of the feature race. Raineri won by a nose.

The season turned into a three-man show between Key, Raineri and Johnny Freitas. Johnny Key had the best year in the short history of the CSCRA; he won a record 7 main events at San Jose and a record 57 on the state circuit on his way to winning that championship.

Raineri led the points at San Jose the entire season until the second to last race, when Freitas overtook him. Freitas won the Hardtop Championship by a mere two points. Clyde Palmer had the second most wins at San Jose with four.

The season ended on November 23 with the Bert Moreland Benefit Race. (Bert had been paralyzed a couple of years earlier at Contra Costa.) This was the first Northern California race to highlight three different sanctions and run four divisional main events. On this freezing day,1,581 hardy fans were in the stands. Al Johnson won the CSCRA main event, Jimmy Day took the West Coast Racing Association Roadster race, Bob Caswell the BCRA Hardtop feature and Tommy Copp was the winner in the BCRA Midgets.

Besides managing and promoting the track, Bob Barkhimer now owned minority interest in the track.

As more people acquired televisions, attendance slowly dwindled. Average crowd counts were down by more than 500 from the previous year.

1953

The *Mercury News* read, "Auto Racing, one of San Jose's favorite sports makes its 1953 debut this afternoon on the third-mile San Jose Speedway oval." The next day the paper stated, "A pair of familiar names, Jolting Johnny Key of Salinas and Jumping Joe Valente of Berkeley, took major honors yesterday afternoon in the combined Hardtop-Hot Rod program at San Jose Speedway before 3519 fans."

George MeHalas (20) hangs on to his Roadster during 1948. The flat track of that year was in complete contrast to the new high banked 1/3-mile built in 1949. *Dennis Mattish Collection*

1950 Roadster shunt. *Dennis Arnold Photo*

Sam Hawks won Roadster races on both the dirt and the high-banked paved track. *Dennis Arnold Photo*

Ed Normi (pictured in 1950) won the first-ever BCRA race held in San Jose. *Dennis Mattish Collection*

CALIFORNIA STOCK CAR RACING ASS'N.

Johnny Key won his first of many San Jose Hardtop races in August of 1949. He won the track championship in 1951. *Jim Abreu Photo*

1950: Ray Raineri was the leading main event winner at the speedway from 1949-1954, with 28 victories and the 1953 championship. *Jim Abreu Photo*

Bad blood had been brewing between Johnny Freitas and Clyde Palmer when the two made contact early in the year. It appeared that Palmer spun Freitas out of contention during the main event. This infuriated Johnny's brother Tony, who then proceeded to attack Palmer. As a result, Tony was suspended for a year. Two months later, there was a special occasion held on the front straight. The feuding drivers shook hands in a "bury the hatchet" ceremony before the start of the main event.

The year belonged to Ray Raineri as he broke out into a quick points lead, winning five main events in the first two months. He then ran away with the points chase, winning a record breaking thirteen main events during the year.

1954

Bob Barkhimer and NASCAR (National Association for Stock Car Auto Racing) had a dialog going on for some time when they got together during the winter. Bill France, founder of NASCAR, and Barkhimer came to an agreement to allow NASCAR to sanction his tracks. CSCRA was absorbed into the national organization, and a new chapter was about to begin in West Coast auto racing history.

The first NASCAR race in San Jose took place on April 4. Al Gaetano won the rain-shortened race. The following Sunday, Fresno visitor Al Pombo was the class of the field, winning his first San Jose main event. The 1951 Kearny Bowl Champion came back the next week and won the first night race of the season. He then announced he would race here on a weekly basis while chasing the State title.

On this same weekend, Johnny Key finished in fourth place during an AAA Sprint Car race in Dayton, Ohio. A month later, he would be dead.

Defending track champion Ray Raineri reeled off four straight main event wins in June.

Three months after Johnny Key died in a racing accident in Ohio, a race in his honor, called "Johnny Key Memorial Gold Cup," was held. At 200 laps, this was the second longest Hardtop race ever held at San Jose. (The longest race was 500 laps held on Memorial Day in 1952. Ironically, Key won that race.) Thirty drivers started the race with five gallons of gas, assuring at least one pit stop. The largest crowd of the year (4,222) saw NASCAR state points leader Danny Graves win the first Johnny Key race. His 31-second pit stop beat second-place Raineri's 61-second stop. Graves' margin of victory was eight seconds.

The Big Cars (Sprint) returned after a three-year absence on June 11. Jack Barney beat both Jack Flaherty and Sam Hawks to the checkered flag.

There was a three-division program held on Labor Day Weekend, featuring the Hardtops, Midgets and, making their first appearance at San Jose, the Jalopies. These were strictly Early Model Stock Cars (1932-1940), the only modifications being for safety purposes. Johnny Colendich won the Hardtop main event by a nose over Raineri. Johnny Baldwin beat Bob Machin and Norm Rapp to the checkered flag in the BCRA Midgets. Johnny Smith won the first Jalopy race at San Jose.

By October, Ray Raineri had won 14 main events, breaking his record from the previous year. Ray also had a commanding points lead with just four races to go. It was the week before Raineri's 14th win that Bob Barkhimer went to Stockton Speed-

Johnny Freitas won the 1950, 1952 & 1956 track championships. *Jim Abreu Photo*

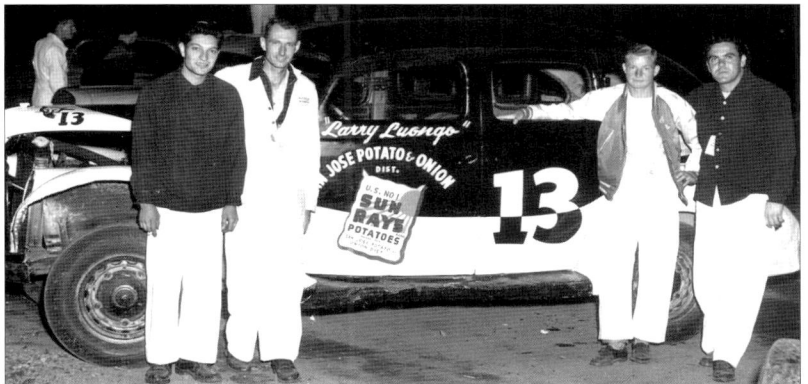

In September, 1950, Larry Luongo (left) won his first main event, setting a track record in the process. He followed it up with another win a month later. *Jim Abreu Photo*

Johnny Freitas (leaning in window) was agitated after this collision with Ray Raineri in 1950. *Jim Abreu Photo*

99

Al Foster, shown in 1950, won the second Hardtop race at the speedway. He would eventually win at least a dozen main events. *Jim Abreu Photo*

With the help of his brother Owen (left), Johnny Key won a record 57 main events in 1952. *Dennis Mattish Collection*

way and negotiated the deal to bring the Jalopy drivers to San Jose as part of a two-division show with the popular Hardtops. The resulting protest and suspensions of the Hardtop drivers cost Raineri the track championship and San Jose Speedway some of its best drivers (complete story on page 75). With Raineri out of the picture, the title chase became a two-man battle between Johnny Colendich and Al Pombo. Pombo overtook Colendich at the final race and won the title by a couple of points. Only 800 people were in attendance for that last points race.

The final race of the season was a Jalopy race. A sparse crowd of 600 was there to see Bert Doty win the feature. Dick Marcell and Howard Kaeding were treated at the local hospital after receiving injuries in separate flips.

After the Jalopies were brought in, attendance dropped. Meanwhile, many drivers were still irate. The disgruntled drivers held meetings that winter and the Western Auto Racing Association (WAR) was founded.

1955

The season started on March 27 under the cloud of the split among its top drivers. Clyde Palmer won the NASCAR main event in front of 2,839 fans.

A week later, the Jalopies ran a race on Sunday. A new rule to the class was the claiming rule under which each Jalopy entered in the program would have a $199.99 Claiming price upon it. The deposit of that amount could purchase any car with the

Larry Rodriguez (22) has a narrow lead in the Trophy Dash. *Bob Mize Photo*

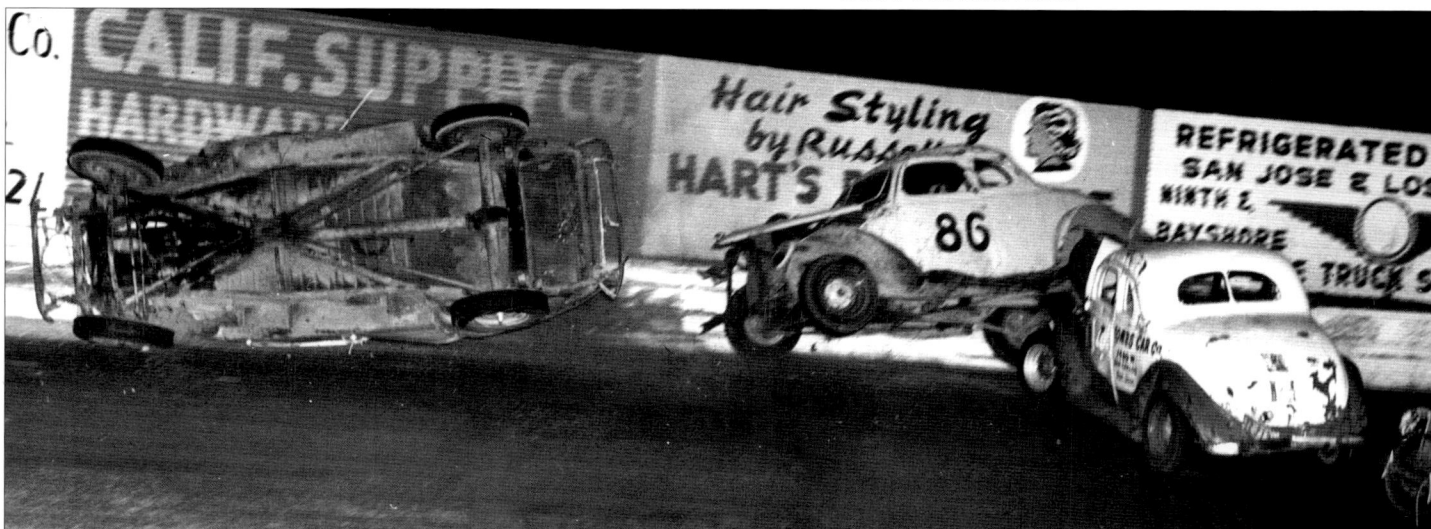

Wild Hardtop action during the 1950 season. Earl Smith is in the No. (86). *Jim Abreu Photo*

referee. The rule was designed to keep Jalopies at an affordable price for the racing enthusiast. Tony Enfantino won in front of 1,102. The Jalopies came back and ran a Thursday night race. A pitifully small crowd of 376 spectators turned out to see Shiner Watkins win that race.

In the Hardtops, Al Pombo won the second annual Johnny Key Memorial race by one lap over Clyde Palmer. It was attended by 2,940, the largest crowd to see the Hardtops during the season.

During a June race, Dusty Fuller lost a wheel after hitting the crash wall. The wheel flew into the grandstands, breaking the leg of a hapless spectator.

Al Foster was badly shaken when he had the most spectacular rollover seen in a Hardtop. He flipped wildly down the front straight, turning over seven times. Al received a severe cut on his arm.

Dub Taylor, who lost his eye in an industrial accident, won three races on the night of his return.

The NASCAR Hardtops turned into a three-man race for the championship between Al Pombo, Johnny Colendich and Johnny Freitas. Leading the list of main event wins with 10 was Al Pombo. But it was Johnny Colendich who won the points championship with five main event wins followed by Freitas with four wins.

Only 800 people showed up for the season final, giving the track an average attendance for the

1950: Al Gaetano won many Roadster races before switching to Hardtops. Al won six San Jose main events during the 1951 season. Gaetano would also go down in history as winning the first NASCAR race in San Jose. *Jim Abreu Photo*

1950: Al Toland won multiple Hardtop main events at San Jose during his career. *Jim Abreu Photo*

Joe Soares (left) with car owners Eva and Tony Goularte in 1950. *Courtesy of the Goularte Collection.*

101

In 1951 a clubhouse and bar was built behind the main grandstands. This would become one of the landmarks of the Speedway. *Ken Clapp Collection*

Elmer George from Salinas, California, set a three-lap track record in the Trophy Dash in 1951. In 1957 George wed Mari Antonia Hulman, daughter of Indianapolis Speedway owner Anton Hulman. They had a son named Tony George. By the end of the century, Tony would be one of the most powerful motor sports figures in the world. *Jim Montgomery Collection*

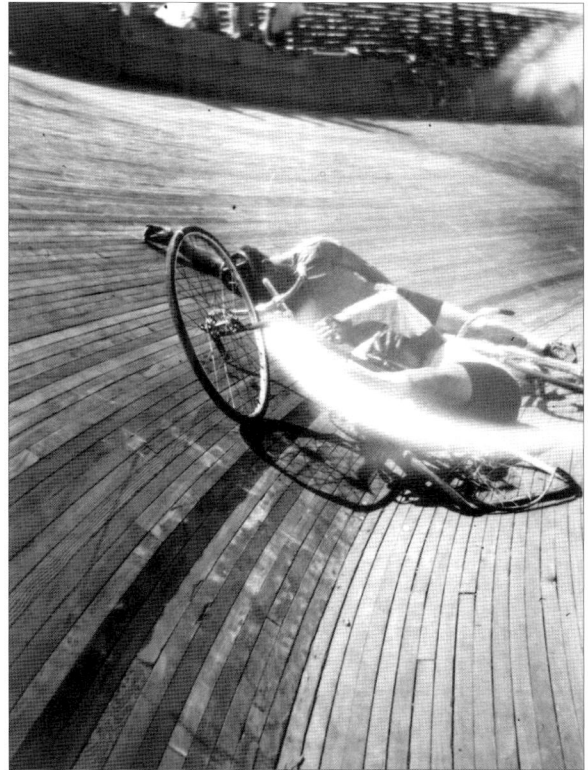

Another landmark of the facility was the 1/10-mile, high-banked wooden bicycle track (Velodrome) that was built outside the north turn during 1950. The pedal pushers held their first race on August 1. *Bob Mize Photos courtesy of Don Mize*

1955: Joe Diaz raced the high banks for over two decades, with his biggest moment coming on in September, 1956, when he won the Main event. *Bob Mize Photo courtesy of Don Mize*

1955: Larry Rodriguez was a fixture at the track, both as a driver and then as a vendor. *Bob Mize Photo courtesy of Don Mize*

Al Pombo won his first of six San Jose titles in 1954. *Bob Mize Photo courtesy of Don Mize*

Saturday night Hardtop action in 1955. *Bob Mize Photo courtesy of Don Mize*

year of under 2,000. NASCAR vs. WAR was taking its toll.

The land that the track sat on was sold to the Brandon Corporation. An agreement was made that would allow the track to be used for five years, rent free.

1956

The season started the same way the previous season ended, with Colendich beating Freitas by a nose in the season opener on March 25. Freitas then reeled off three main event wins in a row. He never looked back as he pulled away to win the points title by a wide margin over second place Reggie Ausmus.

Dennis Arnold, the early points leader in the state, was married to Charlotte Smith on the front straightaway during a June ceremony before the start of a Hardtop main event.

Clyde Palmer inherited the lead on lap 160 when Dave Leroy broke, and then went on to win the Johnny Key Memorial race.

The most ambitious program ever held at the speedway, an "Auto Racing Spectacular," was held on October 14, consisting of five different types of racecars. The feature event was a 150-lap Late Model Stock Car race. A capacity crowd saw Ed Pagan win the Stock Car race behind the wheel of his new 1956 Ford. Also on the card were NASCAR Hardtops, BCRA Midgets, ARA Big Cars and NASCAR Jalopies.

1957

The Hardtops started their season in March, with 91 signed in for the first race, causing the pits to overflow into

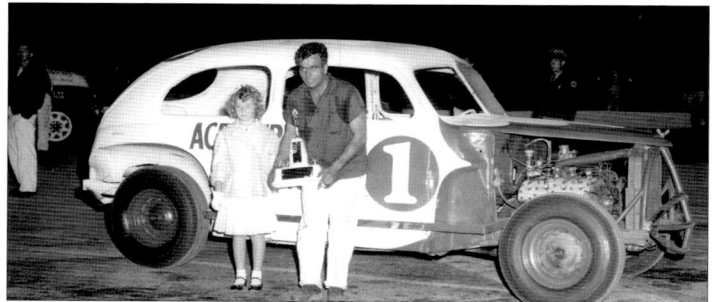

the parking lot with cars. Fresno's Larry Ferrua won his first San Jose feature that day.

Returning to San Jose Speedway during mid-season after a two-year absence while racing at Alviso was Ray Raineri. He won the main event on his second appearance, becoming the first local driver to win. Previously, all the wins had been by drivers from other areas, most notably the Central Valley. Raineri then went on a winning spree, claiming seven out of the next nine main events, including the fourth annual Johnny Key Memorial Race. Because he only raced half the season, Ray was never a factor in the points chase–that belonged to Rick Henderson, who won

both the state and San Jose titles.

Attendance started inching up with Raineri's return.

The last race of the year was a NASCAR vs. WAR shootout. NASCAR driver Dave Leroy won that race. The venom between the two groups was dissipating.

1958

Changes were made to the NASCAR Hardtops during the off-season. The cars were able to run unlimited multiple carburetors along with more cubic inches of displace-

Bob Barkhimer used all kinds of gimmicks to boost attendance. Here is a sampling of some of his "not so politically correct" promotions.

1: Red-head night. "All carrot-tops will be admitted free."

2: Bald-headed night. "All baldies will be admitted at a reduced price."

3: Fat men's night. All men weighing over 220 pounds were admitted at a reduced price.

4: Wild animal races featuring camel, ostrich, and a horse vs. zebra race. There was also a boxing kangaroo.

5: Bloodless bullfights.

6: Female impersonator as trophy girl. The driver was not happy when he found out it was a guy he kissed.

The Kaeding dynasty started in 1954 when Howard won this race in a Jalopy. *Bob Mize Photo courtesy of Don Mize*

Mike McGreevy (99) took the checkered flag first in the 100-lap ARA Big Car race on October 14, 1956. Dave Imorie (95) and Ray Horst (31) were two of his challengers. *Jim Montgomery Collection*

1957: Marshall Sargent (right) & crew.
Bob Mize Photo courtesy of Don Mize

1957: Dave Leroy (aka Dave Moses), after one of his many wins.
Jim Montgomery Collection

Ray Raineri won six of seven main events on his return to San Jose (from WAR) in 1957, including this, the Johnny Key Memorial, race.
Bob Mize Photo courtesy of Don Mize

ment. Certain chassis changes were also allowed which made for better handling. Interestingly, the single-lap track record was not broken during the year.

After a month of rain, the season started in late April. Three thousand sun-soaked fans saw Dave Reed win the opener. The first half of the season had Burt Foland and Rick Henderson battling back and forth for the points lead. Then Burt went up to Capitol Speedway in Sacramento for a BCRA race where he was seriously injured, thus missing the rest of the year. Henderson then coasted to his second title in a row. The fifth annual Johnny Key Memorial race was the highlight of the year for Henderson. After a wheel-to-wheel, three-way battle with Al Pombo and Ray Raineri, Henderson emerged the victor in front of 4,500 satisfied customers.

The season ended with a 100-lap Pacific Coast Championship Early Model Stock Car (formerly called Jalopies) race. The Stock Cars were now allowed to run soft-top convertibles, which a few of them did. Charles Sanchez won the race and clinched the NASCAR Pacific Coast championship.

1959

A newspaper strike shut down the *Mercury News* for 124 days. Information for the first half of the year was obtained from a scab-operated paper based out of a garage, called the *San Jose Reporter*.

The March 22 NASCAR Hardtop opener saw two-time champion Johnny Freitas win the main event in front of 2,800 fans.

Two months later, Larry Ferrua won a special 100-lap Monza-style race. A Monza race is 100 laps, run in three sections: 33, 33 and 34 laps. Thirty-three drivers start inverted (fastest in rear) in each portion. Points are awarded for finishing position. High point total wins.

Another driver having a statement year was Burt Foland with four main event wins.

Once again, Rick Henderson had a banner year, claiming his third track championship in a row, the NASCAR state and national championships (becoming the only Californian to accomplish that feat) and the Belmont and Santa Rosa speedway championships, adding up to five crowns in one year.

The NASCAR Pacific Coast Early Model Stock Cars raced on April 5. Manuel Sanchez powered his 1952 Hudson convertible to victory.

Brandon Enterprises, owner of the land the racetrack sat on, was ready to make a move with the property. (See Chapter 9 for further information on Brandon Enterprises.) Racing would continue for an indefinite period.

1960

Going for four championships in a row Rick Henderson won the March 20 opener. The fol-

Gallery of Hardtop Drivers
Photography by Dennis Arnold

Dennis Arnold

Mike Batinich

Johnny Burton

Johnny Colendich

Al Foster

Johnny Freitas

Al Gaetano

Joe Soares

Al Johnson

Howard Kaeding

Johnny Key

Dick Page

Marshall Sargent

Stan Sinn

Ray Traylor

Dick Whalen

lowing Sunday Marshall Sargent won the main event, and then guaranteed to the media that he was going to win the track championship. Two weeks later, Bill Scott made his own statement by winning a main event and taking the points lead. By the end of June, Henderson had won four feature races to reclaim the points chase, but then Sargent reeled off seven main event wins in a row to reclaim the lead. Dick Whalen stopped Sargent's streak with a win, but that was only a bump in the road for Sargent. Marshall went on to win a record-setting 16 main events (topping Ray Raineri's record of 14 wins set in 1954) on his way to claiming the track championship. During the last race of the year, a spectacular eight-car crash during the semi-main caused serious shoulder injuries to Carl Carr, who was thrown partially out of his car as it was overturning. (Years later, window netting would take care of this problem.)

The NASCAR $99 Claiming races started the season as a support division for the Hardtops but then were awarded their own time slot and switched to Sunday night racing in May, as the car counts grew to 50 per show. The Rough-and-Tumble Division provided thrills and many crashes, but with that came many injuries. On one night, the ambulance made four trips to the hospital. On another night, Mrs. Nicky Simpson was using her husband's Claimer in the Powder Puff Derby. Somehow, she lost control of her car and went flipping into the infield where she hit driver Dink Collins, who was transported to the hospital with serious leg injuries.

On August 28, a 40-car, 100-lap Claiming race was held. Harry Davis survived a 10-car pile-up and then took the lead on the 81st lap on his way to victory. Davis won the championship, while Jim Stewart was runner-up. Other big winners were Jim Clennan and Marty Martin with four wins apiece. Dick Carter was crowned the State Champion.

With a housing development going in around the track, the season ended in a cloud of uncertainty, but then Sunseri, Barkhimer and the Leons bought the track back from Brandon Corp.

1961

Forty-two hundred fans saw Al Pombo win the rain-shortened Modified Sportsman (another word for Hardtop) season opening race on March 19. He followed that up with wins in the next two races. Pombo led the points standing all the way into August. Going into the Johnny Key Memorial race, only one point separated him and Clyde Palmer. Fifty-five hundred fans packed into the speedway and another 1,000 were turned away. The people who were lucky enough to get a seat were treated to one of the greatest races to ever take place at the speed plant. From the drop of the green, Palmer and Pombo raced wheel to wheel for all the 150 laps. Palmer, who just barely won the race, took the points lead and would never look back. He ended the year with nine main event victories and the track championship. Pombo finished in second with six victories and Burt Foland was third with four wins.

The $99 Claimers held their first race on April 16, and Joe Roletto won. The points chase turned into a two-man battle between Roletto and Jim Stewart, with the pair tied for first place with just a month left in the season. Roletto's nine feature wins were enough to clinch the championship over Stewart at the end.

For the first time, motorcycles ran a weekly show. Sanctioned by the United States Motorcycle Club, they used the track on Friday nights. Russ Bordman was the consistent winner of the group. He also set a track record with a very respectable time of 17:98. Unfortunately, on June 9 a four motorcycle pile-up claimed the life of James Williamson. This resulted in the series being cancelled after just four races.

During the winter, residents who moved into the new homes built near the speedway put together a petition drive to try and shut down the race track. The petition, which only had 147 signatures, was presented to the city council. The council sided with the race track, saying that 3,500 people go to the track every week, making it a vital part of recreation. The council also stated that the track had been in operation for 16 years, and that the people built and moved into the houses knowing there was a speedway there. (This was a period of time when auto racing had full support of local government.)

1962

Rule changes for the 1962 season allowed larger and more powerful engines and streamlined bodies.

Rick Henderson won the season opener on March 18 in front of 5,000 racing enthusiasts.

Because of winter floods, Alviso Speedway did not open until mid-June. In the meantime, a number of WAR drivers started competing at San Jose. The two organizations held several meetings, and peace was declared.

Marshall Sargent led the Johnny Key Memorial Race for 130 laps when he was involved in an accident that totaled his car. Clyde Palmer inherited the lead and won the race.

Sargent completely dominated the season in the win column, breaking his record of 16 with a total of 17 feature wins. He didn't win the championship; usually, if he didn't win a race, he crashed or broke. Al Pombo was also out of the points chase because of a lengthy suspension imposed on him by NASCAR. The crown went to Rick Henderson who won an unprecedented fourth San Jose Championship. He edged out Clyde Palmer who finished second.

The Claimers (Claiming Races) enjoyed modest success in their Sunday slot with car counts averaging over 50 and attendance around 1,000. Joe Roletto jumped out to a fast start, winning the first three main events. Ron True won the third annual 100-lap Gold Cup Race. The series switched to Wednesday nights in June.

Injuries continued to mount, with the ambulance making the trip to the hospital nearly every week, often more than once. In many cases, drivers were hitting their heads or faces on the steering wheels after collisions.

During June, the dispute between WAR and NASCAR was resolved. As part of the agreement, the Claimers moved their operation to Alviso Speedway where they would be a support group with the WAR Hardtops. Roletto, with five wins was in first place at the time.

Marshall Sargent (7x) leads the pack in for the start of a 1959 heat race. *Bob Mize Photo courtesy of Don Mize*

There were two open-competition races to close out the year. Rick Henderson and Art Bigiogni won those. Ernie Moniz received a serious leg injury (nearly severed) in a three-car crash. After a number of operations, the lower part of his leg was amputated.

With the track no longer in danger of being developed, the situation with WAR resolved and attendance climbing, the track enjoyed a very good year.

1963

Howard Kaeding won his first local main event during the opener. Five thousand people saw him lead only one lap, the last one. Earlier in the day, Al Pombo flipped his Modified in his heat race. He was okay until he unbuckled his seat belt and fell to the pavement from his overturned car. Clyde Palmer shattered the one-lap track record with a time of 15:70, the first Modified Hardtop under sixteen seconds. This also accomplished a feat which had been considered impossible for years: turn a qualifying lap in a time faster than a Midget race car.

By June, Marshall Sargent had won five main events, making him the winningest driver in SJ speedway history. He was also the most controversial. This is how the *San Jose Mercury News* described an incident in June: "What was described as a near riot ensued when Sargent held up the running of the main event to change a tire on his Hardtop. Extra police assistance was called, but the por-

1959 was a breakout year for George Benson in the Hardtops, winning six main events, including the prestigious 200-lap Johnny Key Memorial race. *Bob Mize Photo courtesy of Don Mize*

Marshall Sargent after one of his record 16 main event wins during his 1960 championship season. *Bob Mize Photo courtesy of Don Mize*

Rick Henderson won his fourth San Jose title in 1961. His career feature win total at the track was 45. *Bob Mize Photo courtesy of Don Mize*

The Sargent (7)- Pombo battles of the 1960s became legendary. *Bob Mize Photo courtesy of Don Mize*

110

tion of the overflow crowd objecting to Sargent's action was kept under control."

Clyde Palmer had the points lead until a back injury sidelined him for the next four months. Joe Leonard drove the Goularte Bros. (10) in his absence. Sargent briefly took the points lead but then was suspended by NASCAR for one week. At that point, Pombo took over. On his return, Sargent was involved in a vicious three-car accident, with his car flipping wildly. He received a back injury, which sidelined him for a couple of more weeks. The title was lost, but on his return, he won the Johnny Key Memorial Race in front of Pombo and Leonard. Sargent went on to win thirteen main events during the year.

Al Pombo, who won six main events, claimed his second San Jose championship by a comfortable margin over Sargent.

Nearly every race during the year was run before capacity crowds.

1964

Two-time national AMA motorcycle champion Joe Leonard made a last-lap pass to win the inaugural event for the Modified Hardtops. Leonard would race another month before heading East to race with USAC. He would become a two-time National Indy Car Champion and a household name by the end of the decade.

Once again, Al Pombo jumped out to an early lead in

the points, winning three straight main events during one March/April stretch. But then Bill Scott came on strong during May and June, winning three in a row and five out of eight at one point to close within a couple of points to Pombo. Scott would hound Pombo right down to the last month of the season, but Pombo's 10 victories for the year were enough for him to clinch his second title in a row and third overall.

Marshall Sargent was in points contention until he was suspended for "conduct unbecoming a driver." He

(continued on page 126)

The 1961 season ended with the first-ever open-competition race. The rulebook was thrown out, and any type of race car (except Midgets) was allowed to race. Art Pollard brought this Super Modified down from Washington and set an all-time single-lap track record of 16.13. Pollard went on to have a successful career driving Indy Cars. *Bob Mize Photo courtesy of Don Mize*

111

Claimers

$99 CLAIMING RACES
and Powder Puff Derby
LADIES FREE
SUNDAY NITE
JUNE 12—8:00 p.m.
Sizzling Competition

NASCAR

SAN JOSE
SPEEDWAY
CY7-6453
On Tully Road Opposite
Hillview Golf Course

Injuries were common in the Claiming class.

Images from 1960 thru 1962 $99 Claiming races. This low budget class of car provided plenty of *slam/BANG!* action. For more information see main text. All photos on these two pages were taken by track photographer Bob Mize.

Midget section
BCRA/USAC

MIDGET RACE

Little Indianapolis

SUNDAY, MAY 29
8:00 P.M.

33 CARS WILL RUN

500 LAPS

"Little Indianapolis Race"

San Jose Speedway

TULLY ROAD

500 LAPS — 500 THRILLS

"Little Indianapolis" Midget Race
1953-1977

One of the premier Midget events in the West was the BCRA-sanctioned, Bob Barkhimer promoted, "Little Indianapolis" race that ran from 1953 through 1977.

Modeled after the Indianapolis 500, the race started 33 Midgets running three abreast for a distance of 500 laps, by far the longest Midget race ever held on the West Coast.

Some notable highlights

Always run on Memorial Day weekend, the first race was held on May 29, 1953.

Johnny Baldwin won the marathon in a time of 2 hours, 44 minutes and 24 seconds.

Two years later, Baldwin won again, this time by an astounding 23 laps over second-place Ross Pollack.

The following year, Bob Machin lead for 398 laps before he slammed into the wall. The Midgets, driven by Mike McGreevy and Ed Normi, then struck his car. After a lengthy clean-up, Tommy Morrow inherited the lead and went on to win by 19 laps over Normi. Finishing third and making his San Jose debut on four wheels was Motorcycle National champion Joe Leonard.

After seven years running as a 500-lap race, the 1960 "Little Indianapolis" was reduced 150 to laps. The fans requested the reduction because all the action happened in the first 150 laps. After that, the field became thinner as more machines were forced to the sidelines. Mike McGreevy took the lead on lap 108, and then held off Chuck Booth for the 1960 win.

The most competitive race was in 1963 when six different drivers held the lead during the 150-lap race.

Rick Henderson pulled a rare double in 1966, winning the NASCAR Modified race on Saturday night and returning to the speedway the following day and winning the annual "Little Indy" Classic.

For some reason there were no "Little Indianapolis" races held from 1969 through 1971. Instead NARC Sprint Cars occupied those dates.

Year 1974 saw Hank Butcher starting last in the 22-car field and then proceeded to work his way through the pack and win a rare non-stop, 150-lap race.

The second longest-running annual Midget race in the West (behind the Thanksgiving Night race in Southern California) died along with the track in 1977.

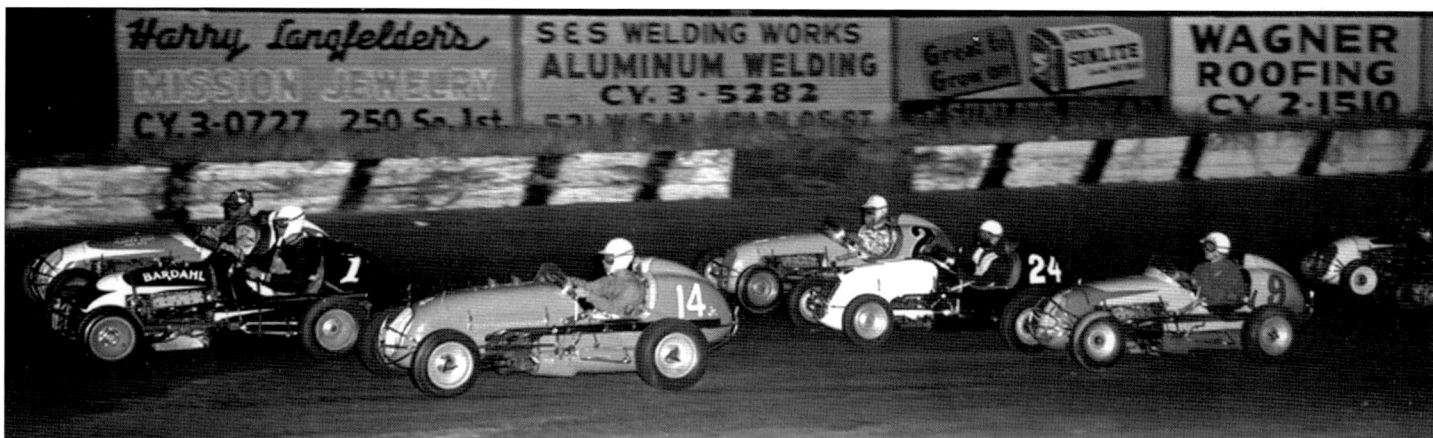

The annual "Little Indianapolis" 500-lap Midget Race was one of the track's biggest draws throughout the years. This was the lineup for the 1955 version, won by #1, Johnny Baldwin. *Dennis Arnold Photo*

"Little Indianapolis" Results

Year	Winner	Laps	Attendance
1953	Johnny Baldwin	500	3,300
1954	Bob Machin	500	
1955	Johnny Baldwin	500	3,591
1956	Tommy Morrow	500	4,221
1957	Bob Cortner	500	
1958	Mike McGreevy	500	2,400
1959	Mike McGreevy	500	
1960	Mike McGreevy	150	
1961	Johnny Baldwin	150	4,500
1962	Bob DeJong	150	3,600
1963	Bob Burbridge	150	
1964	Dee Hileman	150	
1965	George Benson	150	3,200
1966	Rick Henderson	150	
1967	Burt Foland	150	
1968	Dewayne Woodward	150	3,542
1972	Burt Foland	100	
1973	Chuck Gurney	100	2,200
1974	Hank Butcher	150	
1975	Bob DeJong	150	
1976	Larry Patton	100	
1977	Danny O'Neill	100	

Johnny Baldwin (pictured in 1957) won the first Little Indianapolis and a total of three editions of the long distance race. He is one of the most decorated Midget drivers to ever race in San Jose. Not only did he win seven feature events at San Jose, but he also won nine BCRA outdoor and indoor titles. *Jim Abreu Photo*

Bill Vukovich (1), Ronnie Hulse (37), Lloyd Nygren (8) and Jan Opperman (16) fight for position during the 1967 Little Indianapolis. *Jim Montgomery Collection*

USAC National Championship Midgets on parade during 1969. *Jim Abreu Photo*

J. C. Agajanian Presents

Sunday, November 1, 1970

100 LAP - USAC
NATIONAL CHAMPIONSHIP
MIDGET RACES

UNITED STATES AUTO CLUB

The action is always close on the San Jose Speedway, but this traffic jam was more than one could believe. George Benson, No. 94; leads Sonny Ates, No. 30; Dave Strickland, No. 22; Johnnie Anderson, No. 97; Hank Butcher, No. 4; Henry Rossi, No. 24, and Johnny Parsons, Jr., No. 32, during this year's Spring 100-lapper here.

(Larry Wood Photo)

West Coast photographer Larry Wood took this outstanding photo that graced the cover of the November 1970 USAC program. The photo was taken during the Spring 1970 USAC race at the track. *Larry Wood Photo*

USAC National Championship Midgets at San Jose 1956-1977

USAC Midget racing had a rich history in San Jose with a total of 21 National Championship races being conducted there from 1957 through 1977, 13 of those being the opening races of the year for the speedway. The legendary J.C. Agajanian promoted all but two of them.

The lineup of drivers that participated in the races was a Who's Who in the auto racing world, with the most notable being A.J. Foyt, Parnelli Jones, Johnny Parsons, Gary Bettenhausen, Bill Vukovich, Mel Kenyon and Joe Leonard, just to name a few.

The average attendance was 4,500, with a high of 6,118 for the 1970 race and a low of 1,739 for the September race held in 1969. That was the third national event held that year and would account for the low attendance. For a complete list of winners, see Appendix.

Notable Highlights

USAC National Championship Midgets made their first appearance in San Jose on February 10, 1957. Joining the card were the BCRA Midgets, making this the most prestigious Midget race in San Jose history. J.C. Agajanian was promoting the race. Four thousand fans saw National champion Shorty Templeman win the 100-lap race in record time. The star attraction for the 1962 race was 1961 Indianapolis 500 winner A.J. Foyt, who made a late-race charge in the 50-lap affair but just came up short to race winner Bob Wente.

San Jose Speedway opened and closed with USAC National races in 1964. A turn-away, paid crowd of 5,712 saw Johnny Baldwin pass Mel Kenyon on lap 95 and hold on for the win in the February 100-lap race. Mike McGreevy broke the Midget single-lap track record set by Fred Agabashion in 1949, a record that had stood for 15 years.

A star-studded field of Midget drivers participated in the season-ending USAC National Championship race. Parnelli Jones, 1963 Indianapolis 500 winner, lapped the entire field for a record-setting victory in the 100-lap race.

Advanced billing had eight-time Pike's Peak winner Bobby Unser on the 1967 card. Bill Vukovich passed a slowing George Benson on the final lap to win the race in front of 5,540. Vukovich made it two in a row when he also won the 1968 race.

The USAC National Championship Midgets raced an unprecedented three times at the speedway in 1969. Campbell driver George Benson powered his Offy to victory in the season-opening race. He then followed that up with a win in the July 4 race.

February 10, 1957: Promoter J.C. Agajanian (left) presents USAC National Championship Shorty Templeman the first trophy after his victory in the first running of a USAC race in San Jose. *Bob Mize Photo courtesy of Don Mize*

1959: Mr. Excitement Jim Hurtubise raced and won in all types of cars, including Midgets. Jim, who participated in ten Indy 500s, won the Trophy Dash during the 1959 USAC race at San Jose. *Jim Abreu Photo*

1958: Mike McGreevy, one of the Midget driving greats, won two USAC National Championships, four BCRA titles and seven main events at San Jose. *Jim Abreu Photo*

1957: Johnny Boyd had four San Jose victories and two BCRA titles before moving on to the Indianapolis 500 and Big Cars. *Jim Abreu Photo*

A 1958 photo of Bob Wente, who would later win the 1962 race at San Jose and the 1963 USAC National Midget Championship. *Jim Abreu Photo*

Burt Foland spent all night finishing his home-built Midget for the September race. He arrived too late to hot lap, but still set fast time. In the main event, he passed Bob Tattersall late in the race and went on to victory. The feature was marred by the death of Lloyd Nygren from Fresno. He was killed on the first lap when his Midget rode over another car's rear wheel, turned on its side and skidded about 200 feet down the back straightaway, dragging his hapless body on the pavement. It was a short time later that roll cages would be mandatory on Midgets.

Indy car drivers Bettenhausen, Vukovich, Parsons and Snider greeted the capacity crowd on opening day, 1970. Johnny Parsons, Jr., led Johnny Anderson across the finish line and won the annual 100-lapper. The USAC Midgets returned in November and saw Burt Foland do a complete 360-degree spin on lap 32, and without missing a beat, keep right on going to win the race. Three months later Burt won the 1971 race, making him the only driver to win three San Jose USAC races.

Gary Bettenhausen made it look easy in winning the 1972 race but faced a stiffer challenge from Larry Rice in the 1973 contest before making a late-race pass for the win.

Jimmy Caruthers led an overwhelming task force of the new revolutionary Volkswagen-powered Midgets to the finishing flag in 1974. Dave Strickland and Bobby Olivera finished second and third respectively in their VW-powered Midgets. The writing was on the wall for the once mighty Offenhauser.

Jimmy Caruthers, who was undergoing treatment for cancer, led the 1975 race until lap 70, when fatigue took hold. Bobby Olivero took the lead and held on to win. After the race, an exhausted Olivero said, "This is one of the most demanding tracks we race on." Sadly, Caruthers would lose his battle with cancer during the year.

Ron "Sleepy" Tripp survived a dramatic duel with Chuck Gurney and then pulled away for a five-length victory over Larry Patton in 1976.

February 20, 1977, was the last time USAC ever raced in San Jose. Hank Butcher turned back a star-studded field that Sunday evening to win the rain-delayed race. Rich Vogler won the most exciting race of the day, a photo finish in the first heat.

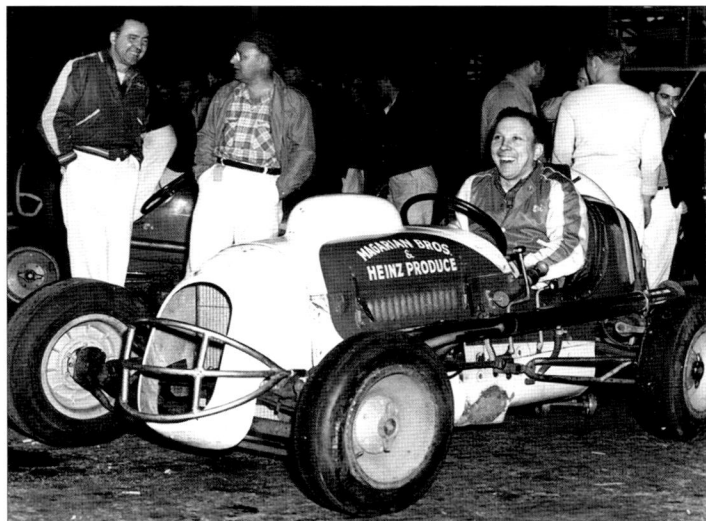

Eli Vukovich enjoys a good laugh in the Magarian V-8 during 1951. *Jim Abreu Photo*

Indy winner Johnnie Parsons, driving the Fred Gerhardt Offy, was one of the entrants for the USAC National Championship race on March 9, 1958. *Jim Abreu Photo*

George Benson won two USAC and two BCRA feature races at San Jose. Benson was also one of the most talented car builders in the Bay Area. *Jim Abreu Photo*

A 1959 photo of Earl Motter who won back-to-back BCRA Midget main events during July and August 1953. *Jim Abreu Photo*

Arguably the greatest American race car driver ever, A.J. Foyt participated in the 1960 Pacific Coast Championship driving an Offy. *Jim Abreu Photo*

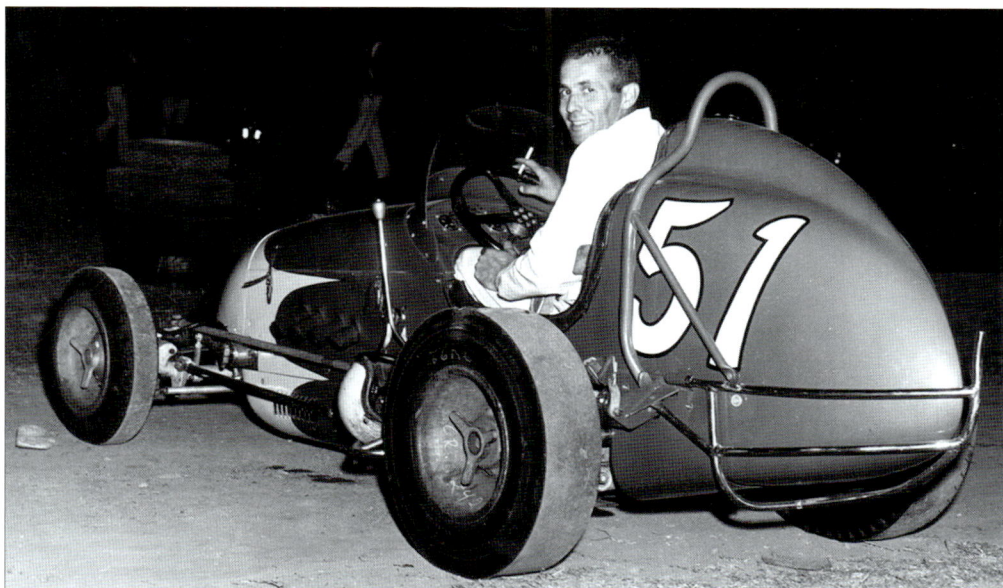

1959: Gene Gurney had a successful career driving Midgets in Northern California. His son Chuck and grandson Chuck, Jr., would also excel at the racing game. *Jim Abreu Photo*

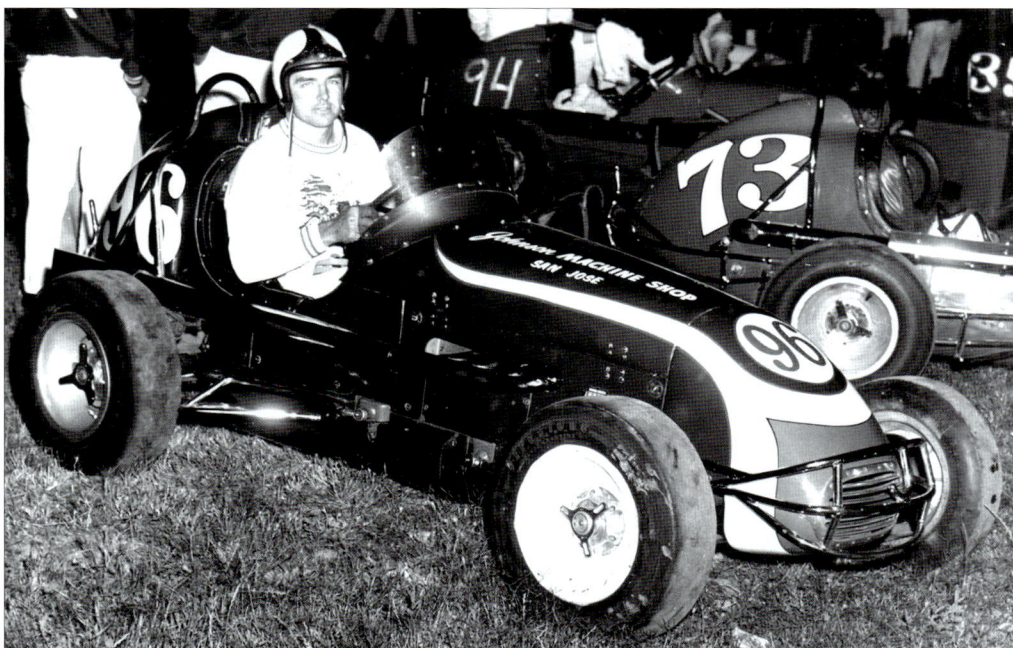

San Jose Hall of Fame driver Joe Leonard at the Midget Auto Racing Pacific Coast Championship in 1960. *Jim Abreu Photo*

1964: Mel Kenyon won 111 USAC National Midget races and 7 championships -- more than anybody in history. *Jim Abreu Photo*

USAC National Midgets returned on October 21, 1962, after an absence of several years. Bob Wente held off a charging Foyt to win the 50-lap affair. Wente sits in the Bob Higman Midget with Parnelli Jones looking on. *Jim Abreu Photo*

Forty years after his father won races at the old 5/8-mile San Jose Speedway, Norm Rapp was winning at the Tully Road track, three in all. *Jim Abreu Photo*

Lloyd Nygren was the fourth person to lose his life at San Jose Speedway. *Jim Abreu Photo*

Burt Foland (pictured in 1967) won more Midget races (18) than any other driver at the speedway. He also set the final track qualifying record with a time of 14.60. Car owner Jack London is standing in front of the car. *Jim Abreu Photo*

Parnelli Jones drove the Marv Edwards Midget to a convincing USAC Midget win on November 8, 1964. J.C. Agajanian gives some words of encouragement before the start of the race. *Jim Abreu Photo*

The star attraction at the 1962 USAC Midget race was 1961 Indianapolis 500 winner A.J. Foyt. *Jim Abreu Photo*

Hall of Fame driver Gary Bettenhausen won the 1972 & 1973 USAC National Midget races at San Jose. Gary, who would start in 21 Indianapolis 500s, won 27 National Midget races and a multitude of Sprint Car and Champ Car races. *Jim Abreu Photo*

J.C. Agajanian and his son Jay (far right), present the Fast Time Award to Chuck Gurney during the 1975 USAC Midget race. *Jim Abreu Photo*

George Benson (pictured in 1970) won five Midget races at San Jose, including two USAC National Championship races in 1969. *Jim Abreu Photo*

Two of the most prominent promoters in West Coast history, J.C. Agajanian (left) and Bob Barkhimer, chatting on the infield during the 1964 USAC Midget race. *Jim Abreu Photo*

1977: San Jose racer Richard Walsh drove Midgets, Sprint Cars and Super Modifieds in San Jose. *Dennis Mattish Photo*

Ron "Sleepy" Tripp (97) won the 1976 USAC race while Gary Bettenhausen (27) came home fifth. *Dennis Mattish Photo*

1970 USAC National Midget Champion Jimmy Caruthers also won the 1974 USAC event at San Jose. *Jim Abreu Photo*

Floyd Alvis (42) races with Stan Lee during the 1976 National USAC event. Alvis won a very impressive six BCRA titles. He also had three Fairground wins in San Jose. *Dennis Mattish Photo*

Racing legend Jan Opperman in a moment of thought at the 1976 USAC race.
Dennis Mattish Photo

USAC Midgets on parade before the start of their National Championship race in February 1975. Eastridge shopping center is in the background. *Dennis Mattish Photo*

(continued from page 111)

then went on the road, racing all over the western states. Although he ran only half the San Jose races, he still managed to pick up five feature wins.

The Johnny Key race was a classic, witnessed by a standing-room-only crowd of 6,800. People were turned away from the full parking lot two hours before the show began. In that race, George Snider passed hometown rival Pombo on the last lap to nose him out for the win. Stan Luhdorff

suffered broken ribs when his car slammed into the wall, rolled sideways five times and burst into flames.

The speedway had another great year with large crowds witnessing an all-star cast of drivers staging excellent shows.

1965

Further advancements were made to the Modified Hardtops during the off-season. The cars were now called Super Modified Hardtops.

Marshall Sargent was suspended for the opening race for participating in a non-sanctioned (outlaw) event in Sacramento. His Australia racing events during the winter climaxed in a riot on his final night down under. A portion of the 30,000 fans destroyed his car during the riot he instigated. It is also noted that he sold his car to a local driver before the races that evening and didn't lose a dime.

Forty-nine hundred fans saw Al Pombo win the opening race on March 28. Pombo then won the next three in a row to jump out to a quick points lead.

On April 24, Marshall Sargent was unhappy with the way flagman Paul Bender was conducting the restarts. When Sargent felt he was cheated, he drove to the flag stand after the race and proceeded to yell at Bender while

1964 program cover featuring (bottom from left) Al Pombo, Marshall Sargent and Clyde Palmer (top) Everett Edlund and Bill Blue.

1964: Bill Hill was the first driver to put a wing on his car at San Jose. *Bob Mize Photo*

1964: Joe Leonard (10) and Clyde Palmer (1) occupy two of the three grooves on the high-banked track. Both cars are Goularte Bros. entries. *Bob Mize Photo courtesy of Don Mize*

Cliff Yiskis accepting one of his many main event trophies he would win at the Tully Road action track, this one in 1964. *Bob Mize Photo courtesy of Don Mize*

1964: Cliff Rogalsky was the third person to lose his life on the high banks. *Bob Mize Photo courtesy of Don Mize*

Tom Haylett was leading a main event in 1964 when his throttle stuck wide open, sending him full speed into the wall. His car exploded into a huge fireball with Tom making a quick exit. As he ran from the burning car with his shirt on fire, he was tackled by the track crew, who then smothered the fire. He suffered only minor burns. *Bob Mize Photo courtesy of Don Mize*

1964 NASACR Modified Hardtop action. Dick Whalen (9), Bill Vukovich (7), Clyde Palmer (10), Al Pombo (3), Art Bigiogni (14), and Stan Eaton (50). *Bob Mize Photo courtesy of Don Mize*

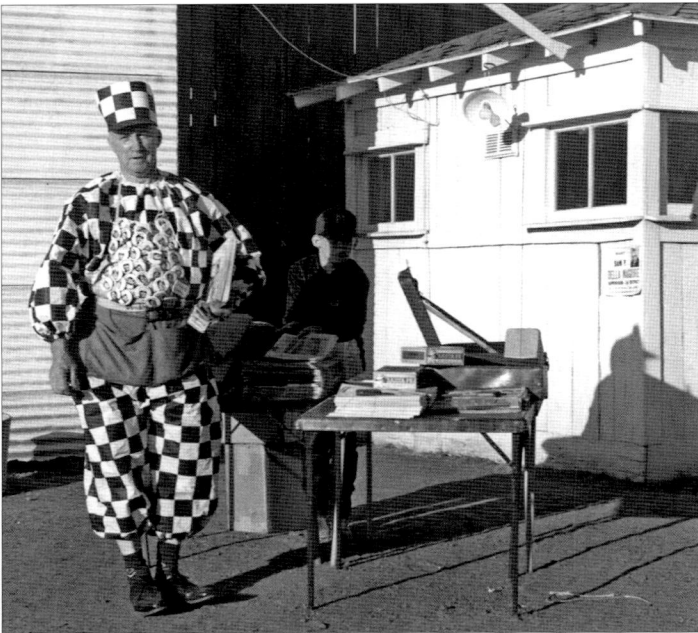

Walt Welton, the program man, was a fixture at San Jose Speedway and later the Fairgrounds for most of its history. *Bob Mize Photo courtesy of Don Mize*

1966 action in turn two. *Bob Mize Photo courtesy of Don Mize*

1966: Vendor Alley behind the front straightaway grandstands. Who could forget the tasty French Fries? *Bob Mize Photo*

200-Lap STOCK CAR RACES

LATE MODEL STOCK CAR CLASSIC

Sunday

March 15

TIME TRIALS 1 P.M.
RACE 2:15 P.M.
CHAMPION DRIVERS ! !

FIRST GREAT AUTO CLASSIC OF 1964 . . All Late Model Cars In Finest condition For Record Speed

ADMISSION
3.00 Children Under 6, 50¢

SAN JOSE **Speedway** TULLY ROAD

OPPOSITE HILLVIEW GOLF COURSE — 251-1401

Take Tully Road East off Bayshore Freeway

Marvin Porter (1) avoided Cliff Garner's overturned Stock Car during the NASCAR Pacific Coast Championship race in 1965. Bill Amick lapped the field twice to score an easy victory in the 200-lap race witnessed by 4,250. Jack McCoy set a Late Model Stock Car track record. *Ken Clapp Collection*

Making a strong showing when he raced in San Jose was Fresno's George Snider. He won three main events in 1964, including the prestigious Johnny Key Memorial Race. *Bob Mize Photo*

Herb Kaeding made his mark in the Claimer Division before moving into the Modifieds. He later became an accomplished off-road racer. His nephew (Brent) adopted the number 69.
Bob Mize Photo courtesy of Don Mize

Bill Vukovich II, son of two-time Indianapolis 500 winner, won a handful of main events at San Jose before moving up to the Indy Car circuit where he competed in 16 Indianapolis 500s.
Bob Mize Photo courtesy of Don Mize

breaking his flagsticks. This action worked the crowd of 4,650 into frenzy, just like in pro wrestling. After much publicity over the episode, there were even more people in the stands the following week. Promoter Bob Barkhimer took notice of this and had a secret meeting with Sargent. It was written years later by Barkhimer that he included extra money in Sargent's payoff whenever he created excitement. Bender didn't have a clue about this agreement.

The following week, Pombo became the first driver to break the 15-second barrier with a time of 14:89. Sargent won that night and would win the next three in a row. The Pombo-Sargent feud was now reaching legendary status (they competed against each other at three different tracks every week, with the same results). The last race in May finished in a dead heat between the pair. After officials had a conference, the victory was given to Pombo. This sent Sargent into a rage of protest, which also stirred up the crowd of 4,900 who were now divided into two camps, half for Pombo and half for Sargent.

Two weeks later, Joe Diaz was unhurt when his machine went over the wall and into the parking lot.

It wasn't until mid-June that someone other than the Pombo-Sargent duo would win a feature race. Rick Henderson, who had not been racing full time, won that race. Rick would race for the rest of the year, picking up eight main event wins.

During a September race, the field was coming in for the green flag when a pile-up occurred. Knocked out of the race was Sargent, who then went into another flag-breaking tirade. The following week he was fined $50 (paid by Barkhimer) and he presented Bender with a new set of flags in front of the crowd. (Not wanting to kill the goose that laid the golden egg, Sargent was no longer being suspended.)

Pombo went on to win 10 main events for the year while picking up his fourth championship, tying him with Henderson in San Jose titles won. Bill Scott finished in second place for the second year in a row. Sargent, with five wins, finished third in points.

The division formerly known as $99 Claimers had evolved into what was now known as the NASCAR Limited Sportsman division. The cars were allowed to modify the engines, bodies, handling and steering. Also, they could no longer be claimed (bought). The stars of the division were Lloyd Beard, Vic Irvan, John Viel, Joe Roletto and Lyle Lister, to name a few. The weekly Friday night series began on April 4. Walt Calkins won the inaugural event. The following week Roletto won on a night when Ray Elder set a six-lap track record. Vic Irvan and Butch Bishop won the following two races. After Watsonville opened up their Friday night season,

Burt Foland after winning the 1965 Johnny Key Classic, his first of two wins in that race. When his career was over, he would be inducted into no fewer than three Halls of Fame.
Bob Mize Photo courtesy of Don Mize

In 1965, the Claiming Division evolved into the Sportsman Division. Vic Irvan (9), father of Daytona 500 winner, Ernie, won a main event in the new class. After a handful of races, the Sportsman Cars left San Jose to concentrate on their own circuit as the featured division at such tracks as Watsonville and Merced Speedways. *Bob Mize Photo courtesy of Don Mize*

SUPER MODIFIED
AUTO RACES

SAN JOSE SPEEDWAY

1966 SOUVENIR PROGRAM 35¢

Everett Edlund (17) leads Clyde Palmer (10) and Al Pombo (3) during 1966 Super Modified main event action. *Bob Mize Photo*

130

it was decided to discontinue the series at San Jose, especially since at all the tracks the Sportsman ran on were dirt (with the exception of Lakeport).

The track was plagued by many injuries during the year. One of the more serious happened when Clyde Palmer went out of control and skidded sideways into the infield, striking Bill Blue. Bill was transported to the hospital with head injuries. He made a full recovery.

1966

During the off-season, $40,000 worth of improvements were made to the speed plant, including a resurfacing of the track.

Because the previous year's Late Model Stock Car race that preceded the Super Modified season caused several thousand dollars' worth of damages to the track surface, it was decided not to run the much heavier cars this year.

San Jose Speedway enjoyed the backing of the city. Here is a statement made by the Mayor of San Jose during opening week. "Whereas speedway racing has long been established as a professional sport, and whereas this sport will begin its 20th year of competition in San Jose on March 19, 1966, and whereas speedway racing has proved to be a top-notch and exciting entertainment having been attended by over 2,000,000 enthusiastic racing fans, now therefore I, Joseph L. Pace, M.D., Mayor of the city of San Jose, do hereby proclaim the week of March 19 as speedway racing week in San Jose and urge that all citizens join in observance of this event."

Fresh off his domination of Australian racing, Marshall Sargent won the San Jose opener in front of 5,114. He then proceeded to win the first four races of the year and take the points lead.

The worst accident in track history took place on April 16. The 1,500-pound Super Modified driven by Joe McGee collided with another racer, climbing his right rear tire. McGee's car shot into the air and then came down and flipped sideways, rolling numerous times. The car then cleared the four-foot crash wall, smashed through a wire fence and then rolled over a crowd of about 70 pitmen who were standing on a raised observation platform. The car continued, landing on top of two pickups parked in the pits. When the dust settled, 18 people were injured. It took five ambulances to transport them to the hospital. By the next day, all but five were released from the hospital and those five would eventually make a full recovery. Miraculously nobody was killed. NASCAR insurance covered all the injured.

Sargent had the best start of any driver in track history, winning 10 of the first 12 main events and setting many track records in the process. Even after that fast start, he still only had a 20-point lead over Al Pombo. On the 13th week, Sargent got caught in a massive 14-car pileup, knocking him out of the race. Pombo won and closed within a couple of points of Sargent.

The following week, Larry Rodriguez and Louis Jacquet were hospitalized when the tire they were working on exploded in the pits.

Aftermath of the 1966 Joe McGee crash. *Bob Mize Photo courtesy of Don Mize*

Burt Foland, driving for Pombo, passed his boss on lap 91 and roared to victory in the Johnny Key Memorial Race. Another turn-away crowd of 6,422 was present to see Foland take his second Key race in a row.

After 27 weeks of racing, Pombo and Sargent were tied for first place. Sargent had 13 wins and Pombo 5. With just three weeks to go in the season, Sargent was knocked unconscious in a five car pile-up. The points he lost to Pombo that night ended up costing him the title.

Pombo won his fourth championship in a row, and fifth overall, surpassing Rick Henderson as the most decorated driver in track history. Other drivers winning several main events were Clyde Palmer, Everett Edlund and Burt Foland.

Drivers from Washington, Nevada and Oregon competed in the biggest open competition race held yet at the speedway. Notable drivers Gary Patterson and Don Edmunds participated, but they couldn't keep up with the locals. Sixty two hundred fans saw Burt Foland win the 100-lap race, his second long-distance win of the year at the track.

1967

Despite cold and threatening weather, 4,903 turned out to see Howard Kaeding hold off a charging Burt Foland to win the mid-March opener. Lem Tolliver suffered acid burns, facial cuts and a concussion in a grinding semi-main crash. Then the weather took over, canceling four out of the next seven races.

Tragedy struck the track on June 3. Twenty-nine year old Cliff Rogalsky was competing in a heat race when the car in front of him blew an engine, spraying the track with oil. Rogalsky slid into the wall, along with Johnny Brazil and Cliff Yiskis. In a freak accident, a piece of magnesium ('mag') wheel broke apart and hit him in the face, killing him. He was the speedway's third death, but the first car driver. Within a week, mag wheels were outlawed.

By July, Marshall Sargent had five wins, but then he was suspended for three weeks for having a disagreement (to put it mildly) with officials at Clovis speedway.

Kaeding had three wins under his belt and the points lead going into the Johnny Key Memorial. In second place was Bill Scott. The pair sat on the front row and proceeded to swap the lead a number of times during the 100-lap race. Scott won the exciting race and took over the points lead.

Marshall Sargent won his seventh main event in September to once again lead in that category. What was significant about that win, it was the last one of his career. On September 16, he was qualifying someone else's car when a tire blew. The car spun around and went into the wall backward at about 80mph. He was transported to the hospital in critical condition with a head injury. He would remain in a semi-coma state for days following the accident. This was the third time in a year that he had been knocked out in a crash. He spent approximately a month in the hospital.

After playing bridesmaid to Pombo for the last two

1966: Clyde Palmer was one of the most versatile drivers to race San Jose, competing in just about every class to have run there. Palmer won the 1961 track championship and 25 feature events in the Hardtops and Super Modifieds. *Jim Abreu Photo*

Fan favorite Al Pombo won an unprecedented six track championships and 104 feature events at San Jose. *Bob Mize photo*

By popular demand, a season ending "Fans Appreciation Day" was held in honor of Marshall Sargent. Sargent, who was still suffering blurred vision and impaired hearing from his September 16, 1967, crash, was presented with a pickup-truck load of gifts and money. People, who used to boo him, were now rallying to help the most colorful and controversial driver in track history. He was very grateful.

years, the roles were reversed for Bill Scott, who picked up his first track championship, winning five main events in the process. Pombo finished second, also with five wins. Kaeding, who led the points race on three occasions only to lose it, finished third with five wins.

The season-ending open competition race was dedicated to the memory of Cliff Rogalski. The 100-lap race, called the "Rogalski Memorial," was billed as the "Battle of Champions" with track champions throughout the West competing. Burt Foland led the first 99 laps, but on the white flag lap he got caught up in a pile-up with lapped traffic. Pombo slipped by the carnage and won the race.

1968

For the first time in two decades, Midget racing was held on a weekly basis. The first race of the Friday night series was held on July 12. Burt Foland feasted on the series, winning seven out of the eight races. Only Dickie Deis was able to stop Foland from a clean sweep. The series was deemed a success.

In the first race for Super Modifieds, Johnny Brazil zipped ahead of track champion Bill Scott on a restart after an accident and held on for a narrow victory. Pombo then took control of the points chase for the rest of the year, winning 14 main events on his way to an unprecedented sixth speedway title. Other drivers having a good year were Burt Foland with five wins and Johnny Brazil and Clyde Palmer with three wins each.

Careful driving and the ability to avoid numerous spins and traffic snarls enabled Howard Kaeding to post his first victory in the 15th annual Johnny Key Memorial Race.

Bill Scott won the third annual open competition race. Although the best drivers in the West entered, they could not keep up with the regulars who raced at San Jose.

1969

After an absence of 15 years, Sprint Cars sanctioned by the Northern Auto Racing Club (NARC) made an appearance on May 30. "Leroy Van Connett and Gary Ponzini ended in a dead heat in the 50-lap Memorial Day pro-

gram," read the *Mercury News*. This may have been the only feature race to end in a tie in San Jose racing history.

Bill Scott drove the brand new Blue Goose Special to a dominating win on opening day. This set the tone for the year. Pombo won the next race, but then Howard Kaeding entered the points chase, winning back-to-back features. In his second win, he had to wrestle the lead from a young Nick Rescino in the closing laps.

Scott started on the pole position and led all 100 laps to record his second Johnny Key Classic win. It wasn't easy, as Johnny Brazil stayed glued to his rear the entire distance and finished a close second.

Scott, who had 13 main event wins, wrapped up the title a month before the season ended. Second in the win column with six was Kaeding.

Making a comeback after his 1967 accident was Marshall Sargent. (He would race for two more months and then park the car.)

NARC Winners at San Jose Speedway	
5-30-1969	Leroy Van Connett/Gary Ponzini *
5-29-1970	Rick Henderson
5-28-1971	Jim Eiland
5-29-1972	Lem Tolliver
10-1-1972	Lem Tolliver
6-22-1973	Chuck Gurney
9-30-1973	Leroy Van Connet
9-29-1974	Lem Tolliver
9-28-1975	Johnny Anderson
* = dead heat finish	

1970

A new era in Super Modified racing greeted the start of the seventies. T-shirted drivers were nowhere in sight. All drivers wore mandatory fire-repellant racing suits that also made them look more professional. The cars continued to evolve into sleek, sophisticated, more powerful machines.

Clyde Palmer, a veteran of over 30 years in racing, was the new chief steward. Palmer was a take-no-crap, rule-with-an-iron-fist kind of guy. During the first race, he levied many fines for infractions committed, getting everybody's attention about the way things would be.

Bill Scott easily won the opener in front of a capacity crowd. At the next race, Scott put a set of Indianapolis Championship Car Firestone tires on his Blue Goose Special Super Modified. He immediately set a track record. The following week, other drivers showed up at the track sporting the new tires. The track record took a beating from Scott five weeks in a row, culminating with a 13:97, thus making him the first driver to qualify less than 14 seconds. As the assault on the track records progressed, the crowds started arriving early for qualifying so they could witness history being made. Scott would go on and set fast time for an unprecedented 16 weeks in a row. Also during that stretch, he won 9 out of the first 14 races and took a sizable points lead. But then mechanical gremlins took control of his car and he did not win a main event for the next three months.

The Roadster-like Super Modified owned by Flyer Tabata and driven by Howard Kaeding made its debut. It took three months to get the bugs worked out, but once that was accomplished, Bill Scott met his match. At mid-season, Kaeding reeled off five straight wins in the new car.

A record crowd of 6,777 attended the 17th annual Johnny Key Memorial race. Kaeding's hard driving style made him his own worst enemy as he tried to pass Scott for the lead on the last lap of the 150-lap affair. He clipped Scott's car and then the two cars got tangled together. Don Epperson, who was running third at the time, could not believe his eyes as he slipped past the pair and claimed the biggest win of his career. He took home the winner's share of the record $11,579 purse (about the price of a modest

1969: The personable Johnny Brazil of Manteca won dozens of main events over the years at San Jose. *Bob Mize Photo courtesy of Don Mize*

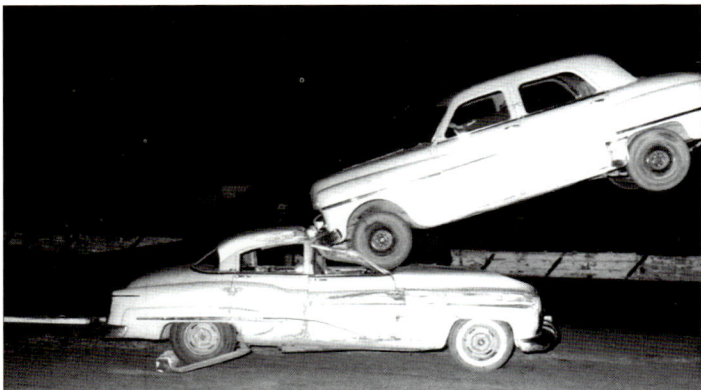

The Auto Daredevils were a regular feature during the history of the track. *Bob Mize Photo courtesy of Don Mize*

There was much talk when Dick Whelan showed up at the track in 1969 with the "Whelan Wedge." He had modest success in the car. *Bob Mize Photo courtesy of Don Mize*

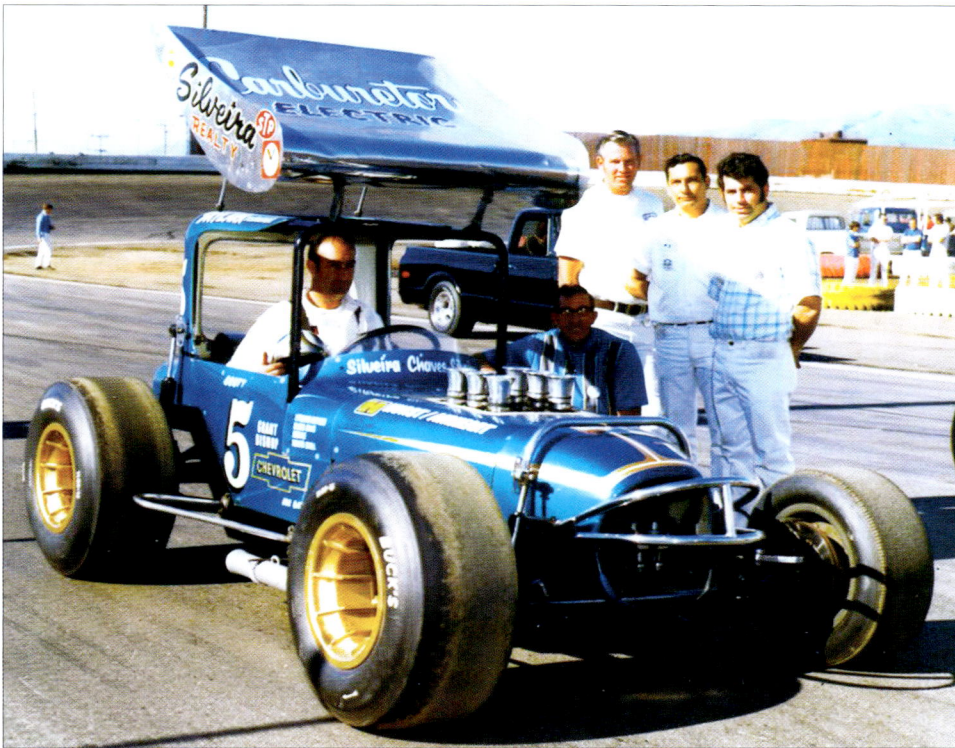

Bill Scott sits in the very successful "Blue Goose Special" during 1970 as car owner Arnold Chaves (four-time Car Owner Champion) and his crew looks on. Scott won 45 main events and the 1967, 1969, 1970 and 1971 track championships. *Jim Abreu Photo*

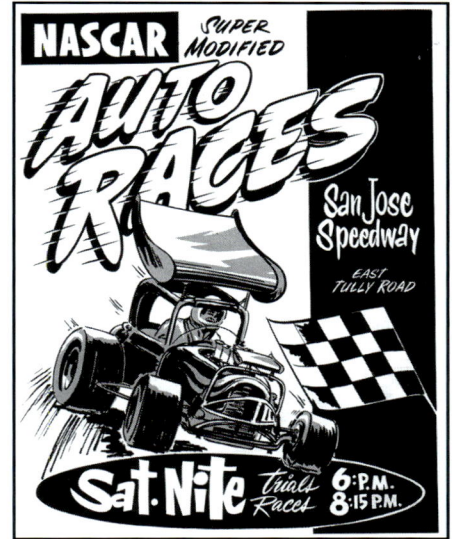

1970: Dick Wallace Metcalfe, host of the *Spotlite on Speed* TV program, has his movie camera aimed at Nick Ringo's trophy celebration. *Bob Mize Photo*

1972: From left: Track announcer Ken Takeuchi prepares to interview racing legends Joe Leonard and Al Pombo. *Bob Mize Photo*

NASCAR Western Grand National Stock Cars line up for the Trophy Dash during their 1971 appearance. Paul Dorrity (15) and Ray Elder (96) occupy the inside. *Bob Mize Photo*.

home in 1970). The following week Epperson flipped end over end down the back straight, destroying his car.

By September, Kaeding had won 12 main events, including the Mission Bell 100, and closed to within 9 points of Scott. But then Scott won two in a row and Kaeding had a stretch of bad luck. Scott held on and won his second championship in a row and third overall.

Car counts for the year hovered around 50 per show.

1971

The NASCAR Western Grand National Stock Cars made their first appearance at San Jose since 1965. Because of rain, the race was delayed for a week, so the teams left their cars at local dealerships. On race day, Johnny Soares muscled his battered 1970 Plymouth to victory over Jack McCoy and Ray Elder in the 150-lap race.

A chilled crowd of 4,900 sat through numerous spins and crashes on a slick track that was swept by strong, gusty winds. When it was over, Howard Kaeding emerged victorious in the Super Modified opener. He then proceeded to win the next five races in a row. Then Bill Scott and Johnny Brazil got hot, winning four main events each during the next nine weeks.

Everett Edlund weaved his way through traffic and mishaps and beat Nick Rescino to the checkered flag in the 18th annual Johnny Key Race.

Showing that he had not softened, Chief Steward Clyde Palmer suspended Art Bigiogni, Nick Rescino and Marshall Sargent during the year.

Kaeding went on to win 15 main events and was crowned track champion. Bill Scott, who switched teams,

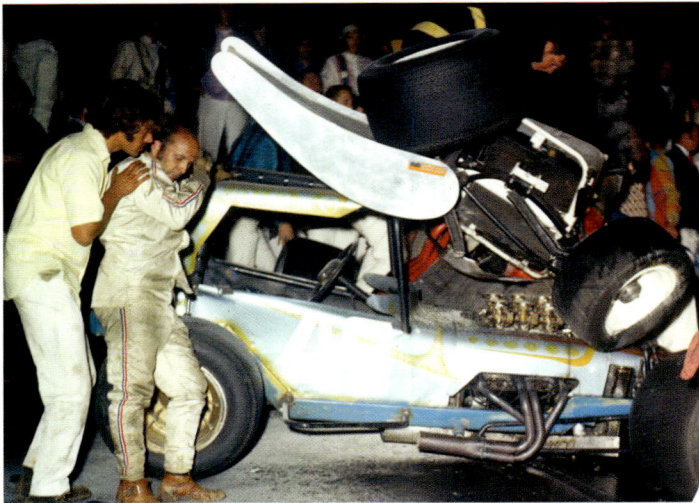

On July 10, 1971, George (Junior) Coppla was racing down the backstretch when his Super Modified bumped with another car and then bounced off the wall hard. The car then rolled on top of the Super driven by Dan Clapp (second from left). When the cars came to rest, Coppla's throttle remained stuck wide open, casting a sickening sound through the air. Clapp, who was seated just inches under the redlining engine, climbed out of his car and shut it off. Coppla was removed from the damaged car unconscious and transported to the hospital where he would remain in a coma for two weeks. He was hospitalized for a month and then faced a long recovery after that. He would never race again. *Bob Mize Photo*

won five mains. Johnny Brazil, who was getting better every year, picked up six wins. Veteran racer Ed Hopper claimed two wins. Making his first trips to victory circle with four feature wins was Nick Rescino, who set fast time at more than half the races.

The first Golden State Classic was held in 1971. This series would develop into the biggest Western states open competition series in history. A term used at that time was "run-what-you-brung," meaning just about any type of race car within reason (Midgets were not allowed) was accepted. The smorgasbord included Super Modifieds, Sprint Cars, offset Roadsters, rear-engined cars, four-wheel-drive cars, Sprint Buggies, Modifieds, Indy Cars and Sportsman. There was even a car with a blower on it–fast as hell down the straightaway, didn't handle very well in the turns. The cars and drivers came from New York, Ohio, Florida and other parts of the USA and Canada.

The series, which raced at four different tracks, was the brainchild of Dick Cinelli, who put up $25,000 of his own money–a huge gamble, especially for a series held in November, the rainy season.

San Jose was the only track hosting two races, the first and last. When the checkered flag fell on the series, it was the San Jose regulars who dominated, taking nine out of the top ten spots. Bill Scott won the first race and was crowned Overall Champion. Howard Kaeding, who won at Lakeport and the last race at San Jose, was runner-up. Bob Seelman from Michigan, drove the same Indy Car Roadster that Troy Ruttman raced in at Indianapolis in 1965, to a seventh place finish, the only non-local to crack the top 10. If people were wondering where San Jose Super Modifieds stood on the national level, this series answered those questions.

In a column by the *Mercury News* sports editor Louis Duino, it was written that auto racing was the most popular sport in the San Jose area. Over the years the speedway had consistently drawn 150,000 annually, making it the most attended sporting event in San Jose.

1972

Once just an afterthought in San Jose racing, Late Model Stock Cars were now making a name for themselves. The San Jose 150 NASCAR Winston Grand National West Late Model Stock Car race was held on March 19. Jack McCoy led wire to wire to win the race, but it wasn't easy, as the father-son duo of Dick and Chuck Bown pressured him all the way. Pre-race favorite Hershel McGriff was sidelined by mechanical problems. Two thousand one hundred spectators were present.

Former Alviso Speedway champion Jack Epperson held off the fierce challenges from Nick Rescino and Howard Kaeding to win the opening day Super Modified race. During qualifying, Marshall Sargent had a throttle stick on his Super Modified, sending him straight into the wall. Sargent, who never regained his form after the severe head injury he suffered in 1967, was rushed to the hospital with another closed-head injury. This accident sent him into permanent retirement. During the main event that day, Steve Bealessio blew his engine on lap 14. His car skidded through his own oil and slammed head on into the wall. He was transported to the hospital in an unconscious state. It took a year for him to recover from his injuries and two years before he would race again.

Nick Rescino passed Howard Kaeding on lap 32 and then lost the lead to Don Epperson on lap 129. He regained the lead on lap 135 in traffic and held off the pesky Epperson for an exciting win in the 19th annual Johnny Key Classic.

Burt Foland drove a Ford-powered Super Modified to victory, the first time in two decades a Ford had won in the Premier Division at the track.

Olympia Beer sponsored a five-race series during the year, each race being 100 laps. Kaeding won that series within a series championship.

The year 1972 was one of the most competitive seasons in track history, with nine different drivers winning main events. Rescino and Kaeding battled right down to the end, with Rescino emerging with the crown.

The second annual Golden State Classic grew in size and stature from the first year. A cast that reads like a who's who in American and Canadian short track auto racing converged on the Golden State. Twenty-three out-of-state drivers were in the San Jose pits for the second race of the series. Howard Kaeding led the local contingent in claiming the first nine positions in the main event. New York's Ollie Silva, who won the first race at Roseville, finished 10th. Nick Rescino won the second race at San Jose and claimed the series championship. The out-of-state drivers had a strong showing in the series this year, especially the rear-engine, four-wheel-drive cars driven by Todd Gibson and Armond Holly.

1973

A new era in racing started this year, as mufflers were now required on all race cars.

The NARC Sprint Cars made their annual appearance on June 22 in a race called the Duane Bonini Memorial. Duane had a commanding lead in NARC points when he lost his life at Calistoga Speedway in 1971. Chuck Gurney, who three weeks earlier had won the Little Indy Midget Race, showed his versatility by dominating the Sprint Cars. He set fast time and won all three of the races he was in. Only 1,000 people were present.

On opening day, Larry Yarimie beat Nick Ringo on the last restart to win his first main event. Few people saw him take the checkered flag, as all eyes were diverted to turn one on the last lap as Howard Kaeding and Ringo crashed violently. They were okay. Kaeding stated that his throttle stuck and he would have gone head on into the wall if Ringo hadn't been there.

"Super Destruction Derby" is what the *Mercury News* labeled the first few races of the year, when only half the field was completing the main events because of crashes. Some of the drivers were bitter about their cars being destroyed and threatened to quit the track.

Nine different drivers, including Roland Wlodyka, won the first nine races. Howard Kaeding beat Nick Rescino by 12 lengths to win the 20th running of the Johnny Key Memorial Race. A standing-room-only crowd of over 6,000 contributed to the record purse of $13,800.

GOLDEN STATE CLASSIC

WORLD SERIES OF SUPER MODIFIED
AUTO RACING

$37,020.00
GUARANTEED TOTAL PURSE
SEVEN RACE SERIES

OCT. 19	8 PM	STOCKTON SPEEDWAY - STOCKTON, CAL.	1/4 MILE PAVED
OCT. 20	8 PM	ALL-AMERICAN SPEEDWAY - ROSEVILLE, CAL.	1/4 MILE PAVED
OCT. 21	2 PM	ALTAMONT RACEWAY - ALTAMONT, CAL.	1/2 MILE PAVED
OCT. 24	8 PM	SHASTA SPEEDWAY - ANDERSON, CAL.	1/3 MILE PAVED
OCT. 26	8 PM	SAN JOSE SPEEDWAY - SAN JOSE, CAL.	1/3 MILE PAVED
OCT. 27	8 PM	SAN JOSE SPEEDWAY - SAN JOSE, CAL.	1/3 MILE PAVED
OCT. 28	2 PM	SAN JOSE SPEEDWAY - SAN JOSE, CAL.	1/3 MILE PAVED

Ron Neal brought this radical (for that time) offset Roadster from Ohio to compete in the 1972 Golden State Classic. Note the blower on top of the engine. It was loud and fast down the straightaway. Photo taken after B-Main win. *Bob Mize Photo*

Todd Gibson from Ohio was the fastest of the out-of-state drivers to compete during the Golden State Classic. His rear-engine, four-wheel drive car easily won this 1972 Trophy Dash. *Bob Mize Photo courtesy of Don Mize*

Early September Kaeding caught and then passed Marshall Sargent's eight-race win streak set in 1962. Kaeding's win streak would eventually be halted at an amazing 14 victories in a row. What makes it more amazing is the feat happened at a time when the fast cars had to start last (inverted) and work their way up through the pack. Not surprisingly, he ran away with the points championship.

The season ended with the third annual Golden State Classic. By the time the series reached San Jose for the final three races, Roy Smith from Canada had won at Altamont Speedway and Jerry McClees from Washington captured the Shasta Speedway (Anderson, Ca.) race.

Then tragedy struck the series. Returning from Redding, Ca., in a Beachcraft Bonanza (a small private plane) were promoter Dick Cinelli, his wife Nancy (who was with child), along with Nancy's parents Glenn and Martha Kelly. The plane, with the five passengers and the purse money from the Shasta Speedway race on board, was approaching Reid-Hillview airport in heavy overcast when the plane lost power and crashed near a residential area, killing all aboard and scattering money and plane parts over a wide area.

Super Modified driver Earl Kelly, who had just lost his parents, sister and brother-in-law in the crash, held a meeting the next day. With a very heavy heart, he authorized the continuance of the series as a tribute to his family. Kaeding won that night, Johnny Brazil the second night and Kaeding finished off the series with another win and the series championship. With the death of the key players, the Golden State Classic would emerge under a different name.

1974

NASCAR made a rule change for the local speed plant during the winter. Up until then, the cars always raced to the yellow flag. For safety reasons, the new rule stated that everybody must slow down when the yellow was displayed and the scoring would resort to the previous lap.

Shot from the grandstands, Kim Beard took this outstanding photo of the last-lap crash involving Howard Kaeding (3) and Nick Ringo during the 1973 opening day race. *Courtesy of Kim Beard.*

This would eventually work, but not at the first race. Lloyd Beard won his first main event that day, but not until he had to pass for the lead four times, only to be set back to second position because of a yellow. Because of confusion, the cars circled the track 97 times to complete the 25-lap race, which took over an hour to run.

Young gun Mike Damron won the second race and took an early points lead. He followed that win with a victory in the Elk's charity race a couple of weeks later. During that race, Al Andrews suffered neck and feet injuries when his throttle stuck wide open. He climbed a wheel and was airborne when he slammed head-on into the wall, spewing a wheel and car parts out into the parking lot where they damaged some cars.

By the end of April, Howard Kaeding had made his move and took the points lead, a position he would hold for the rest of the year. Kaeding was also the King of the Beer, as he won his third successive "Olympia Beer Sweepstakes Championship," a five-race series of 100-lap races. He would once again lead in main event wins, with a total of 10.

Nearly 6,000 fans saw Nick Rescino win an exciting Johnny Key Memorial Classic. Rescino, who began the month of August with four wins, doubled that by the end of the month. He then shattered the track record, becoming the first driver to average over 90 mph on the short oval.

Early Model Stock Car and figure-eight racing started a Wednesday night season on June 12. Dennis Wilson dominated the Early Model oval

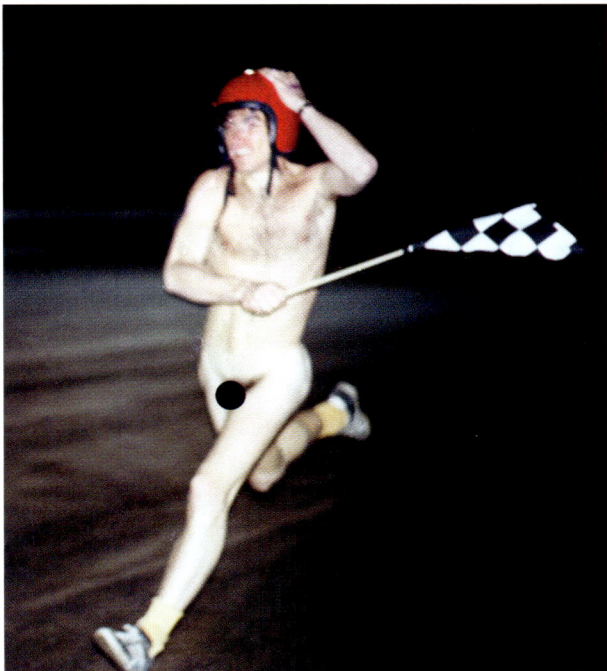

Streaking was the fad of 1974 when promoter Bob Barkhimer paid a San Jose State student to streak around the track on a cold night, much to the delight or dismay of the crowd, depending on how you look at it. *Dennis Mattish Photo*

1972: Lem Tolliver won more Sprint Car races at San Jose Speedway than any other driver, three in all. *Bob Mize Photo courtesy of Don Mize*

1972: Run-what-you-brung was what the Golden State Classic was all about. A rear engine Super Modified , Sprint Car and two Roadsters prepare for battle. *Bob Mize Photo courtesy of Don Mize*

Steve Reyes, one of the nation's premier motor sports photographers, visited San Jose Speedway during 1973 and shot this outstanding photo of Nick Rescino (1) and Bill Scott (5). The cars have unusual reverse-rotation engines. *Steve Reyes Photo.*

Mark Sargent crashed and burned during the 1973 Golden State Classic. He was ok. *Dennis Mattish Photo*

139

track championship, winning eight times.

The figure-eight track was built so the straightaway started at the exit of the turns on the 1/3-mile. This made for a long, fast straight leading into the X. On September 22, Stephen Tarigo lost his life when he was T-boned by race leader Darrel Sandau. The following week the entrance to the X was moved so that the straights were much shorter and slower. Ken Naber and Ken Nott battled right down to the last race before Naber emerged with the figure-eight title.

Earl Kelly took control of the Golden State Classic, a series his brother-in-law and sister started, and renamed it the Golden West Classic. The format was the same but a dirt track (Clovis Speedway) was added to the series. It was thought that Sprint Cars would have an advantage on the dirt, but the top four cars were San Jose Speedway regulars. Dewayne Woodward won the only San Jose race. He inherited the win on the last lap when front-runners Jim Eiland and Rod Furtado crashed each other out of the race. Woodward's win was the foundation for his winning the very competitive series.

The first signs that there was trouble brewing surfaced in September when some drivers and car owners formed an organization and started making demands on NASCAR and the speedway. Coincidently, a short time later, majority speedway owners Joe Sunseri and Joe and Ray Leon agreed they were tired of operating the track after 28 years. They put it up for sale for $1 million.

1975

Harry Goularte started at the back of the pack and proceeded to pass everybody for what was believed to be an opening day main event win in the Late Model Sportsman class. A few days later, NASCAR stripped Harry of his win for having an illegal intake manifold on the Jimmy Whalen-built engine. Defending champion Dennis Wilson took the early points lead before being overtaken by Doug McCoun during the Wednesday night series. Teenage drivers, McCoun and Goularte, traded victories for most of the season before Goularte caught, and then passed, McCoun at the end of the season to claim the championship. Goularte picked up 11 victories, including the 100-lap Silver Cup Classic. Making an appearance at the track during the year was a young Ernie Irvan.

Howard Kaeding held off a strong challenge from second-generation driver Davey Pombo and Nick Rescino on his way to winning the opening-day race, which was witnessed by 4,350 fans.

The points battle turned into a three-way race between Nick Rescino, Johnny Brazil and Howard Kaeding. Rescino used the double-points Johnny Key Classic win as a catalyst to winning the track championship. In that race, he went sideways as he took the checkered flag in front of Everett Edlund. Rescino won 12 features and set fast time at just about every race, thus earning the nickname "Quick Nick."

Nick Rescino drove the Ron Tomasello Super Modified to the fastest lap ever turned at San Jose Speedway during October 1974. His lap of 13.33 seconds was the only time to ever average over 90 mph on the 1/3-mile oval. Tomasello makes some last minute adjustments before Nick goes out to qualify. *Dennis Mattish Photo*

1973: Paul "Red" Bender, Long-time San Jose Speedway flagman, at his post. *Tom Dabel Photo*

NASCAR SUPER MODIFIED
AUTO RACES
SATURDAY
TRIALS AT 7 PM — RACES AT 8:15 PM
SAN JOSE SPEEDWAY
ON EAST TULLY ROAD
(Opposite Eastridge)
Ph. 251-1401
TICKETS:
Adults .. $3.00
Juniors (13-16)
.... $2.50
Under 12 Yrs. $1
Under 6 Yrs. FREE

Jack Epperson, the "Racing Auctioneer," won many main events. *Dennis Mattish Photo*

The most successful car in speedway history, The "Flyers Body Shop Chevy," was driven by Howard Kaeding. Howard won most of his record-setting 112 main events in this car, including a 17 straight-win streak. *Dennis Mattish Photo*

Just like his dad Merv, Rod Furtado won main events at San Jose Speedway. Rod always had nice-looking Super Modifieds.
Dennis Mattish Photo

Dewayne Woodward won the 1974 Golden West Classic.
Dennis Mattish Photo

Joey Iacobitti in 1974.
Dennis Mattish Photo

Having his best year ever at San Jose was Johnny Brazil. He won the Olympia Beer Sweepstakes, winning two of the five 100-lap races. He finished second in the final points standing.

Once again, Kaeding had a strong year, winning nine main events.

Nick Ringo fulfilled his dream by winning the state championship and finishing eighth nationally.

On September 20, Bob Zwemke was hot lapping his Super Modified when apparently something broke on the back of his car and started to drag on the pavement. This caused him to lose control of his car and back it into the wall. The car exploded on impact, sending a wall of fire high into the air, which was visible from over a mile away. As his car slid to a stop, the cars driven by Howard Kaeding and Mark Sargent pulled up to the scene and stopped. Both drivers jumped out of their cars and dashed into the flames to pull the stricken driver out. Zwemkie was rushed to the burn unit with critical burns over 100 percent of his body. Kaeding and Sargent were also treated for burns. Zwemkie clung to life for six days before passing away.

Johnny Brazil won the October 4 Golden West Classic Open Competition race. He followed that up by winning the series championship in the highly competitive multi-track event. The series promoter, Earl Kelly, won the second San Jose race on October 11–his first San Jose win.

The season ended with an open competition race on October 19, with a portion of the proceeds to go to the family of Bob Zwemkie. Burt Foland, who had recently come out of retirement, led flag-to-flag to claim the benefit race. Over $6,000 was raised for the widow and children of Zwemke .

As in years past, attendance continued to be strong, but this would change as the grumbling among some of the drivers and owners continued to grow, leading to the second major split to hit the track in its long history.

The track remained up for sale.

Bob Zwemke during driver introductions. *Dennis Mattish Photo*

Roland Wlodyka set two out of the last three one-lap track records in this car. After Super Modifieds, Roland drove in the NASCAR Cup series and then became a crew chief, winning a NASCAR championship with Dale Earnhardt. *Dennis Mattish Photo*

Cavalcade of Auto Racing
1972-1975

In 1972, fans saw the revival of the "Auto Racing Spectaculars" (from 1956 and 1957) in the form of the "Cavalcade of Auto Racing." All divisions participating were headliners in their own right.

Converging on San Jose Speedway on October 1, 1972, were the NARC Sprint Cars, BCRA Midgets, NASCAR Super Modifieds and NASCAR Sportsmans.

The races were invitational, open to the top 25 drivers in points (or lower down the rankings in order to fill the 25-car field) in their respective classes.

Each class of car ran a Trophy Dash and a 100-lap main event. As you can imagine, this was a race fan's dream come true. To top it off, the races were held on pleasant Sunday afternoons.

Some highlights: 1972: Super Modified driver Nick Rescino climbed into a Midget and won.

1973: In the NARC Sprint Cars, Leroy Van Connett put himself two laps down on the rest of the field after a first-lap tangle. Undaunted, he stormed back through the field to recoup one lap by the 40th go-around and passed George Rogge for the win with just a couple of laps to go.

1975: Johnny Anderson lapped the entire field in winning the BCRA 100-lap race. He then jumped into his NARC Sprint Car and proceeded to win that race, completing the only double in the four-year run.

NASCAR Super Modifieds (above), NARC Sprint Cars (below) NASCAR Stock Cars (right) & BCRA Midgets (right center) on parade during the Cavalcade of Auto Racing. *Dennis Mattish Photos*

The NASCAR Sportsman Division was part of the 1972 & 1973 Cavalcade of Auto Racing. John Cardoza (77), Billy Scyphers (17), Butch Bishop (60), Darwin Ernst (4), Dennis Close (28) and Joe Esperanca (32). *Bob Mize Photos courtesy of Don Mize*

1973 Ad

144

Cavalcade Winners

	1972	1973
BCRA Midgets	Nick Rescino	Johnny Anderson
NARC Sprint Cars	Lem Tolliver	Leroy Van Connett
NASCAR Sportsmans	Ray Campbell	Kirk Edion
NASCAR Super Modifieds	Don Epperson	Howard Kaeding

	1974	1975
BCRA Midgets	Johnny Anderson	Johnny Anderson
NARC Sprint Cars	Lem Tolliver	Johnny Anderson
NASCAR Stock Cars	Dennis Wilson	Nick Foster
NASCAR Super Modifieds	Nick Ringo	Nick Rescino

Johnny Anderson

Two-time NARC champion Mike McCreary (93) races with Pete May (75) during the Sprint Car portion of the 1974 Cavalcade of Auto Racing. *Dennis Mattish Photo*

1976

It was fitting that in Silicon Valley the first computerized scoreboard in the nation for a short track was installed. Jim Foote was the mastermind behind this development.

The BCRA Midgets ran a series of Friday night shows. Hank Butcher, the hottest driver on the circuit during the year, won 11 out of 15 races. Wheeler Gresham, Ken Molica, Johnny Anderson and Danny O'Neill won one each.

The first open competition Stock Car (Super Stocks) race was held on March 7. Promoted by Vic Irvan, the 150-lap race was called the "Spring Championship." Ted Fritz powered his Cougar to victory over an all-star cast of West Coast Stock Car drivers. Don Harper from Oregon won the "Fall Championship Invitational" Super Stock race.

The final open competition Super Stock race was held on October 10. Ernie Irvan set fast time and Dan Reed won the main. Good crowds of about 3,000 attended the first two shows.

The regular weekly Stock Car show joined the Super Modifieds and ran on Saturday nights. Harry Goularte won six main events and defended his crown. Finishing behind him with five wins was Ray Morgan. Jerry DeLoach was in

the hunt until the last month of the season. Ken Naber won eight figure-eight races on his way to claiming his second title in a row at San Jose. Ken Nott won five times.

The Golden State Owner and Drivers Association tried to set up negotiations with Bob Barkhimer and the track owners, who failed to even acknowledge the request for negotiations. The outlaw group then formed the Golden State Racing Association (GSRA) and took their show to the Santa Clara County Fairgrounds (see chapter 11). This was a huge blow for San Jose Speedway, as all the top drivers and owners were part of the GSRA.

Mark Sargent won the Super Modified season opener at San Jose Speedway over a weak field of 15 cars in front of a sparse crowd. All the top teams were running over at the fairgrounds in the GSRA opener at the same time. It was reported that Barkhimer made a trip over to the fairgrounds to see how their show was doing. When he saw 7,200 people in the stands and over 70 cars in the pits, he became irate. (In hindsight, he had reason to be mad. The damage done to local auto racing by the GSRA would take years to recover from.)

Meanwhile, Mark Sargent won the next week and then

1975: Fuel cells became mandatory after this fire involving Bob Zwemke. *Don Mize Photo*

1975: Todd Gibson in the famous Flintstone Flyer. This car was so dominant on the East Coast, it caused all rear engine, four-wheel-drive cars to be banned. At San Jose he was just as fast as the local top dogs. *Dennis Mattish Photo*

1975: Goodyear tires on display before the start of a race. Dick Whalen is in #2. *Dennis Mattish Photo*

Tom Haylett won the 1976 NASCAR Super Modified Championship. *Dennis Mattish Photo*

1976: In the biggest upset in Johnny Key Memorial history, unheralded Tony Ringo put on a superb performance to win the most prestigious race of the year. *Dennis Mattish Photo*

STOCK CAR ♦ **RACING**

ON THE OVAL TRACK PLUS ONE

FIGURE **8** AUTO RACES

X MARKS THE SPOT

AMERICAS MOST EXCITING RACE

WED. NIGHT
8:15 P.M.
Gates open 6:00 P.M.

ADULTS $3 — JUNIORS 13-16 $2

CHILD UNDER 12 — $1

SAN JOSE SPEEDWAY
Tully Rd., opp. Eastridge
251-1401

1975: Mike Amaya takes a chunk out of the wall as Harry Goularte (17) and Ted Stofle (89m) slip by during Late Model Stock Car action. *Don Mize Photo*

1975: Lloyd Keldsen Sr. (1) feels the heat from a wheel-standing Mike Bell (91) during the Figure-8 race. *Don Mize Photo*

1974 Stock Car Champion Dennis Wilson after winning a main event in 1976. *Dennis Mattish Photo*

1976: Long before Ernie Irvan was winning the Daytona 500, he was winning main events at San Jose. *Dennis Mattish Photo*

1975 & 1976 Stock Car Champion Harry Goularte. *Dennis Mattish Photo*

Dan Bishop (61), Ray Morgan (20) driving a convertible, Nick Foster (98) and Stonewall Jackson (93) take it four wide during a 1976 NASCAR Late Model Stock Car main event. All four drivers won main events at San Jose. *Dennis Mattish Photo*

Both Sam Emery (55) and Bob Blake (4) are thrown forward as they slam head-on into the wall at a high rate of speed. Both drivers walked away. *Dennis Mattish Photo*

1977 Late Model Sportsman Champion, Dave Byrd. *Dennis Mattish Photo*

again a couple of weeks later. He held the points lead until mid–season, but couldn't hold on to it because he kept getting suspended (three times) for reckless driving and unsportsmanlike conduct.

As the season wore on, and with the GSRA failing, drivers started to trickle back to San Jose Speedway. The first big name to return was Howard Kaeding. Not a coincidence, the largest crowd of the year (3,500) showed up for his first race. A short time later, Howard became the first driver in track history to score grand slams (winning all events) three weeks in a row. He also dominated the Oly-100 series of five 100-lap open competition races, winning four out of five. By the end of the year he had won a season-high 11 main events.

Tom Haylett used his three main event wins and his consistent top-five finishes as a springboard for winning the Super Modified Track Championship. Finishing second was State Champion Chuck Christian. Mark McCarthy finished fourth in points, the highest ranked rookie in 15 years.

Because Earl Kelly was one of the main spokesmen for the GSRA, the Golden West Classic was not welcome to run at the tracks in Bob Barkhimer's empire. This spelled doom for the series (another casualty of the split). It was now run as a two-night show at the Fairgrounds. Barkhimer started his own annual open competition series, the "California Golden Classic." The format was similar, except only two tracks were involved, and the big names from throughout the country were absent. Nick Rescino won both the Stockton Speedway and San Jose races to win the series.

Attendance-wise, this was the worst year for the track since the 1950s.

At the end of the season, a mobile home park developer approached the speedway owners and said he was interested in the land. But first they had to get the property re-zoned from industrial to residential use, something that would not be a problem. The writing was on the wall.

1977

The BCRA season kicked off at San Jose on April 16. In a cliffhanger, Ron Vines won when race leaders Wheeler Gresham and Mike Smith locked wheels on the last lap and crashed. Gresham flipped and suffered a broken wrist.

On August 6, Hank Butcher won the final Midget race to ever be run on the high banks, 31 years after Swede Lindskog won the first race.

The Stock Cars were upgraded to Late Model Sportsmans, faster, better handling, more streamlined car. This proved true, as the track record for that division was broken four times during the 10-week season. They started out on Wednesday night, but after two shows (won by Ernie Irvan and Dan Reed), they were cancelled off the schedule because of lack of cars. A month later, they were back on the schedule. Ernie Irvan, the hottest Stock Car driver in the state, picked up a couple more wins. When 23 Late Models, 3 Figure Eights and 4 Hobby Stocks signed in for the last race, Barkhimer took away the Wednesday night slot for good. A month later, they

Aerial photos of San Jose Speedway taken in 1976.
Dennis Mattish Aerial Photography

Because attendance was down in 1976, the stands on the back straight were closed. Good thing, because one of the most spectacular accidents in speedway history took place at that time. Ken Bowman (50) launched into a devastating series of flips on top of the crash wall after locking wheels with Dick Whelan (2). Although thoroughly shaken, Bowman was okay but his car was destroyed. Parts of car and pieces of wood flew into the closed stands. Mark McCarthy (99) was also involed. *Color Photo by Don Mize. B&W Photos by Mykeal Clark.*

152

1976: Mark Sargent had many wins in the NASCAR Super Modifieds. *Dennis Mattish Photo*

were added as part of the Saturday night show with the Super Modifieds. Dave Byrd won three main events (out of a 10-race season) on his way to winning the track championship. Vern Anderson was the runner-up. Dennis Wilson, who was plagued with mechanical problems all year, finished third with three wins. Ernie Irvan, who only raced four times at the track, won three of those events. Fourteen years later he would win the Daytona 500.

The NASCAR Winston West Grand National Stock Cars returned to San Jose for the first time in five years on May 21, and 3,800 (the biggest crowd of the year so far) watched Chuck Bown beat Bill Schmitt to the checkered flag in the non-stop 100-lap race.

The NASACR Super Modified season got under way on March 6. Chuck Christian, who started 15th, passed Howard Kaeding on the 16th circuit on his way to winning the feature in front of 2,638.

There were many different winners during the year,

On the last lap of the 1976 Olympia Beer 100, archrivals Howard Kaeding (3) and Nick Rescino (1) had contact. Johnny Brazil (foreground), who had been shadowing the pair, took advantage and shot into the lead and won the race before a vocal crowd. *Dennis Mattish Photo*

The Trophy Dash lineup during the 1976 California Golden Classic. Rod Furtado (9), Howard Kaeding (outside front row), Everett Edlund (1) and Johnny Brazil (100). *Dennis Mattish Photo*

1976: Sheldon Kinser was the first member of the Kinser Clan to race in San Jose. The three-time USAC Sprint Car Champion finished 3rd in the main event on this day. *Dennis Mattish Photo*

Gary Gerould interviews Larry Dickson at the 1976 USAC National Sprint Car race. Gerould went on to become an accomplished TV announcer, most notably with ABC. *Dennis Mattish Photo*

The 1976 season concluded with Tom Bigelow (left) winning the USAC National Sprint Car Championship race which was promoted by J.C. Agajanian (on right). *Dennis Mattish Photo*

In 1977 the San Jose Go-Kart Club held a couple of races on the high-banked track. It proved to be a dangerous adventure, as two drivers were sent to the hospital, one flipped and the other hit the wall. Gary Emmick set fast time at 15.151, good enough to get into a Midget or Sprint Car feature. *Dennis Mattish Photo*

154

R. U. R. A. PRESENTS

AUTO RACING

EVERY FRIDAY NIGHT

RACING AT 8 P.M., QUALIFYING AT 7:15 P.M.

MAY 20 THROUGH SEPTEMBER 16

SAN JOSE SPEEDWAY

TULLY RD. & SWIFT LANE, SAN JOSE, CA

including Earl Stanton and Pat Rose picking up their first wins. But it was Mike Sargent who had a breakout year, winning six main events, and the track and state championships.

A week after the July 30 Key race, it was announced that the San Jose City Council had cleared the way for construction of a mobile home park and storage sheds on the 28-acre site. That sealed the deal for the sale of the land. The last race was set for September 3.

On the last night, 4,930 showed up to watch Earl Kelly rout the open-competition field. He took the lead on lap 54 (of 100) and lapped everyone with the exception of second place Chuck Christian.

The *San Jose Mercury News* read the Monday after the race, "It was ironic that Earl Kelly, the man who was a key figure in the insurrection among drivers and owners at San Jose Speedway last year, would win the track's final race over the weekend. Track owners had alluded to the after-effects of last year's boycott as at least a secondary reason for disposing of the speedway. A number of cars and drivers did return after the revolt. But, the track lost many spectators to other forms of entertainment."

Kelly, the lanky airlines pilot, conceded the split in the Super Modified ranks the previous year hastened the sale of the track. "The split didn't help and I'll agree with Barky (Bob Barkhimer) that getting tied up with Silas Carter (the dissidents formed a rival association headed by Carter) was a mistake."

But Kelly emphasized that the split at San Jose was primarily because of treatment, not the money. You felt like you weren't wanted. "We couldn't talk to the man (Barkhimer). If he had sat down and talked to us, all the problems might have been avoided."

A newspaper article printed during that final week stated "Joe Sunseri pointed out with justifiable pride that 17 of the 33 starters in this year's (1977) Indianapolis 500 once raced at San Jose."

(continued on page 158)

1977: Switching from its customary off-road dirt racing, Roads Unlimited Racing Association (RURA) held a series of Friday night races on the paved, high banks of San Jose Speedway. Over 50 cars checked into the pits for its May 20 opener. The series proved to be a modest success.

(Above) John Johnson (82), Tim Callaway (13), TT Sprint Buggy Champion Ken Snarr (2) and Rick Zermani (27) during main event. *Dennis Mattish Photo*

(Left)1600cc Super Sedan Champion Dalye McIntyre (37) gets some advice before taking to the track for qualifying. *Dennis Mattish Photo*

Defending State Champion Chuck Christian won on opening day 1977. Trophy Kids Michelle and Richie Davis would make many more appearances before the camera in the coming years. Their parents, Sandy and Richard, owned Davis Motorsports and were sponsors at the track. *Dennis Mattish Photo*

Talented USAC and BCRA Midget driver Danny O'Neill proved his versatility when he won the biggest race of his career, capturing the 24th annual 150-lap Johnny Key Memorial Race before a great turnout of 5,750 vocal fans. The turning point in the race came on lap 144 when race leader Everett Edlund was clipped by a hard-charging Howard Kaeding, knocking both cars back into the pack. O'Neil and Tony Ringo slipped by to finish first and second. Rich and Sandy Davis make the presentation. *Dennis Mattish Photo*

1977: Mike Sargent won the last championship before the track closed. Following in the footsteps of his father Marshall, who had won the championship at the same track in 1960, the Sargents were the only father-son combo to win the championship at San Jose Speedway. *Dennis Mattish Photo*

Wally Pankratz was a regular during the open competition races, driving the Piper rear-engine Super Modified. *Dennis Mattish Photo*

Hank Butcher won the final USAC race in San Jose on Feb. 20,1977, and the final BCRA Midget race held at the paved track, which was on August 6, 1977. His eleven wins there rank him among the greats. *Bob Mize Photo.*

Ed Evans from Reno had a most unusual sponsor, a brothel from his home state of Nevada. The car also had a full race 427 cubic inch Chevy engine with tons of horse power. *Dennis Mattish Photo*

Rob Carlotto had just taken the checkered flag for a win in his heat race when his throttle stuck wide open. The resulting impact shattered his arm. *Tom Cory Photo*

Heat race, Opening Day 1977. *Dennis Mattish Photo*

Final night. *Dennis Mattish Photo*

(continued from page 155)

The racetrack that was a proving ground for the big time was now a memory.

Nowadays, if you drive by the site, you will see a mobile home park and storage sheds.

Earl Kelly wins final SJ Speedway race. *Dennis Mattish Photo*

SAN JOSE
SPEEDWAY
RACING EVERY SAT. NITE

SUN MAR 13
NASCAR
SUPER MOD
OPEN 11 AM

Above and right: The final destruction of San Jose Speedway. Some people say this is progress. I say it is a crime.
Dennis Mattish Photos

158

San Jose Speedway
Final point standings
1949-1977

California Stock Car Racing Association (CSCRA)

1949

Hardtop
1. Dave Carter
2. Mike Batinich

1950
1. Johnny Freitas

1951
1. Johnny Key

1952
1.	Johnny Freitas	522
2.	Ray Raineri	520
3.	Johnny Key	----

1953
1.	Ray Raineri	845
2.	Dean Holden	729
3.	John Colendich	586
4.	Mike Batinich	565
5.	Bobby Barg	520
6.	Johnny Freitas	511
7.	Clyde Palmer	462
8.	Al Johnson	438
9.	Al Toland	399
10.	Al Foster	372

National Association Stock Car Auto Racing (NASCAR)

1954

Hardtop
1.	Al Pombo	1298
2.	Johnny Colendich	1292
3.	Danny Graves	1118
4.	Johnny Freitas	848
5.	Al Gaetano	810
6.	Rick Henderson	720
7.	Marshall Sargent	446
8.	Al Foster	412
9.	Al Toland	396
10.	Joe Guisti	388

1955
1.	Johnny Colendich	1280
2.	Johnny Freitas	1210
3.	Al Pombo	1044
4.	Cliff Yiskis	1038
5.	Joe Soares	904
6.	Harvey Borba	850
7.	Fred Hunt	848
8.	Dave Lee	768
9.	Howard Kaeding	744
10.	Clyde Palmer	592

1956
1.	Johnny Freitas	1194
2.	Reggie Ausmus	918
3.	Joe Soares	898
4.	Dave Leroy	844
5.	Harvey Borba	832
6.	Johnny Colendich	714
7.	Larry Rodriguez	712
8.	Ray Traylor	678
9.	Dave Reed	610
10.	Burt Foland	588

1957
1.	Rick Henderson	938
2.	Paul Barsotti	864
3.	Dave Leroy	822
4.	Lee Humphers	766
5.	Dave Reed	760
6.	Lloyd Silacci	714
7.	Jerry Reed	680
8.	Joe Soares	598
9.	Johnny Freitas	568
10.	Burt Foland	510

1958
1.	Rick Henderson	1114
2.	Dean Holden	994
3.	Johnny Freitas	974
4.	Ed Andrews	876
5.	Stan Sinn	770
6.	Johnny Colendich	740
7.	Clyde Palmer	646
8.	George Benson	616
9.	John Smith	600
10.	Bill Scott	594

1959
1.	Rick Henderson	1341
2.	Johnny Freitas	1300
3.	George Benson	1038
4.	Bill Scott	906
5.	Clyde Palmer	888
6.	Dick Overstreet	866
7.	Burt Foland	860
8.	Marshall Sargent	832
9.	Ed Metro	802
10.	Johnny Colendich	715

1960
1.	Marshall Sargent	1405
2.	Rick Henderson	1330
3.	Johnny Colendich	1168
4.	Bill Scott	1089
5.	Burt Foland	1025

6.	Cliff Yiskis	961
7.	Clyde Palmer	833
8.	Stan Sinn	830
9.	Dick Whalen	808
10.	Lee Humphers	797

1961

1.	Clyde Palmer	1291
2.	Al Pombo	1081
3.	Burt Foland	979
4.	Rick Henderson	920
5.	Bill Scott	845
6.	Johnny Colendich	842
7.	Cliff Yiskis	801
8.	Dick Whalen	793
9.	Herb Kaeding	648
10.	Larry Rodrigues	609

1962

1.	Rick Henderson	1462
2.	Clyde Palmer	1416
3.	Marshall Sargent	1373
4.	Bill Scott	1049
5.	Cliff Yiskis	1038
6.	Herb Kaeding	1036
7.	Gary Johnson	908
8.	Dick Whalen	748
9.	James Stainton	712
10.	Al Pombo	708

1963

1.	Al Pombo	1482
2.	Marshall Sargent	1156
3.	Joe McGee	960
4.	Dick Whalen	910
5.	Howard Kaeding	885
6.	Clyde Palmer	829
7.	Bill Hill	815
8.	Rick Henderson	807
9.	Bill Scott	758
10.	Cliff Yiskis	681

1964

1.	Al Pombo	1551
2.	Bill Scott	1409
3.	Clyde Palmer	1385
4.	Howard Kaeding	1207
5.	Gary Johnson	1139
6.	Dick Whalen	1109
7.	Burt Foland	1026
8.	Marshall Sargent	935
9.	Art Bigiogni	843
10.	Joe McGee	832

1965

1.	Al Pombo	1398
2.	Bill Scott	1365
3.	Marshall Sargent	1213
4.	Howard Kaeding	1212

5.	Rick Henderson	1188
6.	Joe Lobbia	1182
7.	Clyde Palmer	1130
8.	Dick Whalen	1126
9.	Johnny Brazil	1021
10.	Burt Foland	841

1966

1.	Al Pombo	1687
2.	Marshall Sargent	1578
3.	Clyde Palmer	1325
4.	Everett Edlund	1245
5.	Dick Whalen	1146
6.	Dewayne Woodward	1141
7.	Cliff Yiskis	1127
8.	Howard Kaeding	1054
9.	Dick Overstreet	1037
10.	Burt Foland	1003

1967

1.	Bill Scott	1446
2.	Al Pombo	1352
3.	Howard Kaeding	1287
4.	Johnny Brazil	1159
5.	Clyde Palmer	1117
6.	Dewayne Woodward	1109
7.	Everett Edlund	1082
8.	Cliff Yiskis	1019
9.	Joe McGee	872
10.	Marshall Sargent	773

1968

1.	Al Pombo	1696
2.	Clyde Palmer	1585
3.	Everett Edlund	1547
4.	Howard Kaeding	1514
5.	Bill Scott	1407
6.	Johnny Brazil	1337
7.	Joe Lobbia	1071
8.	Burt Foland	1036
9.	Art Bigiogni	956
10.	Bob Bakeman	927

1969

1.	Bill Scott	1806
2.	Johnny Brazil	1524
3.	Everett Edlund	1245
4.	Junior Coppla	1178
5.	Steve Chambers	1132
6.	Howard Kaeding	1123
7.	Jerry Thompson	1057
8.	Cliff Yiskis	1012
9.	Don Epperson	1004
10.	Al Pombo	847

1970

1.	Bill Scott	1931
2.	Howard Kaeding	1797
3.	Johnny Brazil	1499

4.	Don Epperson	1476
5.	Steve Chambers	1207
6.	Junior Coppla	1155
7.	Nick Rescino	1010
8.	Ted Witt	976
9.	Ed Hopper	968
10.	Cliff Yiskis	819

1971

1.	Bill Scott	1890
2.	Ed Hopper	1595
3.	Johnny Brazil	1589
4.	Howard Kaeding	1547
5.	Everett Edlund	1506
6.	Nick Rescino	1461
7.	Al Andrews	1226
8.	Ken Molica	1197
9.	Don Epperson	1080
10.	Ray Otis	1007

1972

1.	Nick Rescino	1510
2.	Howard Kaeding	1382
3.	Everett Edlund	1076
4.	Don Epperson	1038
5.	Nick Ringo	971
6.	Johnny Brazil	905
7.	Bill Scott	778
8.	John Pearson	748
9.	Ray Otis	742
10.	Ted Witt	708

1973

1.	Howard Kaeding	1733
2.	Nick Rescino	1444
3.	Don Epperson	1198
4.	Ed Hopper	1057
5.	Terry Chalker	1032
6.	Roland Wlodyka	1010
7.	Johnny Brazil	864
8.	Joe McGee	730
9.	Wendell Chambers	723
10.	Mike McCann	721

1974

Super Modified

1.	Howard Kaeding	1709
2.	Nick Rescino	1343
3.	Mike Damron	1252
4.	Lloyd Beard	1194
5.	Roland Wlodyka	1105
6.	Mike Sargent	1047
7.	Don Epperson	1025
8.	Ed Hopper	947
9.	Dick Whalen	785
10.	Johnny Brazil	708

Early Model Stock Cars

1.	Dennis Wilson	937
2.	Bill Veyl	796
3.	Ray Morgan	743
4.	Ted Stofle	619
5.	Mitch West	547
6.	Dave Fowler	505
7.	Mel Bentson	462
8.	Tony Capote	460
9.	John Van Hooser	442
10.	Bob Hedrick	428

Figure Eight

1.	Ken Naber	1028
2.	Ken Nott	948
3.	Lloyd Keldsen Sr.	930
4.	Darrel Sandau	876
5.	Lloyd Keldsen Jr.	856
6.	Pat Norris	622
7.	Les Grimes	548
8.	Mike Bell	546
9.	Mel Bentson	504
10.	Randy Glover	454

1975

Super Modified

1.	Nick Rescino	1393
2.	Johnny Brazil	1308
3.	Howard Kaeding	1294
4.	Nick Ringo	1118
5.	Mike Damron	997
6	Lloyd Beard	866
7.	Dick Whalen	749
8.	Mike Sargent	728
9.	Tom Haylett	644
10.	Ed Hopper	637

Late Model Stock Car

1.	Harry Goularte	1281
2.	Doug McCoun	1114
3.	Ray Morgan	930
4.	Tony Capote	776
5.	Pat Norris	759
6.	Rich Johnson	716
7.	Dave Alonzo	646
8.	Nick Foster	630
9.	Dave Fowler	604
10.	Mel Bentson	568

Figure-eight

1.	Ken Nott	1312
2.	Pat Norris	1242
3.	Ken Naber	1228
4.	Darrel Sandau	1146
5.	Lloyd Keldsen Jr.	1084
6.	Lloyd Kelden Sr.	886
7.	Randy Glover	838
8.	Rich Johnson	722
9.	Mike Townsley	486
10.	Vernon Anderson	476

1976

Super Modified
1. Tom Haylett — 1024
2. Chuck Christian — 953
3. Jack Epperson — 935
4. Mark McCarthy — 766
5. Jay Smith — 756
6. Mark Sargent — 723
7. Art McCarthy — 712
8. Jerry Robertson — 578
9. Dan Haulot — 578
10. Howard Kaeding — 576

Late Model Stock Car
1. Harry Goularte — 1120
2. Ray Morgan — 1031
3. Jerry DeLoach — 996
4. Pat Norris — 890
5. Ken Nott — 885
6. Larry Jackson — 873
7. Dan Bishop — 836
8. Nick Foster — 811
9. Jeff Prescott — 770
10. Vern Anderson — 715

Figure Eight
1. Ken Naber — 946
2. Lloyd Keldsen Jr. — 864
3. Ken Nott — 826
4. Pat Norris — 804
5. Lloyd Keldsen Sr. — 798
6. Darryl Sandau — 740
7. John Keldsen — 580
8. Jerry Mostek — 360
9. Vern Anderson — 322
10. Ed Olive — 284

1977

Super Modified
1. Mike Sargent — 917
2. Howard Kaeding — 696
3. Chuck Christian — 629
4. Nick Ringo — 621
5. Earle Stanton — 579
6. Tom Cox — 546
7. Pat Rose — 475
8. Dana Stahl — 456
9. Jack Epperson — 454
10. Art McCarthy — 450

Late Model Stock Car
1. Dave Byrd — 545
2. Vern Anderson — 537
3. Dennis Sargent — 465
4. Dennis Wilson — 403
5. Ray Morgan — 397
6. Jerry Mostek — 328
7. Dell Todd — 310
8. Tony Capote — 284
9. Hal Bushaw — 264
10. Don Hutchinson — 218

Hobby Stocks
1. Jim Booth — 100
2. Guy Pacheco — 92
3. Scott Brown — 48
4. Larry Noel — 46
5. Dan Princeau — 46

San Jose Speedway
One-Lap Track Records on 1/3-Mile
1949-1977

Midget
Year	Driver	Time
1949	Marvin Burke	16.40
1949	Bob Sweikert	16.34
1949	Fred Agabashion	16.22
1964	Mike McGreevy	15.73
1964	George Snider	15.44
1965	Dick Atkins	15.34
1966	George Benson	15.27
1966	Burt Foland	15.11
1967	Burt Foland	15.09
1968	Bill Vukovich	15.07
1968	Burt Foland	15.02
1968	Burt Foland	14.87
1970	Burt Foland	14.62

Roadster
Year	Driver	Time
1949	Ed Huntington	16.88
1949	Ed Elisian	16.74
1949	Ed Elisian	16.63
1949	Bob Machin	16.61
1949	Bob Machin	16.50

Big Car /Sprint Car
Year	Driver	Time
1950	Dave Carter	17.91
1969	Leroy Van Connett	15.50
1970	Rick Henderson	14.48
1976	Tom Bigelow	14.221

Late Model Stock Cars
(NASCAR Pacific Coast Grand National to Winston West)
Year	Driver	Time
1949	Frank Phillips	20.99
1950	Fred Steinbroner	20.69
1964	Bill Amick	17.78
1971	Dick Bown	16.23
1972	Jack McCoy	16.152
1977	Jim Reich	15.505

Jalopies / Early Model Stock Car / Late Model Sportsman
Year	Driver	Time
1954	Irwin Lee	20.44
1958	Charles Sanchez	19.71
1959	Charles Sanchez	19.08
1974	Dave Alonzo	18.342
1974	Dennis Wilson	18.067
1974	Dave Alonzo	17.815
1974	Billy Veyl	17.381
1974	Dennis Wilson	17.305
1974	Billy Veyl	17.115

1974	Billy Veyl	17.055
1975	Dan Reed	16.989
1975	Harry Goularte	16.961
1976	Harry Goularte	16.919
1976	Ken Nott	16.849
1976	Ray Morgan	16.834
1976	Ken Nott	16.731
1976	Ray Morgan	16.657
1976	Ray Morgan	16.635
1976	Ray Morgan	16.572
1976	Dennis Wilson	16.403
1976	Nick Foster	16.294
1976	Stonewall Jackson	16.088
1977	Ernie Irvan	16.050
1977	Dennis Wilson	15.952
1977	Ernie Irvan	15.849
1977	Vern Anderson	15.846

Super Stocks/ Open Competition Stock Cars

1976	Bill Schmitt	15.687
1976	Jim Thirkettle	15.228

TT Sprint Buggies

1977	Ken Snarr	16.073
1977	Ken Snarr	15.546
1977	Ken Snarr	15.137

1600cc Super Sedan (VW)

1977	Dalye McIntyre	16.351

Go-Kart

1977	Gary Emmick	15.151

Hardtop/ Modified /Super Modified

1949	Dave Carter	20.00
1950	George Boerstler	19.65
1950	Mac Margolatti	19.48
1950	Mac Margolatti	19.40
1950	Ray Raneri	19.05
1951	Al Gaetano	18.94
1951	Ray Raineri	18.84
1951	Al Gaetano	18.62
1951	Joe Soares	18.62
1951	Johnny Smith	18.59
1952	Al Gaetano	18.57
1952	Johnny Key	18.47
1952	Johnny Freitas	18.42
1953	Dean Holden	18.35
1953	Ray Raineri	18.31
1953	Dean Holden	18.30
1953	Ray Raineri	18.23
1954	Ray Raineri	18.16
1955	Al Pombo	18.15
1957	Dee Hileman	18.06
1957	Rick Henderson	18.02
1957	Hugh Purdy	17.98
1957	Dave Leroy	17.90
1957	Paul Barsotti	17.69
1959	Rick Henderson	17.66

1959	Paul Barsotti	17.58
1960	Lee Humphers	17.42
1960	Rick Henderson	17.35
1960	Marshall Sargent	17.27
1960	Marshall Sargent	17.15
1960	Al Pombo	17.10
1961	Burt Foland	17.07
1961	Al Pombo	16.74
1961	Clyde Palmer	16.68
1961	Al Pombo	16.66
1961	Art Pollard	16.13
1962	Rick Henderson	16.02
1962	Al Pombo	16.00
1963	Clyde Palmer	15.70
1963	Al Pombo	15.55
1964	Herman Hutton	15.51
1964	Bill Scott	15.42
1964	Marshall Sargent	15.35
1964	Bill Scott	15.33
1964	Al Pombo	15.29
1964	Al Pombo	15.21
1965	Al Pombo	14.89
1965	Al Pombo	14.82
1966	Marshall Sargent	14.71
1966	Marshall Sargent	14.66
1966	Al Pombo	14.47
1967	DeWayne Woodward	14.39
1969	Bill Scott	14.36
1970	Bill Scott	14.33
1970	Bill Scott	14.19
1970	Bill Scott	14.13
1970	Bill Scott	14.00
1970	Bill Scott	13.97
1971	Nick Rescino	13.86
1971	Nick Rescino	13.74
1972	Howard Kaeding	13.702
1973	Howard Kaeding	13.689
1974	Roland Wlodyka	13.578
1974	Roland Wlodyka	13.511
1974	Roland Wlodyka	13.401
1974	Nick Rescino	13.333

Chapter 12

Santa Clara County Fairgrounds
1941 - 1999

In 1940, Frank Mitchell, first president of the Santa Clara County Fair Association, offered $35,000 to Kirk MaComber to buy his 97-acre Mira Monte Ranch located at Tully Road and Monterey Highway. During the previous 24 years, the property had been used as a stock farm for racehorses, using the old San Jose Driving Park one-mile oval as its training ground. To Mitchell's and his colleagues' surprise, McComber accepted. The foundation was set for the next Santa Clara County Fairgrounds. The first fair was staged in 1941 and was marked by canvas tents and dusty grounds. The six-day October event drew 55,661 patrons, including California Governor Culbert Olsen.

Although there were only a few bleacher seats available, a fair-sized (pun intended) crowd attended the horse and harness races on the oval. Two months later, World War II broke out and all but halted activity at the facility.

1976 aerial photo showing the mile, half–mile and speedway motorcycle track. The track in the bottom right is for horses.
Dennis Mattish Aerial Photography

J. C. AGAJANIAN and LARRY SUNSERI
Present

AAA

National Championship
100 MILE AUTO RACE

OCT. 21, 1951

Sanctioned By

AMERICAN
AUTOMOBILE
ASSOCIATION

OFFICIAL
SOUVENIR
PROGRAM

PRICE
25¢

TONY BETTENHAUSEN
—*O'Dell and Shields Official Indianapolis Photo*

Santa Clara County Fairgrounds   **San Jose, California**

Tony Bettenhausen was on the cover of the program for the 1951 race. It was only fitting because he dominated the race, one of eight he would win in 1951 on his way to the AAA National Championship. *Mattish Collection*

1951

The Fairgrounds would expand in size by the time the first motoring event took place in August, an American Motorcycle Association (AMA) sanctioned, national championship motorcycle race. Making his San Jose racing debut that day was a young rider named Joe Leonard. Forty-two hundred spectators watched the 18-year-old Leonard set a new track record with a time of 44.68 during qualifications. Gene Thiessen went into the history books as the first feature winner on the renamed track.

October 21: The last time AAA raced on the one-mile oval was July 4, 1915, when it was the San Jose Driving Park. The last time AAA raced in San Jose was October 8, 1933, at the San Jose Speedway on Alum Rock Avenue. So when AAA scheduled a sanctioned race for October 21, they already had a rich history in San Jose, having sanctioned 51 races between 1909 and 1934 in the garden city.

J.C. Agajanian and Larry Sunseri co-promoted the National Championship race featuring Indianapolis cars. Some of the 27 cars that were entered were brand new and making their debut in preparation for the Indy 500 the following May.

Driving the pace car was 1924 AAA San Jose winner, Ralph DePalma.

Bleachers had been added to the front of the new grandstands to increase seating capacity, and 8,697 fans packed those seats on race day.

Tony Bettenhausen sped around the one-mile dirt oval in 36.41 seconds at a speed of 98.02 mph in qualifying to shatter Joe Leonard's short-lived track record. He followed

The crowds file in to the still-young Fairgrounds facility for the 1951 race. *Mattish Collection.*

AAA Big Cars (Sprint Cars) line up for their National Championship Race. It was only a matter of time before the infield pond was removed . My father took these color photos in 1951 from the stands. *Bill Mattish Photo*

The first car race on the mile since 1915 took place in 1951. Houses were yet to be built next to the track. *Bill Mattish Photo*

A packed house watches Tony Bettenhausen (pole) and Jim Rigsby (26) lead the pack in for the start of the 1951 100-miler. *Mattish Collection*

Troy Ruttman sits in the Kurtis 4000 on race day 1951. The following year, Troy won the Indianapolis 500. He would ultimately win three National crowns during his Hall of Fame career. *Courtesy of the Imlay Collection*

Two-time Indianapolis 500 winner Roger Ward at San Jose in 1951. *Mattish Collection*

Joe James poses in the John Zink Kurtis prior to the 1951 race. (He would later lose his life while leading the 1952 race at the Fairgrounds.) *Courtesy of the Imlay Collection*

Johnnie Parsons (3) prepares to move past Jim Rigsby (26) on his way to finishing seventh in 1951. *Mattish Collection*

1952 program marking the 50th anniversary of AAA-sanctioned racing. *Mattish Collection*

that up with a dominating victory in the grueling 100-mile race. Following over 100 yards back were Paul Russo, Henry Banks, Jack McGrath and Jim Davis, in that order.

After the successful race, Agajanian stated he would be back.

1952

The best Late Model (1949-1952) Stock Car drivers in California converged on the Fairgrounds for the 100-mile Pacific Coast Championship race held on March 23.

Some 3,000 Stock Car fans watched Dick Meyers lap the entire field in his 1949 Dodge on his way to victory. Finishing second, more than a mile back was Lee Humphres. Jim Morgan crossed the finish line third, then hit a rut and flipped. The lap before that, Mike Batinich did the same thing in the same turn. Batinich received a deep head gash, requiring hospitalization. Pole sitter Marvin Panch led the first seven laps before dropping back. Johnny Soares won the Trophy Dash.

May 11 – A brand new regulation (horse track distance) half-mile dirt oval was carved out in front of the grandstands, and the first to test the track were the Hardtops. Johnny Soares took the lead from Joe Guisti on lap 33 and never looked back. Rod Zanoline and Ed Normi rounded out the top three in the 30-car feature. Fifteen hundred fans were in attendance to watch the crash-infested show (thanks in part to the east turn coming apart).

J.C. Agajanian returned to promote the AAA 100-mile championship on November 2. Agajanian's own #98 Special won the Indianapolis 500 and was an early favorite to win this race with Billy Vuckovich behind the wheel.

A crowd of 7,900 watched the stellar field of open wheel drivers muscle their 340-hp iron steeds around the track. Joe James and Bobby Ball were having a spirited duel for the lead when disaster struck on lap 47. James was leading when a collision took place ahead of him. Track officials began slowing traffic when James climbed the wheel of a slowing Duane Carter. It was speculated that James was blinded by low sun at the end of the front straight and didn't see Carter slow down. James' car then did a couple of flips and landed on top of him. He was rushed to the hospital in grave condition.

Once the race resumed, Ball had things his way, cruising to an easy victory. Mike Nazaruk, Paul Russo and Jack

170

Bobby Ball drove the Blakely Oil Special to victory in the 1952 100-mile race. *Mattish Collection*

McGrath followed in that order. Vukovich was disqualified when he would not obey officials' orders to come to the pits to have his car examined after hitting the railing and stalling.

Joe James succumbed to his injuries in San Jose hospital three days later.

This was the last time that AAA would ever race in San Jose. Because of the many deaths in auto racing, and especially the 1955 crash at Le Mans that killed 82 people, the American Automobile Association decided to distance itself from auto racing and get out altogether. The United States Auto Club (USAC) would replace them.

1954

The first sanctioned road race (Sports Car) in San Jose history took place at the Fairgrounds on July 18. The race meet was for the benefit of Santa Clara County Youth Center Building Fund and was sponsored by the Sports Car Club of America. (SCCA)

To hold the races at the Fairgrounds, it was necessary to build a special mile-and-a-half course, which used the tarmac already in place. The track snaked its way around the grandstand and out to the stables. Donations covered the $12,000 price tag for setting up the track.

All the top West Ccoast drivers from SCCA and the Pebble Beach Road Race were entered, including the Pebble Beach winner, Sterling Edwards.

Twenty-thousand people, the largest crowd to ever

LOOK WHO'S BEHIND YOU—Like a jackrabbit trying to catch a greyhound, Dr. Leon Becker, Santa Clara surgeon, noses his little Cooper Formula II Grand Prix racer up to Bill Behel's Jaguar XK-120-M in this bit of action during yesterday's sports car road races at County Fairgrounds. Behel came in first with Dr. Becker not far behind. The little Coopers have very small engines which burn methanol instead of gasoline.—Staff Photo by William Regan.

NO CRACK-UPS IN 11 EVENTS

20,000 Watch Sports Cars Race Around Fairgrounds

171

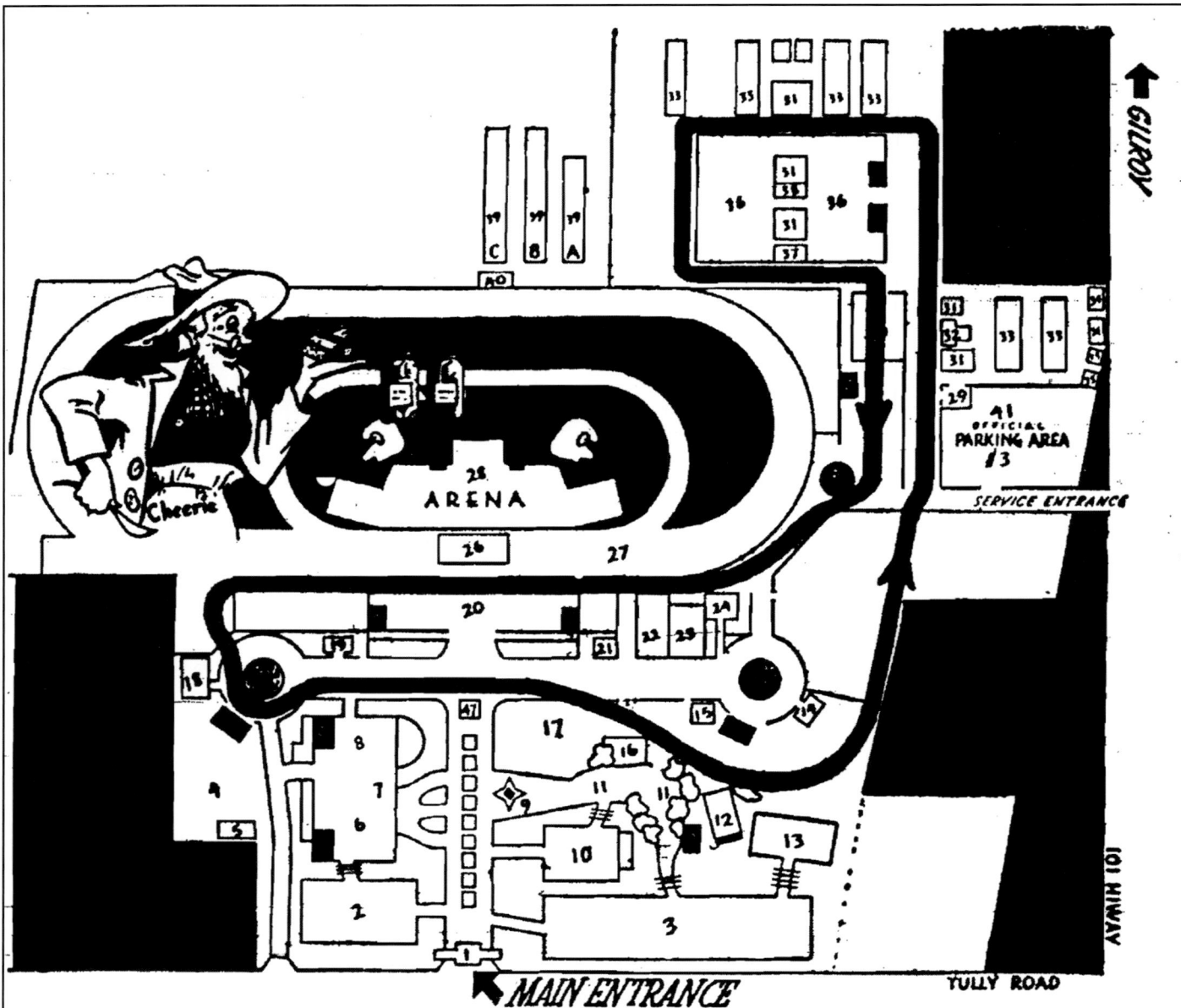

HERE'S ROAD RACE COURSE — This is the special mile and one-half road race course over which tomorrow's Youth Center program of 11 races will be run. This course was built with donated equipment, materials and labor, and according to Chairman Patrick J. Ryan of the Youth Boosters Club committee, represents a $12,000 investment. Since the course is comparatively short for road races, skill and maneuverability will be main factors in deciding winners.

Sports Cars Race Here Tomorrow

attend a motor racing event in San Jose, watched 146 sports cars race in 11 events. The racing was safe with plenty of thrills and near misses as an occasional car veered into the hay bales, creating a mess. George Sawyer won the 20-lap final in his 1000+cc Kurtis-Chrysler. The event was a huge success and the money it brought in helped build the youth center (Watzit Club) on Newhall Avenue in Santa Clara.

1955

The first local race for WAR since the split with NASCAR was held on the one-mile oval on May 1. This was the biggest track that the Hardtops had attempted to run on in Northern California. Racing veteran and former Hardtop Champion Mike Batinich was the promoter. With the backdrop of the two associations despising each other, the race went forward at the Fairgrounds, just two miles down the road from San Jose Speedway on Tully Road.

Delayed one week because of rain, a large field of cars signed in to the pits for the 50-car, 50-lap main event. There was much anticipation as the day began, but that would turn to dread by the end of the day. The following day the headline on page one of the *Mercury News* read "Death Mars WAR Race." The first paragraph read, "Frank Rose nosed out Art Viat by half a car length Sunday as one death marred an abbreviated Western Auto Racing Association main event opener before 3,300 persons at the one-mile Fairgrounds track."

The racing began on that day with Ray Raineri setting fast time with a lap of 47.8 seconds. He followed that up with a win in the Trophy Dash.

Things spiraled downhill from there, as the track didn't seem to suit the Hardtops.

On lap four of the main event, rookie driver Reco Whitton and Ed Middleton, sped into the east turn side by side, both suddenly losing control of their cars without touching. Both cars crashed through the rail fence. Whitton's 41 Mercury turned on its side and skidded into a tree. A huge limb broke off the tree and smashed through his windshield frame, killing Whitten instantly. The race was stopped while a crew of county firemen was called to cut the wreck open with welding torches. Middleton, whose car also turned over, crawled out without injuries. On lap 29, Earl Smith and Johnny Smith were battling for the lead when they locked wheels in the same place as the Whitten accident. Earl's car flipped wildly off the track while Johnny went through the railing. (This is the kind of railing that you see at horse racing tracks.) Johnny escaped injury when a fence rail ripped through his front windshield and narrowly missed him. Earl was transported to the hospital with a head concussion. After the Smith incident, Frank Rose inherited the lead and then held off a fast-charging Art Viet at the checkered. Because of the numerous delays during the day, the race was shortened to 35 laps because of darkness. By the end of the day, most of the railing in the turns had been knocked down by the 20 accidents that marred the program. Only 21 cars finished the feature.

What was supposed to be a statement race aimed at San Jose Speedway turned into a disaster.

Sprint Cars (Big Cars) took to the Fairgrounds dirt on

FIRST TIME IN CALIFORNIA
HARDTOPS ON MILE TRACK

HARDTOP RACES

TOMORROW
SUNDAY, MAY 1
Santa Clara County
FAIR GROUNDS
MILE TRACK . . .

50 MILES 50 CAR
MAIN EVENT

70 CARS ON TRACK
DRIVERS YOU KNOW AND ADMIRE . . .
THRILLS EVERY SECOND

Benefit FOR THE BLIND
Time Trials 9 a.m. on.
First Races 2:15 p.m.

WESTERN AUTO RACING AUTHORIZED

Crash Kills Young Driver During Fairgrounds Race

Hardtop
Skids Off
The Track

20 Accidents
Mar Main Event;
San Josean Hurt

1955: Qualifying in turn four within the confines of the dangerous horse railing. *From the Collection of Don Radbruch*

Jack Gardner waits his turn to qualify during the 1955 ARA race. *Courtesy of Ken Clapp*

The ARA Big Cars/Sprint Cars take the green flag in front of a sparse crowd on September 25, 1955. *Bob Mize Photo*

ARA Sprint Cars race through turn four on the mile during 1955. *From the Collection of Don Radbruch.*

BCRA Midgets made their first appearance at the Fairgrounds on September 14, 1957. This artistic drybrush shows Ken Martin (left) and Sullivan on the half-mile that day. *Jim Montgomery Collection*

September 25. Sanctioned by the American Racing Association, the race was scheduled for 50 miles on the one-mile oval.

Nick Valenta, from Los Angeles, powered his Offenhauser to victory in front of 1,500 fans. Johnny Baldwin came in second. The race was stopped when Bill Peterson flipped his car and was pinned under it. Because of darkness, the race was shortened to 20 laps.

1957 - 1967

During 1957 a new $100,000 roof was installed on the 80 ft. x 400 ft. grandstand. The first to use the new roof in July was the AMA crowd. National champion Joe Leonard won the race and set three new track records in a dominant performance. Leonard went on to win his second national championship that year.

Stepping away from their normal environment of paved road courses, Sports Cars held a race on the mile dirt oval during July, 1958. Jaguars, led by Gene Thomas, took the top three spots.

Mario Andretti headlined an indoor car show at the fairgrounds in March, 1966.

Promoter Harold Murrell presented a series of successful AMA flat track motorcycle races on the half-mile oval during 1967.

In November, 1967, motorcycles made their debut on the tenth-mile paved oval in the Exposition Building.

Live closed-circuit TV made its debut in 1965 at the County Fairgrounds Exposition Hall. Twenty-four hundred people jammed into the building to watch Scotland's Jimmy Clark win the Indianapolis 500 on May 31.

The last day of the 1957 County Fair featured the NASCAR Late Model Stock Cars, which ran a 100-mile race on the half-mile oval. The race was scheduled for 200 laps, but came to a grinding halt when nine cars piled up on the 117th lap. The car driven by Dick Gitty flipped in the turn and then was plowed into by other cars. Gitty was hospitalized with minor injuries. The race was called at this point and Marvin Porter (below), who was leading at the time of the crash, was declared the winner. *Photos Courtesy of Ken Clapp*

1958: *Bob Mize Photo*

Destruction Derby

The biggest attraction at the annual Santa Clara County Fair for 40 years was the crowd-pleasing Destruction Derby. The Derby was usually held on the last day of the fair and was nearly always witnessed by capacity crowds of 6,000-plus.

The 100-car mass Destruction Derby was promoted by Bob Barkhimer and it would prove to be one of his most successful promotions.

Some highlights

Gerald Chase won the 1963 Derby in front of nearly 7,000 people. It was the car that came in second place that drew the attention of the crowd. Andy Brown smashed his rare 1937 Pierce Arrow to the runner-up spot.

Seeing a good thing, NASCAR started sanctioning the Destruction Derby in 1965 and it was an immediate hit. The stands sold out early and hundreds were turned away at the door.

Joe Reyes, the best crasher in the history of the Destruction Derby at the Fairgrounds, picked up $500 for winning the 1968 event in front of the capacity crowd. He would win five out of the next six Derbies, a feat that was never matched.

The last Fair Derby took place when the track closed in 1999.

1958: *Bob Mize Photo*

1987: *Dennis Mattish Photo*

1968

The last year for indoor Midget racing at the Oakland Exposition Building was 1967. Promoter Bob Barkhimer made arrangements to move the series to the very tight 1/10-mile asphalt oval in the Exposition Building at the Santa Clara County Fairgrounds in San Jose. The motorcycles had already run six races on their indoor campaign, which meant that everything was already in place for the BCRA midgets when they made their debut on January 6. Dickie Deis drove the Caves Offy to victory in the 25-lap main event which was witnessed by 1,250. Burt Foland had moved up through the pack to challenge for the lead when he broke. Zeke Maldonado was the first driver to flip on the indoor surface. Pleased with the results of the first night "trial run" on the small track, Barkhimer scheduled another show in two weeks and then two more in February.

Gary Ponzini and Hank Butcher won the next two races, leading up to the SJ Indoor final on February 10. Only 12 points separated the top three, Deis, Butcher and Bob Dejong.

Burt Foland flipped his car in the final heat that night, and then returned to action for a smashing victory in the main event. In the feature, Dejong passed Deis and finished second. That maneuver gave him just enough points to win the championship over Deis.

After four races, everybody came to the conclusion that the track was just too small for a successful indoor season like the kind they enjoyed in Oakland. Also, the building was so narrow that only small grandstand seating would fit. With a small seating capacity, it just wasn't profitable, so Barky moved the series to Santa Rosa for the remainder of the indoor season.

Dick Deis does a wheelie on his way to winning the first indoor Midget race in San Jose on Jan 6, 1968. *Jim Montgomery collection*

Hank Butcher driving the Jim Montgomery Offy to victory on February 3, 1968. *Jim Montgomery Collection*

A packed house witnesses a pile-up during a February, 1968, BCRA main event involving Bill McCormick (10), Bob Yuhre (30), Dick Whalen (98x), Dave Bostrom (39) and Tom Clark (89). *Larry Wood photo from the Jim Montgomery collection*

The series had car counts from a low of 27 to a high of 33 cars per show.

By special request of local race fans, the 1969 indoor season started in San Jose on December 6, 1968. Defending Champion Bob DeJong dominated the BCRA field, winning his heat race, the dash, and the 30-lap main event.

The series then moved to the Cow Palace for one race and then finished the season in Santa Rosa.

1969-1971

In the motorcycles, riders making a name for themselves were Jim Rice, Gene Romero, Dick Mann and Gary Nixon on the outdoor tracks and Mark Brelsford on the indoor track.

Making his first appearance in San Jose as an amateur in 1969 was future World Champion Kenny Roberts.

On October 31, 1971, ABC televised the special AMA Race of Champions motorcycle race for its *Wide World of Sports* program.

1968: Don Sparks (20) bicycles inside of Larry Ferrua (29) and Hank Butcher on the very narrow indoor track.
Larry Wood photo from the Jim Montgomery collection

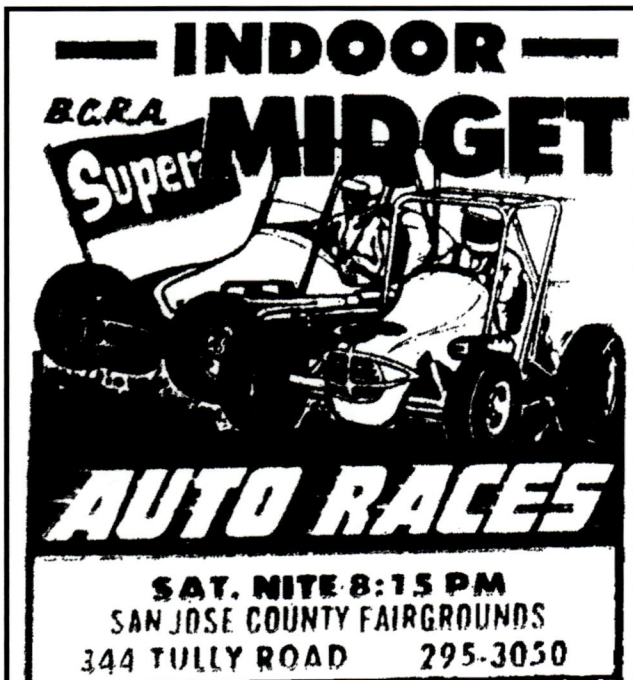

1973 Advertisement for the last Indoor Midget race held in San Jose.

During the 49 years that motor racing was held at the Fairgrounds, 15 of those years featured motorcycles only. Those years were 1953, '56, '59, '60, '61, '62, '63, '64, '65, '66, '67, '69, '70, '71 and '74.

1972

On April 30, Sprint Cars made their first appearance at the Fairgrounds since 1955. Titled the Northern Auto Racing Club (NARC) Championship Sprint Car Auto Races, the cars were divided between Southern California-based California Racing Association (CRA) and NARC. Three-thousand spectators were in attendance to see Southern Californian Rick Goudy take home over $1,000 for winning the 100-lap race. Goudy had to hold off the challenge from Frank Secrist and Leroy Van Connett. The program was delayed because of spins, wrecks, stalls and the continuous grooming of the track to keep the dust down.

ABC television was back in October, this time providing live coverage of the AMA "Race of Champions" on the mile. The Fairgrounds mile was now recognized as one of the premier motorcycle tracks in the country. Two national races were held annually, one on the mile and one on the half-mile. The mile proved to be twice as exciting and drew twice the crowd.

1973

Encouraged by the car count and crowd size of the 1972 race, NARC was back for year two in April.

Two-time NARC champion Leroy Van Connett sped to victory over Jimmy Oskie and Rick Horton. The big story was the race was cut from 50 to 30 laps because of dust and poor track conditions. This infuriated the crowd. NARC would not return until 1977.

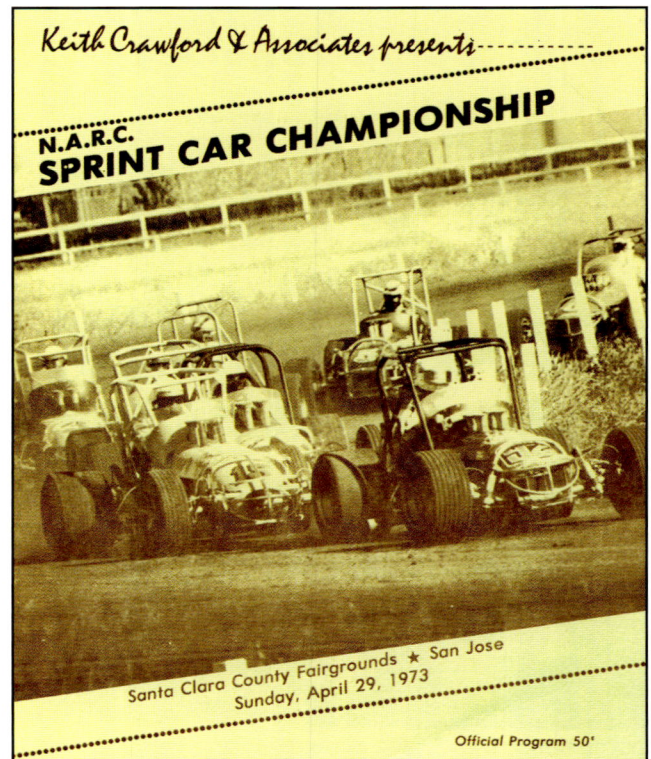

Program cover photo is from 1972 SJ NARC race.

A 3/4-mile, dirt, closed course, off-road racing track was built for the November 1974 Western Sprint Sport Championship race sanctioned by Roads Unlimited Racing Association (RURA). Rick Mears of Bakersfield, a nationally prominent off-road racer, was the headliner. Mears won two races on the program. He would go on and win four Indianapolis 500 races.

On May 20 Kenny Roberts shattered Scott Brelsford's one-lap AMA track record during qualifying with a time of 26:08 on the half-mile. A month earlier, Jimmy Oskie turned a lap at 25.27 in a Sprint Car.

The main event turned tragic when rider Lloyd Allen Houchins nosed out rookie rider Pat McCaul at the checkered flag during a heat race. As the pair crossed the finish line, their motorcycles locked handlebars. The two then crashed to the ground. Houchins then slid into one of the posts for the railing that circled the track, used for horse racing. He was dead on arrival at Alexian Brothers Hospital. The July 1974 AMA race sent seven riders to the hospital with injuries.

Returning to the indoor oval on November 3 after a five-year absence was the BCRA Midgets. Scheduled for a six-race series, they only ran one race. Ken Nichols won that race.

1975

Speedway motorcycles made their debut on a specially constructed seventh-mile track in front of the grandstands. The series was run by Harold Murrell and ran on Thursday nights.

RURA held a short series of Mini Sedan races on the indoor 1/10-mile oval in December and January. The races on the tight track were generally crash-filled affairs. Car counts averaged about 15 and the crowds were small.

1976

A repeat of 1954 (when WAR split with Bob Barkhimer and San Jose Speedway) took place in this Bicentennial year. Called the "Revolution in the Dirt," a large group of disgruntled owners and drivers, led by Silas Carter, broke away from San Jose Speedway and formed the Golden State Racing Association (GSRA). After negotiations with the Fair Board, contracts were signed, improvements were made and the Fairgrounds

Flyer for the much-anticipated GSRA races in 1976.

GOLDEN STATE
RACING ASSOC.
PRESENTS

REVOLUTION
IN THE
DIRT

DATES
FEBRUARY 22
FEBRUARY 29
MARCH 7
OTHER DATES
TO FOLLOW

SANTA CLARA
COUNTY FAIRGROUNDS

half-mile became their home track. The first race was February 22, in direct competition to San Jose Speedway's opening race.

Classified as an open competition race, the field consisted of Sprint Cars and Super Modifieds. Eighteen of the top twenty drivers in points from the 1975 season who had raced at San Jose Speedway were present. All the top NARC drivers were there as well as the Ohio traveler, Rick Ferkle.

The grandstands were jam-packed with 7,200 spectators who watched the 70-car field put on the most thrilling race yet on the half-mile oval. Leroy Van Connett and Rick Ferkle put on a show as they diced for the lead in the closing laps of the main event. Ferkle just edged out Van Connettt at the stripe as the crowd went wild. Mike Sargent finished third in his Super Modified. Four of the top five positions went to Sprint Cars. The track stayed in good shape throughout the show, and the event was a huge success. More races were scheduled. Meanwhile, at San Jose Speedway, just three miles up the road, they had the lowest car count and attendance for an opener on record.

One hundred cars signed in for race number two on February 29, when 6,000 people saw Jimmy Boyd, Van Connett, Gary Patterson and Johnny Anderson put on a show while battling for the lead of the main event. Boyd emerged victorious. Sprint Cars took the top three spots, followed by Davey Pombo, Howard Kaeding and Nick Rescino in Super Modifieds. Larry Rice finished seventh.

Thirty-two hundred showed up on March 13 to watch

Rick Ferkle leads a pair of Super Modifieds during the debut race for the GSRA. It was an SRO event (the front bleacher seats were vacant for safety reasons). *Dennis Mattish Photo*

The landmark Santa Clara County Fairgrounds archway in 1976. *Dennis Mattish Photo*

1976: The start of the GSRA main event. *Dennis Mattish Photo*

Don Hicks scatters dirt and lumber during a 1976 GSRA show. *Dennis Mattish Photo*

1976: Leroy Van Connett (01) and Rick Ferkle (outside) battled for the lead for most of the main event before Ferkle emerged with the win in a very exciting opening race for the GSRA. *Dennis Mattish Photo*

Rising star Sammy Swindell (71A) sits in his Sprint Car alongside Howard Kaeding (1X) in a Super Modified before the start of the 1976 Golden West Classic main event. *Dennis Mattish Photo*

Gary "the Preacher" Paterson (left) and Rick " The Buckeye Traveler" Ferkle were real Outlaws in the truest sense, racing wherever and whenever they wanted. Photo taken at the 1976 Golden West Classic. *Mattish Photo*

Bobby "Scruffy" Allen has the all-time single-lap track record on the half-mile. Here he is after winning the WoO Trophy Dash in 1978. *Dennis Mattish Photo*

Johnny Anderson win the first night race on the half-mile by 12 lengths over Jimmy Boyd. Fifty-four cars signed in for the final combination Sprint Car/Super Modified show. (The Supers would be on their own just as the series was starting to lose steam.)

Two weeks later, Mike Sargent won the first Super-Modified-only GSRA main event. Sargent took home the winner's share of the $4,000 guaranteed purse, with 2,000 people in the stands on this cold night.

After one race as a Super-Modified-only show, the format was switched back to open competition on May 2. Terry Chalker powered his Super Modified past a slowing Jimmy Sills on the last lap to win the 25-lap main event.

This was the last GSRA event to be held at the Fairgrounds. The series moved to Altamont Speedway for the rest of the year, where it would die a slow death because of dwindling car counts and crowds. The split from Bob Barkhimer would help drive the nail into the coffin of San Jose Speedway, a situation that nobody won!

The third annual Golden West Classic made its first appearance at the Fairgrounds on October 8 and 9. The Classic was previously a series of races at many tracks, San Jose Speedway acting as its home track.

Gary Howard, a California Racing Association (CRA) driver from Los Angeles, stalked Rick Ferkle for much of the 50-lap main event before passing him enroute to the win. Howard took home $2,000 in front of a crowd of 5,000.

1977

The first race of 1977 for NARC took place at the Santa Clara County Fairgrounds in February. Twenty-eight hundred sprint car fans saw another good show on the half-mile. The main event turned into a three-car battle between Johnny Anderson, Leroy Van Conett and Jimmy Boyd. Van Conett and Boyd hounded Anderson for 24 laps before Anderson had a slight bobble. That's all it took, as the pair slipped under Anderson with six laps to go. The three would finish under a blanket in that order before an appreciative crowd.

October 8: This was the second California Golden Classic, but the first at the Fairgrounds (the prior Classic was held at San Jose Speedway in 1976). Different from the Golden West Classic, this race was promoted by Bob Barkhimer and Ken Clapp.

What started out as a local event was now an East vs. West shootout. Pre-entered were Jan Opperman, Sammy Swindell, Rick Ferkle, and Bobby Allan from Pennsylvania.

In qualifying, Jimmy Boyd shattered the track record, but it was Allan who showed the rest of the field the fast way around the track when he won by a full straightaway over Boyd, Gary Patterson and Nick Rescino. He was so dominant in his home-built car that he lapped everybody but the top three. The locals were finding out just how fast these guys from Pennsylvania were. Over 90 cars timed in

1977: NARC Sprint Cars on the half-mile. Gary Patterson (56) leads Chuck Gurney (outside), Tommy Astone (89) and Gary Ponzini (85) during the dash. Patterson won. *Dennis Mattish Photo*

before a crowd of 5,400.

1978

After the final race was held at San Jose Speedway on September 3, 1977, Bob Barkhimer almost immediately started looking for another site for a weekly show. Fremont Raceway and Morgan Hill were discussed and then rejected. Ken Clapp, who in December of 1977 had just become the majority owner of Bob Barkhimer Associates (BBA), and Barkhimer (Ken's mentor) then entered into negotiations with the Santa Clara County Fair Board. They proposed to hold weekly NASCAR Super Modified and Stock Car races. Once the local residents heard about the talks, there was strong opposition to any racing taking place at the Fairgrounds. There were even threats of lawsuits. (It is noted that the racetrack was there long before the houses were.) In January, the Fair Board granted the track six trial races, one motorcycle and five auto races. The objective was to check for dust and noise levels. A 10:30 p.m. curfew was also imposed on the track

The races were to take place in April and May. The first order of business was to carve out a new 1/4-mile dirt oval inside the 1/2-mile, using the front straightaway of the mile

Promoters Ken Clapp (left) and Bob Barkhimer negotiated a deal to bring weekly NASCAR racing to the Fairgrounds.
Photo Courtesy of Ken Clapp

1979 WoO "A" feature winner, Shane Carson.
Dennis Mattish Photo

track as the common link between the three tracks.

But then a huge wind and rainstorm struck the track and tore half the massive roof off the grandstand and tossed it over the backside. To make matters worse, it was discovered that there was wood rot in the remaining section of the roof. It was going to cost $200,000 to repair, so the decision was made to just remove it altogether. More storms followed, turning the track into a swamp area. This set opening day back three months while they cleaned up the mess and waited until things dried out. The first 1/4-mile oval was flat and would be challenging for the Super Modifieds, which were still basically pavement cars.

Finally, after over two months of delays, the next phase of auto racing (weekly racing) started at the speed plant on June 10.

A field of 20 Supers and 19 Stock Cars greeted the 4,000 spectators who attended that first event. Davey Pombo (Al's son) was the pre-season favorite to win the track championship, and he showed why on opening night. Right out of the gate, Pombo set the automatic track

NASCAR Super Modified champion Davey Pombo after one of his three main event wins during 1978. *Dennis Mattish Photo*

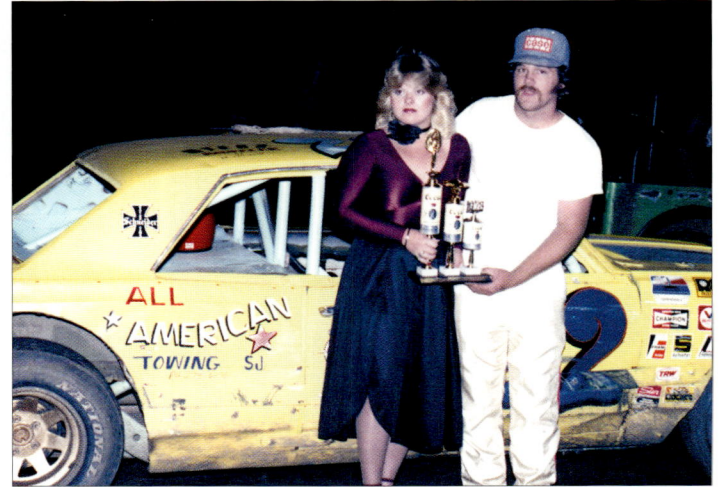

1978 Late Model Stock Car champion Larry Lundin. Larry had 16 career main event wins at San Jose. *Dennis Mattish Photo*

Davey Pombo drove the Jim Bowman Chevy-powered Super Modified to the 1978 state and track championships. *Mattish Photo*

record in qualifying. Nick Foster established the first Stock Car record.

Pombo dominated the Modified main, becoming the first winner on the new track. Mitch West won the first Late Model Stock Car race.

The 25th annual Johnny Key Memorial Race was won by Johnny Brazil, who started last in the 100-lap, 26-car race. What was amazing was he had to win the semi in order to transfer to the Key race, becoming the first person to win both on the same night. Attendance was 6,000.

Dave Pombo won the track championship with three wins during the short 11-race season. Finishing close behind was Lloyd Beard, also with three wins.

1979: Lloyd Beard was one of the premier drivers to have raced in San Jose. He won 27 NASCAR Super Modified main events in his career before his untimely death at Calistoga. There were 19 Lloyd Beard Classic races run in his honor between 1980 and 1999. *Dennis Mattish Photo*

1979

Despite his dazzling set of statistics that saw him win nearly half of the 20 features and set fast time nearly two-thirds of the time, former San Jose pavement champ Mike Sargent had to battle right down to the wire to win the Super Modified title. Sargent was pushed all the way by veteran Lloyd Beard, who won four main events. At one point during the season, the rivalry between the two camps became so heated that both sides were fined and put on probation for fighting.

Mark Sargent was suspended for a year after several incidents, the last of which was Howard Kaeding taking out 90 feet of sound barrier when he ran out of room while racing with Mark.

Mike Parker from Fresno won a Super Modified main event during 1979. *Dennis Mattish Photo*

Hot laps during 1979. *Dennis Mattish Photo*

Brent Kaeding after one of his six NASCAR Super Modified victories in 1980. *Dennis Mattish Photo*

The buy-a-ride was in its early stages in 1980. The first to do this at the fairgrounds was T.J. Winningham (97), renting the Larry Rodriguez Super Modified. Winnigham then had the misfortune of performing a series of end-over-end flips down the back straightaway and heavily damaging the rental (below). Art McCarthy (19) (above) races wheel to wheel (literally) with T.J. *Dennis Mattish Photos*

Howard Kaeding won his third Johnny Key Memorial Race, this one by 10 lengths over Lloyd Beard. It was a family affair for Kaeding, as his son Brent won the semi-main. Six-thousand fans were in attendance.

In the Stock Cars, Dave Byrd and Ray Morgan had a seesaw battle for the championship. Byrd's seven feature wins were enough to edge out Morgan for the title.

Tragically, Lloyd Beard lost his life in a freak Sprint Car crash during the final race at Calistoga Speedway during the year.

1980

As the Fairgrounds track grew in status, more top-notch drivers were joining the weekly Super Modified programs, which in turn drew bigger crowds. Joining the series this year were Sacramento Champions John Viel and Nick Rescino. Also joining the fray was Howard Kaeding's son, Brent. These three drivers dominated the season, winning 18 of the 20 main events. Nick Rescino won the track championship with seven feature victories. His old West Capitol Raceway adversary, John Viel, finished second with five main event wins. Brent Kaeding had a sensational year, picking up six wins, while Mike Sargent won twice. Ninety-two drivers competed in the Supers with the car counts averaging 40 and the final two races drawing over 60. Twenty-five of those Super Modifieds flipped during the year.

On May 4, Hank Scott rode his Harley to victory in the 17th running of the San Jose mile in front of 17,000 spectators and the ABC Wide World of Sports program.

A memorial race in honor of Lloyd Beard was held on May 31. Nick Rescino avoided a huge rut in turn one (and the persistent challenges from Brent Kaeding) on his way to winning the 100-lap Memorial Race as 6,700 looked on.

On March 31, 1979, Donna Walton (right) led the Late Model Stock Car main event for 12 laps. What was significant about this is she was the first woman driver to lead a NASCAR main event in San Jose. This presentation commemorates that event. *Dennis Mattish Photo*

In the 27th running of the Johnny Key Classic, Brent Kaeding passed John Viel on a lap-95 restart and then beat him to the checkered flag. Kaeding pocketed $3,500 in the biggest win of his young career.

The Stock Cars were just as successful, with 106 drivers making appearances. Watsonville's Ray Morgan won the title with three main event wins. Bob Link, a mechanic on Morgan's pit crew, was struck by a wheel that came off a Super Modified during their feature race. Link, who was in the pits (which were located in turns one and two on the half-mile) was rushed to the hospital in critical condition. Soon after, the pits were moved to the back of the track.

Engineer gone wild. Dan Clarke designed this unique-looking offset, slant-six cylinder Super Modified in 1980. The car did not live up to expectations. *Dennis Mattish Photo*

1980: Gary Willey used the guardrail to shorten his Super Modified. *Dennis Mattish photo*

Leland McSpadden (center) won all four races (two at SJ and two at Watsonville) on his way to winning 1980's California Golden Classic. Car owner Sam Bailey (left) and car builder Chuck Delu share the moment. *Dennis Mattish Photo*

NASCAR great Bobby Allison (waving) and his son Davey paid a visit to San Jose during 1981. Davey would also go on and win many NASCAR Winston Cup races. Track announcer John Trussler did the interview. *Dennis Mattish Photo*

187

During the season, a single-engine Cessna airplane crash-landed on the front straightaway of the mile. Although the pilot was okay, the plane was heavily damaged when it tore through the guardrail.

San Jose continued to be the best-drawing NASCAR track west of the Mississippi (number two in the nation), averaging a weekly attendance of over 4,000. Counting the motorcycles, over 100,000 people went through the turnstiles.

1981

Nick Rescino and Mike Sargent battled right down to the wire for the crown, with Rescino winning his second straight championship on the final night of racing. It wasn't easy, as a lap-six accident sent Rescino to the pits for repairs. He finished the race mid-pack, just enough to edge Sargent for the crown. During the year both drivers won four main events while third place finisher, John Viel, won six times.

Brent Kaeding, who was racing both Sprint Cars and Super Modifieds in the state, had an eventful year. He won four main events at San Jose, but he was also suspended twice for rough driving. On the second suspension, which was for 10 weeks (the rest of the year), other prominent drivers came to his defense. Bill Gazaway, NASCAR Director of Racing Operations in Daytona, lifted the suspension after two weeks and put Brent on probation. He was back in time for the Key race.

Mike Sargent took the lead on lap 51 and then held off the persistent challenges from Nick Rescino to win the biggest race of his career, the 28th annual Johnny Key Classic. A record standing-room-only crowd of 7,300 were on their feet for the last lap as Rescino pulled next to Sargent going into turn three, but Sargent was carrying enough speed out of turn four to win the thrilling 100-lap race. He took home the winner's share of the record $20,000 Johnny Key purse.

Nick Ringo had a pair of main event wins on the fairgrounds dirt to go along with his six wins at the old paved track. *Dennis Mattish Photo*

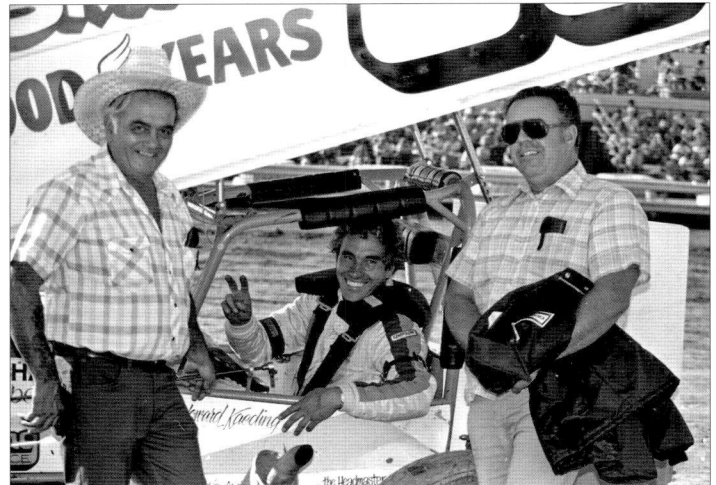

Three San Jose Speedway legends pose for the camera in 1981. (L to R) Al Pombo, Howard Kaeding and Marshall Sargent. *Dennis Mattish Photo*

Ernie Rose won four Super Modified main events, including the 1983 Lloyd Beard Classic. *Dennis Mattish Photo*

Jimmy Boyd will always be remembered for winning the first WoO race in 1978. At San Jose he broke the one-lap track record on the half-mile on three different occasions. *Dennis Mattish Photo*

By 1981 San Jose Fairgrounds Speedway was the number one short track in attendance west of the Mississippi, number two in North America. *Dennis Mattish Photo*

San Jose Speedway was famous for having the biggest wings in the country in the early eighties. John Viel (12) battles with his archrival Nick Rescino (1) in this 1981 photo. *Dennis Mattish Photo*

Jimmy Sills won three out of four main events, including the two at San Jose, on his way to winning the 6th annual California Golden Classic series title in 1981. This was the second year in a row the Bailey Brothers Sprint Car dominated the series. *Dennis Mattish Photo*

1981: Hall of Fame driver Jack Hewitt raced in San Jose with the WoO. *Dennis Mattish Photo*

Super Modifieds await push trucks before a race during 1981. *Dennis Mattish Photo*

Robert Miller (left) and Jim Pettit II would have stellar careers in both Stock Cars and Grand American Modifieds. Both drivers were 16 years old when this photo was taken in 1981. *Dennis Mattish Photo*

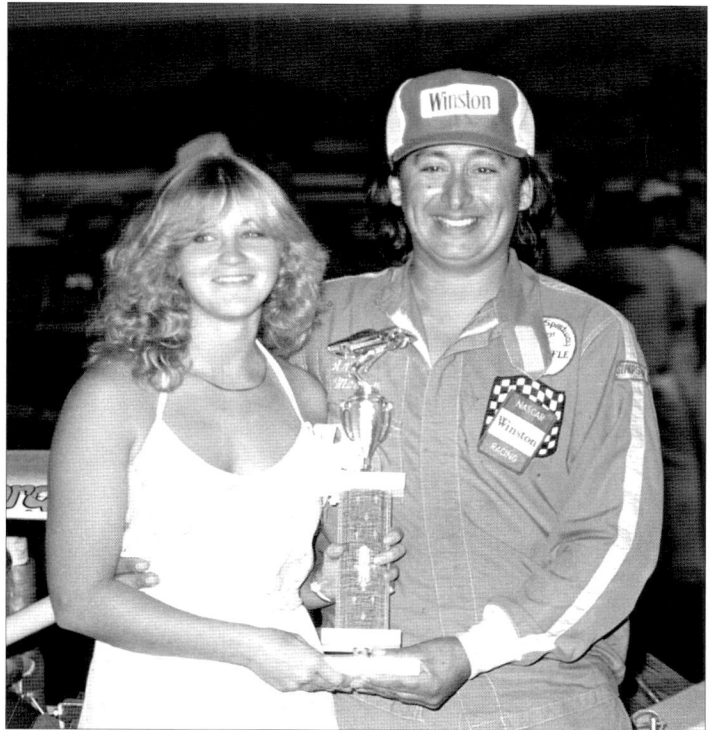

Ray Morgan was the 1980 & 1981 San Jose Stock Car champion. *Dennis Mattish Photo*

NASCAR Late Model Stock Cars on pace lap during 1981. *Dennis Mattish Photo*

New to San Jose in 1981 was an event called "Super Pull," or Tractor Pull as it is more commonly called. This is an event where trucks or tractors pull a sled with a sliding weight. The object is to see who can pull it the farthest. The farther it is pulled, the heavier the sled gets. *Dennis Mattish Photo*

1982: "Little Indian" John Keldsen won 13 Stock Car main events and was a threat to win the track championship on several occasions. *Dennis Mattish Photo*

Four-time San Jose Stock Car Champion Ed Sans. *Mattish Photo*

Ray Morgan successfully defended his crown in the Stock Cars, claiming six wins. His closest challenger was Dave Byrd with five wins.

Larry Lundin had the most spectacular Stock Car flip ever seen at the fairgrounds when he barrel-rolled eight times at the end of the front stretch.

The weekly show itself broke all attendance records as 110,000 paying fans flocked to the Fairgrounds to watch 23 weekly shows. This was the pinnacle for the 73-year-old track.

1982

John Viel won a record 11 feature races to become the fourth different Fairgrounds Super Modified Champion in five years. Viel finished ahead of arch-rival Nick Rescino, who had four wins. Mike Sargent finished third and had his finest year since 1979 with seven victories and seven fast times.

Total prize money for the year exceeded $166,000.

Tom Henry led 24 laps before Howard Kaeding passed him for the lead of the third annual Lloyd Beard Classic. Kaeding then led 69 laps and was only seven laps from victory when his steering failed. Mike Sargent inherited the lead and held off John Viel in front of 6,503 fans.

The big news for the Stock Cars was the announcement of the $25,000 regional point fund put up by Winston. The winner got $10,000 and a shot at the National title, worth another $10,000.

1982: Second-generation driver Jerry Freitas won three Super Modified main events at the Fairgrounds track. *Dennis Mattish Photo*

An All Star lineup in a 1981 Trophy Dash. Howard Kaeding (68), John Viel (12), Mike Sargent (7) and Nick Rescino (1). Every one of these drivers won multiple San Jose championships. *Dennis Mattish Photo*

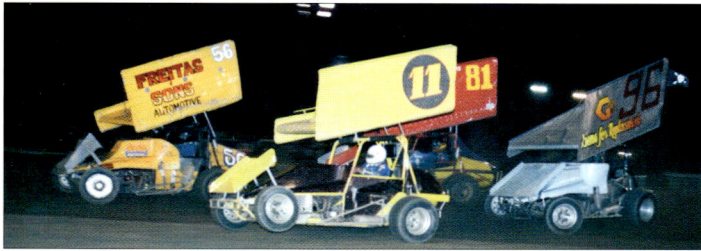

1982: Dan Smith (11), Jerry Freitas (56), Nick Ringo (96) and Ernie Rose (81). *Dennis Mattish Photo*

1982: Joe Moniz (92) makes life exciting for this photographer as he slams into an infield tractor tire just a few yards away. Ray Cotta is (90). *Dennis Mattish Photo*

1982: Four-time Watsonville Sportsman Champion Jerry Cecil moved up to the Super Modifieds and won a main event at San Jose. *Dennis Mattish Photo*

1983 Stock Car action involving Ed Oliveria (5) and Joe Chapman. Bill Wesenberg (85) slips by on the inside. *Dennis Mattish Photo*

1983: Nick Rescino, six-time San Jose champion (1972, '75, '80, '81, '83 & '84), six-time Johnny Key Classic winner and one-time Lloyd Beard Classic winner.
Dennis Mattish Photo

1981 Johnny Key Classic Trophy Dash. Brent Kaeding (69), Nick Rescino (1) & Mike Sargent (7).
Dennis Mattish Photo

1982: Tom Henry won his first of nine career main events at San Jose on June 27, 1982.
Dennis Mattish Photo

1982: Mike Sargent–1977, 1979, 1985 and 1986 track champion. He earned 43 feature wins. *Dennis Mattish Photo*

1982: John Viel–1982, 1987 & 1988 track champion. He, too, earned 43 feature wins. *Dennis Mattish Photo*

Rich Voss, as seen in 1982, won the 1985 Johnny Key Classic and 7 feature events in his short career at the Speedway. *Dennis Mattish Photo*

1984: Roger Fosdick, Jr. (31) leads the charge into turn one during a 1984 NASCAR Super Modified heat race. John Lott (08) is in close pursuit. *Dennis Mattish Photo*

1983: Gary Dillard (nose up) had a bad night after climbing the right rear wheel of Jim Telfer (53). *Dennis Mattish Photo*

1984: Ernie Rose keeps his right rear tire spinning as he tries (unsuccessfully) to correct the situation. *Dennis Mattish Photo*

Ed Sans, Jr., became the first driver to win the San Jose championship without winning a single feature race. A number of drivers enjoyed success during the year in the Stock Cars. John Keldsen started the year out with back-to-back wins. The following week Jim Pettit II became the youngest driver at 17 to win a Stock Car main event in San Jose. San Josean Robert Miller became the second 17-year-old to win a main event, then he did it three weeks in a row.

1983

Nick Rescino and John Viel continued to dominate the Winston Racing Series Super Modified events in 1983 finishing one-two in the series for the third time in four years and winning 18 of 20 features.

The year clearly belonged to "Quick Nick," as he nabbed 10 main events and posted 11 fast times, including a sizzling new track record of 13.665 on June 18. This beat Tim Green's Sprint Car record of 13.875. Rescino joined Al Pombo as the only five-time San Jose champion in 37 years of competition. Defending champ Viel also had a fine season, winning eight features.

Mike Sargent received the 11th suspension of his career.

After starting on the pole the previous two years, John Viel finally won his first Johnny Key Classic. Viel ran second to Rescino for 67 laps until his motor blew. Viel then held off Mike Sargent and Rich Voss, the only other driver to complete the 100 laps. A crowd of 7,000 contributed to a purse of $24,600.

Cheryl Robertson became the first woman Super Modified driver to race locally. Husband Jerry gave up his car so his wife could fulfill her dream, and she did, winning the C Driver points title and finishing in the top 10 in semi-points.

The NASCAR Stock Car division took on a new look in 1983, with fiberglass bodies, spoilers and wider tires. The increased speed was immediately evident as track records were shattered. The close racing that characterized the division continued.

Ed Sans was the track champion for the second

straight year, catching Greg Williams with a furious late-season charge and winning the title on the final night.

The average weekly attendance was 4,185, keeping the speedway the number one short track west of the Mississippi.

1984

The largest crowd to ever witness a weekly auto race in San Jose history showed up for the opener on March 10. A standing-room-only crowd of 8,000 watched John Viel take home the winner's share of the $15,750, a record purse for a weekly show.

Nick Rescino had virtually re-written the San Jose NASCAR record book over the previous five seasons and notched an unprecedented sixth San Jose Super Modified driving title.

John Viel's title hopes were dashed when he suffered burns on a May 31 crash. While leading the race and lapping a slower car, contact was made, sending Viel into a wild series of flips. His car then burst into flames. He missed the remainder of the season while skin grafts healed.

The Stock Car Division saw Ed Sans, Jr., enjoy a record-smashing season. He became the first driver in Fairgrounds history to win three consecutive track championships. His seven feature wins tied the record for most wins in a season, four of them coming in a row.

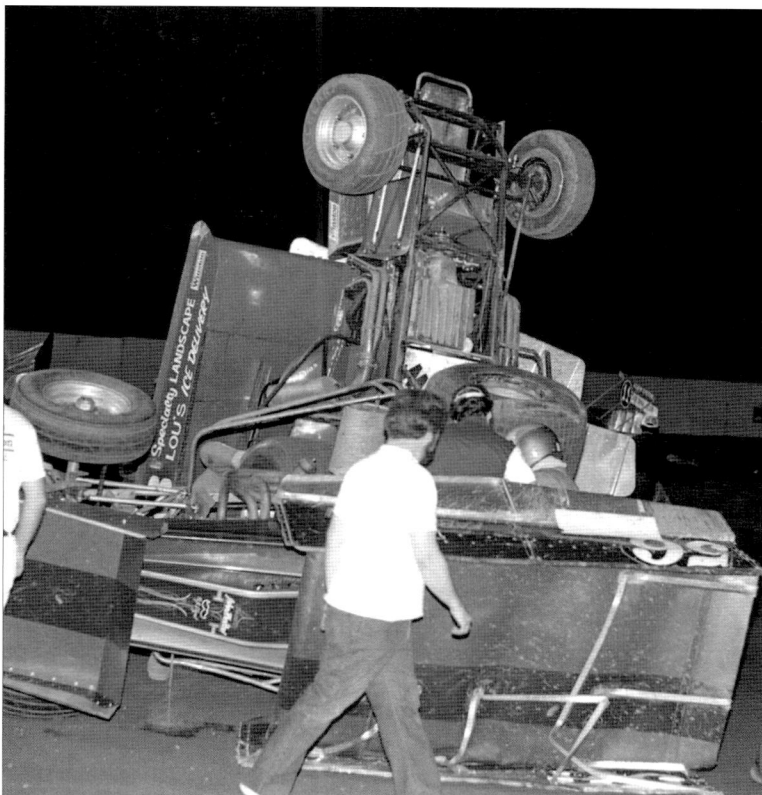

Paul Dias' Super Modified appears to be ready for launch after this 1984 incident. This photo was on the cover of the *National Speed Sport News'* 50th Anniversary issue. *Dennis Mattish Photo*

The track continued to attract over a 100,000 spectators a year in 1985. *Dennis Mattish Photo*

Brad Doty during driver introduction before the start of the 1986 WoO Main. Doty won 11 "A" Feature WoO races before his career was cut short in a paralyzing crash in Ohio. These days he is a TV commentator.

Northern California Sprint Car driver Dave Bradway, Jr., before the start of the 1986 WoO feature race.

Gallery of Open Wheel drivers.
Photos by Dennis Mattish

Johnny Key was not related to the original Johnny Key, but his father named him after the legendary driver. Key lived up to the name with three main event wins in the tough NASCAR Super Modified class.

Doug Wolfgang is number four on the WoO win list with 107. He has two preliminary main event wins at the fairgrounds.

Chuck Miller won the 1993 & 1994 Johnny Key Classics. He also won the 1984, 1994 & 1995 Lloyd Beard Classics along with another half dozen main events during his very successful racing career at the fairgrounds.

1987: Joe Von Schriltz, who looks more like a rock star than a race car driver, became a winning Sprint Car owner after his driving days ended.

1981: San Jose driver Joey Santos had a 30-year career driving in a variety of open wheel classes.

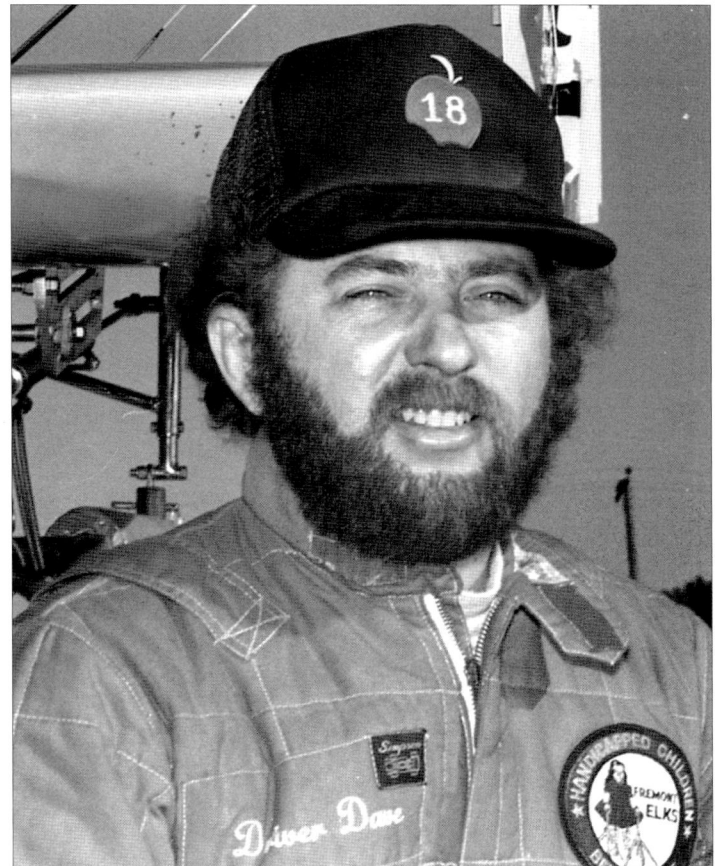

Driver Dave Thompson had his best year in 1989 when he won a feature race and was fastest qualifier three times.

Larry Lundin had an impressive year, winning six main events, and on August 25 he broke the track record set in 1979 by Dave Byrd with a time of 16.928.

Bob Link, who was critically injured in 1980 and received brain damage, filed a lawsuit against the track. The track's insurance company settled.

Over 104,000 fans attended the 24 events.

1985

Mike Sargent won his third NASCAR Winston Racing Series San Jose Super Modified Championship in 1985. Sargent was in complete control of the point standings virtually all season long. After taking the opening night feature race win, Sargent then added six more victories before season's end, including the seventh annual Lloyd Beard Classic. He was the first two-time winner of that event.

Bursting into the winner's circle in a big way was Rich Voss with five main event wins. Voss won the crown jewel of Super Modified racing, the 33rd running of the Johnny Key Classic. He took home a record $10,000 for winning that race, witnessed by 6,500. He also led the Beard race for 77 laps before a back marker put him in the wall.

The ageless Howard Kaeding picked up his 118th San Jose win on March 30, followed by Mark Sargent's winning his first Fairgrounds race the following week.

Robert Miller completely dominated the Stock Cars, winning a record 11 feature race wins in 18 events, including a record five in a row. His closest challenger was second place finisher Mike Petruzzi with two wins.

(above & below) Scene from the 1986 Mark Sargent–Howard Kaeding incident. See main text on page 201 for complete story. *Dennis Mattish Photos*

1986

Mike Sargent edged Jim Perry, Jr., by a scant five points to win his fourth NASCAR Super Modified title. It was the closest point finish in the 33-year history of NASCAR Modified racing in San Jose. Sargent joined Rick Henderson, Al Pombo, Bill Scott, Howard Kaeding and Nick Rescino as the only drivers to win back-to-back championships.

It was one of the most competitive seasons in history as four different drivers exchanged the points lead nine times. The season produced seven different winners with Perry leading with seven. Sargent posted five wins and Rescino four. Rescino became the first driver to win over $100,000 at the Fairgrounds.

In the Stock Cars, Mike Williams easily won the championship, winning three times. It was a family affair, as his brother Greg won four features and the pair finished one-two twice.

On April 5, controversy struck during the Super Modified main event when coming out of turn four, and battling for the lead, Mark Sargent and Howard Kaeding made contact. Kaeding's car catapulted the guardrail, launched about 20 feet into the air and came down on the catch fence that separates the track from the stands. If the rear wheels hadn't caught one of the cables that ran the length of the fence, the car would have ended up in the stands. With the car in a precarious position and fuel running under the stands, the Sheriffs' Department cleared the area and halted the racing for the night. Sargent was declared the winner, which didn't sit well with Kaeding or some of the fans. NASCAR Daytona intervened, disqualified Sargent for rough driving and set him back to 18th position. He was also suspended. Rod Spencer was awarded his first main event victory.

In a race reminiscent of the old days at the paved track, Nick Rescino and Howard Kaeding battled for the lead of the seventh annual Lloyd Beard Classic over the last 50 laps. The roar from the crowd of 5,000-plus, who were on their feet, could be heard over the noise of the cars, as the two traded the lead in the closing laps in what was perhaps one of the most exciting races ever staged on the oval. The only big race that Kaeding hadn't won was now his. This was Kaeding's 31st 100-lap main event victory.

On October 11, the grand reopening of the 1/2-mile (last used in 1979) took place, featuring the NARC Sprint Cars and Late Model Stock Cars. By now it was common knowledge that the track was closer to five-eighth of a mile than half a mile .

Jac Haudenschild, who was in town a week early for the World of Outlaws show, won the Sprint Car portion of the program.

Making their first appearance since 1957 on the 1/2-mile dirt track were Late Model Stock Cars. Ed Sans, Jr., had a big payday, winning the feature in front of 4,000.

Over $300,000 in prize money was paid out during the year for the car races.

1987

John Viel won six main events on his way to winning his second championship. Viel joined Rescino and Sargent in the $100,000 Fairgrounds club.

Mike Williams (8) passes Mike Petruzzi (43) and Joe Glade (9) on his way to winning the 1986 Late Model Stock Car championship. *Dennis Mattish Photo*

World Heavyweight Boxing Champion George Foreman (left) shares a laugh with NASCAR champions Howard Kaeding (center) and John Viel. Foreman, who enjoyed the races, was also there promoting his upcoming fight. *Dennis Mattish Photo*

1987: John Lott, first cousin of San Francisco 49er Ronnie Lott, won his first NASCAR Super Modified main event on April 2, 1988, becoming the first African American to accomplish this. *Dennis Mattish Photo*

Daredevil Brian Carson attempted to jump three semi trucks and a string of cars during the 1987 WoO show. He went up the ramp okay, then flew through the air 80 yards and missed his target, slamming into the ground. He was thoroughly shaken . *Dennis Mattish Photo*

Blair Pine was the fastest Super Modified qualifier on this night in 1987. *Dennis Mattish Photo*

August 15 was undoubtedly the most destructive night in the 1/4-mile's history as no fewer than nine cars flipped, half of them violently. Three drivers were sent to the hospital with moderate injuries.

In the Stock Cars, Robert Miller of San Jose won his second San Jose championship in three years. Miller, who had three wins, had to hold off the fierce challenges from runner-up Ed Sans, Jr., who won seven times.

With the Stock Car counts down, the division was now designated an official Winston Racing Series division. This was done in hopes of bringing in more cars and fans. The warning was given if there were fewer than 20 cars, their purse would be cut in half. If there were fewer than 15 cars, the division would be discontinued at San Jose. They made it to the end of the year.

Street Stocks, Late Models, Super Modifieds and Sprint Cars held an open competition race on the half-mile. Rick Downey was first in the Open Wheel cars, Jim Pettit II took the Late Model Stock Car race and Ron Parker won the Street Stock feature.

Auto racing attendance had been in a gradual decline for the last couple of seasons. It is also noted that there were nights when dust problems prevailed. Spectators could be heard complaining about the problem, especially if the wind blew from the south into the stands.

1988

Early in January, NASCAR officials from Daytona, including Bill France, Jr., came to San Jose and lobbied to bring big-time Stock Car racing to the Fairgrounds. The International Speedway Corporation, which included track promotor Ken Clapp, met with all five supervisors, key members of the fair board and Mayor Tom McEnery.

They explained that San Jose was the number one choice to replace Riverside International Raceway as the primary track in the West for the premier Stock Car division, the Winston Cup. They proposed to spend $12 million dollars to turn the Fairgrounds into a super speedway, complete with seating for 40,000 and garages on the infield for the cars–all this at no cost to the city. Racing would be reduced from 33 nights a year to four weekends, which would be better for the local residents. Studies conducted by NASCAR and confirmed by Clapp, showed there would be a $200 million economic impact on the economy.

The first San Jose 500 would be in October, 1989.

The Pacific Outlaw Super Stock Enterprise (POSSE) brought their wild-looking Stock Cars down from the Pacific Northwest and put on an entertaining show in 1987. *Dennis Mattish Photo*

1987 NASCAR Super Modified Trophy Dash consisting of Ernie Rose (81), Mike Sargent (7), Rod Spencer (22) and Jim Perry, Jr. (15). Perry had won a dozen main events at the Fairgrounds by the time this photo was taken. *Dennis Mattish Photo*

Ray Terri's 1987 Sprint Car makes a nice backdrop for an aspiring model. *Dennis Mattish Photo.*

The reaction of local officials ranged from enthusiasm to concern about the impact of traffic and noise on nearby residents. It wasn't long before a local group called "Citizens against NASCAR" was formed. The spokesman said they did not want to breathe the air or hear the noise from the races. Later it was rumored that Sears Point Raceway was behind one of the groups that opposed the project. Sears Point's thinking was, "If San Jose doesn't get the race, we will." They were right.

Some of the local drivers, who knew how the fair board thought, were skeptical that the track would ever be built. They said the fair board was more concerned about the few horses that were housed in the barns on the backside of the property. The horses used the track for exercise, and the board would never approve paving over the dirt.

As the year wore on, the dream of building the speedway became more distant. An obstacle course of neighborhood opposition and government regulation stalled the process. An environmental study was dragging on and talks came to a standstill.

Susanne Wilson was the only supervisor who showed strong interest in the proposal, but she was outnumbered. Other visionary politicians voicing support were Don Cortese and Senator Al Alquist, but they didn't have a vote.

When supervisor Zoe Lofgren attended a rally against the plan to build the speedway, NASCAR in Daytona took note. It was that rally that helped influence the decision of NASCAR to throw in the towel. So in March of 1989, the project was dead. The actions of a few cost the local economy hundreds of millions of dollars over time. It wasn't long before NASCAR became the second biggest spectator sport in America.

During the off-season the track was enlarged to one-third of a mile and more banking was added, making it a much faster track.

John Viel became the seventh man to win back-to-back championships in the 38-year history of San Jose NASCAR Modified racing. Making his presence known was second place Rod Spencer with four wins. "Rod Spencer leads only 2 laps but wins controversial Key Classic," read the headline of the story the following day. The 35th running of the Johnny Key Race turned into a three-way battle between Spencer, Howard Kaeding and Mike Sargent. On lap 98 Sargent and Kaeding were battling for the lead when contact was made. Sargent, who had led for 81 laps, ended up on his side, and he wasn't happy about it. He immediately announced his retirement, later to be rescinded. On the restart, Spencer moved by Kaeding and went on to win the biggest race of his short career.

Ed Sans, Jr., had his finest season as he won half (eight) of the Stock Car main events. Sans also won the Winston Racing Series Pacific Coast Region title and the Watsonville crown. He far outdistanced second place Ken Haskell, who had two wins.

Because advertised WoO drivers didn't show for the Western Spring Open in February, refunds were given out to the fans. Jimmy Sills took home $3,000 for the win.

Because it was felt that the mile was going to be paved, the 33rd running of the San Jose Mile was advertised as the last. (It wasn't.) Steve Morehead won the event.

Fairgrounds rival track Baylands Raceway Park (aka Fremont Raceway) closed for good at the end of the season.

What could have been. Artist rendition of what the Fairgrounds Super Speedway would have looked like. The then-existing grandstand was to be incorporated into the new plan.

204

1988 was the Tenth Anniversary year of weekly racing.

Larry Tachovsky was okay after flipping end over end during a 1988 heat race. *Dennis Mattish Photo*

The team cars of Wayne Katen (99) and Robert Silva (19x) during 1988. *Dennis Mattish Photo*

The San Jose 500, as it was advertised, was held on October 8, 1988. The only 500-lap race ever held at the Fairgrounds proved to be a long, grueling race featuring 100 equally prepared passenger cars. Late Model Stock Car driver John Brazil, Jr., outlasted everybody to win the Enduro. *Dennis Mattish Photo*

205

1989

The changing of the guard took place in 1989 as new blood occupied the top positions in the final point standings. Rod Spencer won the title on consistency, and finishing second was sophomore driver Rick Martin. Both drivers won one main event. Scott Luhdorff finished third with five main event wins. Only seven points separated the top three.

1988: Versatile racecar driver Bobby Hogge won half a dozen Late Model Stock Car feature races at San Jose. He also won many Sprint Car and Modified races during his racing career. *Dennis Mattish Photo*

Tragedy struck the speedway during the main event on May 27 when Frank Carlotta sped into turn one and never slowed down. He slid sideways into a huge tractor tire that guarded a wall and light pole. The impact threw the tire 15 feet into the air. His car then bounced off the concrete barrier. Carlotta died of multiple traumatic injuries. His was the first death on the smaller track. Ironically, the light pole was never a concern when the track was smaller. A year later it was moved to the infield.

Notably absent this year were the Late Model Stock Cars.

1990

Rod Spencer won five main events on his way to winning back-to-back championships. For the second year in a row Rick Martin was the bridesmaid, this time losing the title by a mere one point.

Frank Carlotta

1989 hot lap session, looking toward turn one with Oak Hill Cemetery in the background. *Dennis Mattish Photo*

1991

Rick Martin was crowned the track champion on the final night of the year after a close battle with Terry McCarl, who had entered the last race with a seven-point lead but then blew his engine in qualifying. He worked his way up through the C and B mains, only to have mechanical problems in the main cost him the title.

There were two separate incidents away from the track during the year that involved local race car drivers.

(Continued on page #216)

SAN JOSE
SUPER SPRINTS
1990 SEASON OPENER
THIS SATURDAY NIGHT!

Winston   **MARCH 17th**   *Coors*

— GRANDSTAND OPENS 5 PM • RACING 7 PM —
PWB MATCH RACE! NEWLY GROOMED 1/3 MILE CLAY OVAL!
NEW FOOD CONCESSIONS! NEW FAMILY DISCOUNT TICKET!

CALL 24 HOUR HOTLINE 294-RACE

SPEEDWAY

The cars evolved from Super Modifieds to Super Sprints (essentially a Sprint Car) for the 1990 season.

Danny Olmstead, who had just turned 18, drove like a veteran when he outran Brent Kaeding to win his first main event, the 37th annual Johnny Key Classic on August 18, 1990. *Dennis Mattish Photo*

Rick Martin shown during his rookie year in 1988. From Rookie of the Year he would go on and win the 1991 & 1994 track championships, the 1995 Johnny Key Classic and 1989 & 1990 Lloyd Beard Classics. *Dennis Mattish Photo*

Second-generation driver Scott Luhdorff (11x) had a very successful driving career at San Jose. Along with his 11 feature wins were victories in the 1989 & 1992 Johnny Key Races and a triumph in the 1993 Lloyd Beard Classic. *Dennis Mattish Photo*

1988: Larry Petterson (63) takes a wild ride after contact with Dwane Larson. *Dennis Mattish Photo*

207

The San Jose Mile was the most famous of all the tracks at the Santa Clara County Fairgrounds. The track held races over a 90-year span, starting in 1909. Top photo was taken in turns 3 & 4 during the AMA race in 1990. Bottom photo (1989) shows part of the standing-room-only crowd that was common at the AMA Motorcycle races. Decisions by the Fair Board would put an end to one of San Jose's biggest events, the San Jose Mile Motorcyle Race. *Dennis Mattish Photos*

1990: Kevin Pylant (14p) first raced at the Fairgrounds in the Stock Car class but it was in the Sprint Cars that he made a name for himself. Mike Manthey (21M) was one of many drivers who started in the Quarter Midgets and then worked his way up to Sprint Cars. The personable driver had multiple wins in the 360 Sprint Car ranks. *Dennis Mattish Photo*

Undeniably the best Sprint Car driver to ever come out of the San Jose area, Brent Kaeding won 13 WoO, GSC and NARC Sprint Car main events to go along with a dozen NASCAR wins on his home track. Brent has an unprecedented 13 GSC and 11 NARC Championships at this writing. *Dennis Mattish Photo*

Randi Turner (4q) wheelies out of turn two in hot pursuit of Lindsey Casto during the 1991 season. *Dennis Mattish Photo*

Darrell Hanestad (17) and Steve Kent (2) in a 1990 GSC race. Both drivers were GSC main event winners at SJ. *Dennis Mattish Photo*

Rod Spencer (left) and John Neese (car owner) teamed up to win back-to-back track championships in 1989 & 1990. *Dennis Mattish Photo*

Terry McCarl missed winning the 1991 track championship by just a few points on the final night of the season. He has his hands full in this photo after winning the 1991 Johnny Key Classic, thus adding his name to the prestigious list of former winners. *Dennis Mattish Photo*

Terry McCarl (88) and Randy Hannagan (1) race down the front stretch during the 1991 season. In a few years both drivers would be accomplished WoO drivers. *Dennis Mattish Photo*

Oops! Sometimes the infield isn't the safest place, as this aftermath photo shows. Stan Luhdorff lost control of his car in 1991 and hit the pace vehicle which was in the middle of the infield. *Dennis Mattish Photo*

Super Sprints in action during 1991. *Dennis Mattish Photo*

1991: The awesome sight of Sprint Cars on dirt. *Dennis Mattish Photo*

Pat Rose (22) and Scott Luhdorff (11x) finish first and second respectively in the 1992 points championship. This photo shows them battling for the lead of the main event during the Santa Clara County Fair. *Dennis Mattish Photo*

The Wingless Warriors of the Southern California-based California Racing Association made their first appearance at the Fairgrounds in October 1991. Leland McSpadden (91) was one of their top performers. *Dennis Mattish Photo*

1992: Jamie Hood won two feature races at the fairgrounds Speedway. *Dennis Mattish Photo*

Four abreast in turn two during a 1991 show proves there was plenty of room to pass at San Jose. Battling for position are Jason Statler (00), Charlie Caraccilo (87), Eric Rossi (4R) and Tom Henry (17T). All have won multiple main events on this track. *Dennis Mattish Photo*

211

World of Outlaws at the Fairgrounds
A few Highlights

A new Sprint Car association called the World of Outlaws made its first appearance at the Santa Clara County Fairgrounds in October, 1978. Hailed as the "greatest show on dirt," the Outlaws were unmatched in speed and talent from anywhere in the world. The group was part of the third annual California Golden Classic, which instantly elevated the race to a higher status.

The weekend started with Bobby Allan breaking his own half-mile track record and ended with Steve Kinser winning the A Feature on Saturday (he also won the Friday preliminary race). Rick Ferkle and Jack Hewitt chased him across the finish line. The most thrilling race of the night was Jan Opperman making a last-lap pass to win the B Main and earn a transfer to the A Main. Before a crowd of 7000 (standing room only), 80 cars timed in.

The following year 7,000 people again packed the stands for the fourth edition of the race. The weekend started with Doug Wolfgang shattering the track record on the well-prepared oval. During Saturday's A-main, Shane Carson inherited the lead with four laps to go when Steve Kinser had a gearbox failure. Carson then ran out of gas just as he crossed the finish line first. Gary Patterson and Wolfgang followed in that order. After the race Carson said, "This track is so big [the biggest half-mile in the country] you use a lot of fuel."

After a four-year absence, the WoO returned to San Jose in September, 1983. It was stop two of the four-track WoO California Gold Rush Tour. Sixty-nine hundred witnessed Steve Kinser win the main event over arch-rival Sammy Swindell. Nick Rescino was running second to Kinser early in the main event before mechanical problems on his Super Modified caused him to drop out. It was four years earlier that Rescino had beaten the Outlaws driving a Super Modified, the only driver ever to accomplish that feat.

One year later "Slammin" Sammy Swindell lived up to his name as he slammed Steve Kinser out of the way in the closing laps to take the lead and win in the A Main event. He would back it up with a win in the 1985 event also.

On October 18, 1986, Steve Kinser clinched his seventh WoO championship at San Jose when he won the A Feature race on Saturday. Bobby Allen reclaimed the track record that he had set 10 years earlier on the larger-than-a-half-mile track. His speed was well over 100 mph.

Nearly 9,000 people saw Steve Kinser blow away the competition during the February 1988 show on the quarter-mile. He came back and did the same thing on the half-mile in October.

March, 1989: Because of a split with the World of Outlaws, top drivers like Steve Kinser and Sammy Swindell were not present for this show. They joined the rival United Sprint Association that was racing in Alabama the same weekend.

During the A Feature, Jeff Swindell and Jack Hewitt were swapping the lead in the closing laps when they collided coming out of turn four on the last lap. That provided just enough opening for Brent Kaeding to slip by for the win. The hometown crowd was ecstatic.

The Outlaws were back together for the 1991 season, when 8,347 spectators witnessed history being made as Steve Kinser won his historic 300th WoO main. Eighteen-year-old San Jose driver Danny Olmstead set fast time over the Outlaws. The two-day March show attracted 13,000.

On March 7, 1992, a week of rain saturated the track and made it a challenge, even for the best drivers, but Stevie Smith was able to find the smoothest line around the sloppy track and win the WoO main event.

Future NASCAR driver Dave Blaney caught Steve Kinser on lap 28, then passed him to win the 1994 WoO main event. Blaney repeated in 1995.

Mark Kinser won all four main events (two preliminary and two A Features) driving for his father, Karl, during 1996 and 1997. In 1996 he broke the track record on the 1/3-mile oval with a time of 13.383 (90 mph), a record that would stand until the track closed. Mark went on to win the 1996 WoO Championship.

There were a total of 21 A-features held on three different tracks between 1978 and 1999. It was only fitting that Steve Kinser, the "King of the Outlaws," the greatest Sprint Car driver in history, would win the most with six.

The "King of the Outlaws" Steve Kinser won his 300th A Feature WoO race during 1991, and it happened in San Jose. *Dennis Mattish Photo*

Steve Kinser at SJ during 1992. *Dennis Mattish Photo*

Dave Blaney won the 1994 and 1995 WoO A Feature races at San Jose. He would use this talent as a springboard to the NASCAR Cup series. *Dennis Mattish Photo*

Danny Lasoski (83) and Kevin Gobrecht (93) battle for the lead of the 1999 preliminary WoO main event. *Dennis Mattish Photo*

Sammy Swindell won the 1998 WoO event at San Jose, his third A Feature win there. His son Kevin takes part in the victory celebration. In a matter of years the roles would be reversed and Sammy would be celebrating Kevin's victories. *Mattish Photo*

World Of Outlaw Winners

Date	Winner	Track
10-6-1978	Steve Kinser	Half-mile
10-7-1978	STEVE KINSER	Half-mile
10-5-1979	Doug Wolfgang	Half-mile
10-6-1979	SHANE CARSON	Half-mile
9-11-1983	STEVE KINSER	Quarter-mile
9-23-1984	SAMMY SWINDELL	Quarter-mile
9-24-1985	SAMMY SWINDELL	Quarter-mile
10-16-1986	Doug Wolfgang	Half-mile
10-17-1986	Bobby Allen	Half-mile
10-18-1986	STEVE KINSER	Half-mile
2-27-1987	STEVE KINSER	Quarter-mile
10-16-1987	Steve Kinser	Half-mile
10-17-1987	STEVE KINSER	Half-mile
3-3-1989	Bobby Davis Jr.	Third-mile
3-4-1989	BRENT KAEDING	Third-mile
9-7-1989	Bobby Davis Jr.	Third-mile
9-8-1989	Jeff Swindell	Third-mile
9-9-1989	KEITH KAUFFMAN	Third-mile
3-3-1990	Danny Lasoski	Third-mile
9-7-1990	Steve Kinser	Third-mile
9-8-1990	JOE GAERTE	Third-mile
3-2-1991	Craig Keel	Third-mile
3-3-1991	STEVE KINSER	Third-mile
3-6-1992	STEVIE SMITH	Third-mile
9-11-1992	Sammy Swindell	Third-mile
9-12-1992	JAC HAUDENSCHILD	Third-mile
9-10-1993	Stevie Smith	Third-mile
9-11-1993	STEVIE SMITH	Third-mile
9-9-1994	Steve Kinser	Third-mile
9-10-1994	DAVE BLANEY	Third-mile
9-8-1995	Stevie Smith	Third-mile
9-9-1995	DAVE BLANEY	Third-mile
9-6-1996	Mark Kinser	Third-mile
9-7-1996	MARK KINSER	Third-mile
9-15-1997	Dave Blaney	Third-mile
9-16-1997	MARK KINSER	Third-mile
8-28-1998	Sammy Swindell	Third-mile
8-29-1998	SAMMY SWINDELL	Third-mile
8-27-1999	Danny Lasoski	Third-mile
8-28-1999	JAC HAUDENSCHILD	Third-mile

Lower case – Preliminary main event winner
ALL CAPS – "A" Feature winner

Johnny Key Classic

For more than four decades, the Johnny Key Classic was considered one of the most prestigious short track races in the West. Arguably the greatest driver of his time, Johnny Key haled from Salinas, California. The 1951 San Jose champion won an unprecedented 57 main events during 1952. Eight of those wins came in a seven-day period. Tragically, he lost his life at the peak of his career during a Midget race in Ohio in 1954. This Memorial race has been held in his honor ever since then. The first 24 races were held at San Jose Speedway and the rest at the Fairgrounds track. For more information see the main text in Chapters 11 and 12.

Danny Graves (kneeling) won the first Johnny Key Memorial Race in 1954. *Dennis Mattish Collection*

1986: Nick Rescino won the most Key Classics with a total of six between the two tracks. *Dennis Mattish Photo*

Johnny Key Classic Winners

San Jose Speedway

1954	Danny Graves
1955	Al Pombo
1956	Clyde Palmer
1957	Ray Raineri
1958	Rick Henderson
1959	George Benson
1960	Marshall Sargent
1961	Clyde Palmer
1962	Clyde Palmer
1963	Marshall Sargent
1964	George Snider
1965	Burt Foland
1966	Burt Foland
1967	Bill Scott
1968	Howard Kaeding
1969	Bill Scott
1970	Don Epperson
1971	Everett Edlund
1972	Nick Rescino
1973	Howard Kaeding
1974	Nick Rescino
1975	Nick Rescino
1976	Tony Ringo
1977	Danny O'Neill

Fairgrounds Speedway

1978	Johnny Brazil
1979	Howard Kaeding
1980	Brent Kaeding
1981	Mike Sargent
1982	Nick Rescino
1983	John Viel
1984	Nick Rescino
1985	Rich Voss
1986	Nick Rescino
1987	Howard Kaeding
1988	Rod Spencer
1989	Scott Luhdorff
1990	Danny Olmstead
1991	Terry McCarl
1992	Scott Luhdorff
1993	Chuck Miller
1994	Chuck Miller
1995	Rick Martin
1996	Bud Kaeding
1997	Craig Smith
1998	Ronnie Day
1999	Eric Rossi

Lloyd Beard Classic

A cornerstone on the San Jose schedule for 20 years was the Lloyd Beard Classic. Beard, from Los Banos, was a Watsonville Speedway Sportsman Champion in the 1960s, Madera Speedway Super Modified Champion during 1974 and NASCAR State Champion that same year. He was one of the best San Jose drivers when he lost his life in a freak Sprint Car crash at Calistoga Speedway in 1979. San Jose Fairgrounds Speedway held this race in his honor until the track closed in 1999. More information about Lloyd Beard and the race named after him can be found throughout this chapter.

Lloyd Beard Classic Winners

1980	Nick Rescino
1981	John Viel
1982	Mike Sargent
1983	Ernie Rose
1984	Chuck Miller
1985	Mike Sargent
1986	Howard Kaeding
1987	John Viel
1988	Howard Kaeding
1989	Rick Martin
1990	Rick Martin
1991	Rod Spencer
1992	Eric Rossi
1993	Scott Luhdorff
1994	Chuck Miller
1995	Chuck Miller
1996	Bud Kaeding
1997	Mark Monico
1998	Ronnie Day

1998: Ronnie Day won the last Lloyd Beard Classic race. *Dennis Mattish Photo*

Jim Perry, Jr., after winning the 1987 Elks charity race.
Dennis Mattish Photo

Mike Damron won the first Elks Charity Race in 1974.
Dennis Mattish Photo

Elks Charity Race

For 14 years, San Jose Speedway and San Jose Fairgrounds Speedway ran a charity benefit race put on by the Milpitas Elks Lodge, and then later, the Fremont Elks. The event was known as the Cerebral Palsy Benefit Race and "Aiding Physically Handicapped Children."

The driving force behind the first race at San Jose Speedway in 1974 were Super Modified driver Jack Epperson and track official Jim Christman both members of the Milpitas Elks.

Held until 1988, the race raised a significant amount of money for the charity.

Elks Charity Race Winners

	Super Modified	Stock Car
1974	Mike Damron	
1975	Johnny Brazil	
1976	Mark Sargent	
1977	Howard Kaeding	
1979	Mike Sargent	
1980	Nick Rescino	Dave Byrd
1981	John Viel	John Keldsen
1982	Mike Sargent	John Keldsen
1983	Nick Rescino	Larry Lundin
1984	Larry Rudolph	Greg Williams
1985	Scott Luhdorff	Greg Williams
1986	John Viel	Mike Williams
1987	Jim Perry, Jr.	Ed Sans, Jr.
1988	Tony Bettencourt	Todd Souza

215

Randy Hannagan celebrates his first career main event win in 1992. Track announcer George Hague (right) was there to make the call. *Dennis Mattish Photo*

killing his wife. Her body was never found, and the charges were dropped because of lack of evidence.

On October 12, a special "San Jose Speedway vs. NARC" race was held. San Jose drivers took three out of the top four spots with Rick Martin winning in front of 6,124 fans.

1992

The evolution from Super Modified to Sprint Car was complete. The division now was called the NASCAR Sprint Car.

Pat Rose, who was Rookie of the year in 1977, teamed up with two-time champion car owner John Neese and proceeded to win the Sprint Car title.

Consistency paid off, as Pat's ten top-five finishes and one main event win proved to be enough to hold off Scott Luhdorff for the title.

CRA returned for the second year in a row. On Friday night, Richard Griffin passed Randy Hannagan with a few laps to go to win the curfew-shortened race.

On Saturday, San Jose drivers completely dominated the Southern California-based CRA, taking the top five

Tom Henry was hospitalized briefly with burns after this major engine explosion in 1992. *Rich Davis Photo*

(Continued from page 207)

Sprint Car driver Bobby Buhler was convicted of manslaughter when he killed three teenagers while driving under the influence. He was sentenced to 15 years to life in prison.

Super Modified driver Rob Carlotto was charged with

View of the track from Oak Hill. *Dennis Mattish Photo*

positions in the main event. Tim Green won, followed by Luhdorff, Rose, Kaeding and Martin. This was amazing considering San Jose drivers never run without wings. The vocal crowd voiced their approval as the top cars stopped on the front straightaway after the race.

During the year, County Supervisors Zoe Lofgren and Ron Gonzales stated, "Tobacco advertising must disappear from the Santa Clara County Fairgrounds." This created a problem because auto racing was the most lucrative event taking place at the Fairgrounds, and it was called the NASCAR Winston Racing Series. (Winston Cigarettes is a division of R.J. Reynolds.) Eventually the supervisors got their way, Winston was removed from the scoreboard, and the banners disappeared. The article from the *Mercury News* that this information was obtained from also quoted the supervisors as stating that of all the events that take place at the fairgrounds, auto racing and gun shows were the least desirable. Ten years later, with the racetrack gone, the fairgrounds would be in a fiscal crisis.

Pat Rose, 1992 NASCAR Sprint Car Champion. *Mattish Photo*

1993: Pat Rose (22) bicycle. *Dennis Mattish Photo*

Track champion Pat Rose hot lapped the Budweiser Sprint Car on the mile during the 1992 AMA race. This was the first time a car had turned the mile at speed since 1955.
Dennis Mattish Photo

Randy Hannagan (third from right) stands next to his brother and car owner Terry (center) for the 1993 championship photo after clinching both the 360 and 410 cubic inch Sprint Car titles. *Dennis Mattish Photo*

217

WoO on parade for the 1993 race. *Dennis Mattish Photo*

Stevie Smith (right) with car owner Al Hamilton after winning the 1993 WoO race. He also won the spring 1992 race at San Jose. *Dennis Mattish Photo*

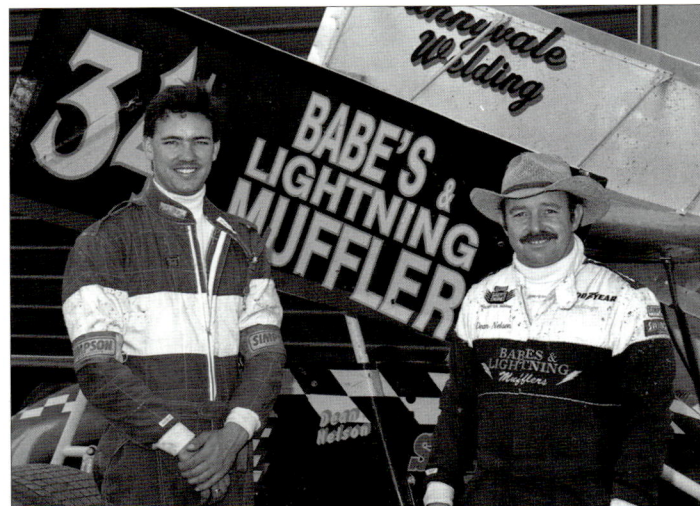
The father-son Sprint Car team of Kurt (left) and Dean Nelson. *Dennis Mattish Photo*

1993

Introduced as a budget class and stepping stone, 360 cubic inch cast iron engine Sprint Cars made their debut. They would act as the supporting division to their big brother, the more powerful 410 cubic inch aluminum block Sprint Car.

Randy Hannagan ran both categories of Sprint Cars and the results were the same, winning the championship in both divisions. He dominated the 360 class, winning 10 out of 11 races. He won the 410 title on the last night of the season, just edging out Rick Martin. On four different nights, he won both feature events.

Scott Parker and Ricky Graham traded the lead six times on the last three laps before Parker crossed the line first. This was Parker's unprecedented eighth AMA San Jose Mile win in a row. It was also the last time AMA would race on the mile.

1994

Three divisions of cars competed in 1994. Joining the 410 and 360 Sprint Cars were the Late Model Stock Cars.

Two-time defending NASCAR Pacific Coast Champion Steve Hendren won the Stock Car track title. Kimberly Myers was the Late Model Rookie of the Year. What was amazing about this accomplishment was not the fact that she was female, but that she had cystic fibrosis. During one race late in the year, she was leading with just a couple of laps to go, closely followed by three-time champion Ed Sans. With the crowd on its feet cheering her

Disc jockey Paul Tonelli from radio station KJSO blew out both right side tires after slamming into the elevated berm during a celebrity race. *Dennis Mattish Photo*

1994: Chuck Miller (24) and Lee Brewer (5) battle for position. *Dennis Mattish Photo*

Kimberly Myers was the 1993 National "Real heroes of NASCAR" awards winner. Myers won on the basis of her community involvement and motivational messages to children with cystic fibrosis, a disease she herself had. She was also a very good race car driver. *Dennis Mattish Photo*

1994: John Silva (59) and Kimberly Myers (65Roses) battle for the lead of a heat race. Myers would prevail. *Dennis Mattish photo*

Third-generation driver Kirk Sargent (son of Mike, grandson of Marshall) won his first San Jose Sprint Car main event during the 1993 season. *Dennis Mattish Photo*

1994: San Jose Speedway was one of the tracks Paul McMahan cut his teeth on before becoming a regular on the WoO circuit, where he has seven A Feature wins as of this writing. *Dennis Mattish Photo*

1993 & 1994 top ten driver Bob Cooney. *Dennis Mattish Photo*

1995: Jason Statler from San Jose won Sprint Car main events at San Jose and on the WoO circuit. *Dennis Mattish Photo*

1994 Late Model Stock Car Champion Steve Hendren. *Dennis Mattish Photo*

on, Sans slammed his way past her, knocking her out of the groove. Instead of wilting, she charged back up and put the bumper back on him. Although she lost the race, the crowd gave her a very loud standing ovation after the race. Sans received the exact opposite.

Rick Martin won his second 410 Sprint Car title, this time handily.

Mark Chaves, son of prominent car owner Arnie, won the 360 championship.

"Gone forever is the motorcycle race referred to simply as 'The Mile,'" stated the *Mercury News*. The Santa Clara County Fair Board decided to lease the land that turns one and two sat on, for a flea market.

There was a recurring problem during the year of bad tracks. Some nights there were dry, dusty tracks, and other nights there were ruts a foot deep. The drivers became very vocal about the situation. Meanwhile, the attendance was dwindling.

Bud Kaeding (69) tries to avoid a charging Dan D (33) during the Micro Midget main event. Held on a small track carved out on the infield of the 1/3-mile, the little cars held ten races in 1995. Many Sprint Car drivers, including Bud, got their start in this class. *Dennis Mattish Photo*

1994 & 1995 360 Sprint Car Champion Mark Chaves. Chaves drove the only Ford-powered Sprint Car (5) during his two year championship run. He also won 16 main events during that time. *Dennis Mattish Photos*

221

1999 Johnny Key and 1992 Lloyd Beard Classics winner Eric Rossi (left) and 1995 410 Sprint Car Champion Lindsey Casto. *Dennis Mattish Photo*

Dave Blaney won the 1995 WoO A Feature. Former ABC announcer, *National Speed Sport News* editor and publisher emeritus, Chris Economaki, did the post race interview. *Dennis Mattish Photo*

Bud Kaeding (29) and Rick Williams (6) fight for the lead of the main event and 1996 track championship. After a season-long battle, Kaeding emerged the champion. *Dennis Mattish Photo*

1995

Lindsey Casto drove the Al's Roofing Special to the 410 Sprint Car title while Mark Chaves successfully defended his 360 Sprint Car championship with his unique Ford-powered car. Mark won five of eleven races.

When the attempt failed to merge into a touring series NASCAR and Petaluma Speedway's Late Model Stock Cars, San Jose elected to still run their series dates as open comp races and managed to draw solid fields. Feature wins in the three races went to Richard Papenhausen, Larry Damitz and B.J. Pearson.

A special track was built on the infield for the Micro Midgets. Their seven events were won by Russ Husman with three, Eric Ferreira won twice, and Roger Paulson and Jim Christian picked up one each.

When the flea market deal fell through, the Fair Board approached promoter Harold Murrell about bringing back the San Jose Mile. Murrell was happy to oblige, but AMA was tired of the games the Fair Board was playing and declined.

There was a split in the CRA organization, with most of its members breaking away and forming the Sprint Car Racing Association (SCRA). San Jose was one of their stops, and Cory Kruseman was the winner.

1996

As the number of 410 Sprint Cars in the state and San Jose dwindled, and the popularity of the 360 Sprint Cars grew, the decision was made to elevate the 360s to the feature division. The 410s were discontinued.

Never in the history of San Jose racing has a rookie had a season like Bud Kaeding did. Bud not only won the track championship, he also won the three biggest 360 Sprint Cars races on the West Coast. His first big win was in the 17th annual Lloyd Beard Classic. He followed that up with a win in the 43rd annual Johnny Key Classic, becoming the third Kaeding to do so. His

Tim Kaeding looks on as his brother Bud celebrates his 1996 Johnny Key victory. *Dennis Mattish Photo*

222

1996: Brad Furr raced the San Jose Fairgrounds before becoming a full-time WoO driver, where he had three A Features wins. *Dennis Mattish Photo*

1992 Rookie of the Year Chris D'Arcy shown in 1995. *Dennis Mattish Photo*

Car owners Virgel and Ann Owen with the All Weld Sprint Car team. Tim Green (center) was the driver. *Dennis Mattish Photo*

Former WoO driver Tim Green became a regular at San Jose during the mid 1990s. Green has nine Outlaw A feature victories on his resume to go along with his dozen wins at San Jose in NARC-, GSC-, and NASCAR-sanctioned events. *Dennis Mattish Photo*

Nearly 90 years after the first race was held on this very same piece of real estate, dust problems were exactly the same (for a day race). Only the lead car has a clear view in this very rare day race held in 1996. *Dennis Mattish Photo*

223

The 1996 NARC season final found Mark Monico (21) literally driving over the car containing Brad Furr. *Dennis Mattish Photo*

"Cowboy" Craig Smith took his mount for an untamed ride during the 1996 season. Number 57 is John Golobic. *Dennis Mattish Photo*

Likable "Cowboy" Craig Smith from Montana won the 1997 Johnny Key Classic. *Dennis Mattish Photo*

Dwarf cars were a regular part of the San Jose schedule from 1995 until the track closed in 1999. These miniature cars, powered by a 1200 cc engine, are capable of reaching speeds of 100 mph. They are built from scratch to resemble the 1930 – 1940 era of the American Automobile. Ken Jordan (32), Gary Byroads (11), Gilbert Tosti (8) and John Massie (76) shown in 1996. *Dennis Mattish Photo*

Three generations of Kaedings gather to honor Howard. (L to R) Joel, Bud, Howard, Tim and Brent. Howard's 140 San Jose main event victories (pavement & dirt tracks) were far more than those of his closest pursuer, Nick Rescino, who had 84. *Dennis Mattish Photo*

grandfather Howard (1968, 1973, 1979 and 1987) and his dad Brent (1980) also won the Key Classic. A Kaeding had won the Key race in four different decades. Bud capped the season off with a win in the 360 Pacific Sprint Nationals. Obviously, Bud won the NASCAR Rookie of the Year award.

The biggest opponent that auto racing has ever faced in San Jose history surfaced in 1996. The *Mercury News* article read "County Supervisor Blanca Alvarado has proposed that NASCAR racing, Drag racing, Sprint Car racing, Truck racing and Motorcycle racing –– in other words, nearly all attractions offered at the Fair's San Jose Speedway –– be removed from the list of 'acceptable uses' for the County-owned Fairgrounds."

This was the biggest shot taken yet at local racing.

In another article, it was revealed that racing alone brought in over $250,000 in revenue to the Fairgrounds annually.

1997

Consistency paid off for Charlie Caraccilo, as his 12 top-five finishes and two main event wins was enough for him to win the track championship.

Making their debut at San Jose was a new touring group called the Civil War Series, featuring 360 Sprint Cars. This group would grow in stature and prestige in the coming years. Ronnie Day won the June race while Randy Hannagan claimed the September feature.

This is what TV announcer Bobby Gerould had to say

(Continued on page 230)

Mark Monico (center) won the 1997 "Outstanding Contributor to Motor Sports" award given by the Motor Sports Press Association for his charity work in raising funds for the St. Jude's Children's Hospital. Mark's tireless work between 1994 and 1999 raised over $400,000 for St Jude's. Monico was also an outstanding driver, winning the 1997 Lloyd Beard Classic. *Dennis Mattish Photo*

Mark Kinser won the 1996 & 1997 WoO A Feature races and the 1997 Trophy Cup. *Dennis Mattish Photo*

BCRA Midget Racing at the Fairgrounds
(outdoors)

The first Midget race at the Fairgrounds took place on September 14, 1957, during the Santa Clara County Fair. Bay Cities Racing Association (BCRA) staged a 25-lap main event on the half-mile oval, where a capacity crowd saw Tommy Copp pass Bob Cortner on the final lap to win the main event.

Midget racing would not return to the outdoor track until the 1970 County Fair. The race was performed on a specially-constructed 1/6-mile dirt track in front of the main grandstands. Bill McCormick was the first winner in what became an annual BCRA event. An extra race was added in 1971, making the event a two-day show. They were the last two days of a six-day tour to five different tracks. Bob DeJong and Hank Butcher took home the first place trophies. The final races on the 1/6-mile oval were held in 1974. Crowds averaged about 4,000 during the five-year run.

The Midgets held an annual race (which lasted for three years) called the Gold Cup. The first race took place on September 4, 1977, and was held on the half-mile, 20 years after their previous race on that track. This was one of the few times the little cars raced on such a big track, and the drivers were excited about it. USAC driver Tommy Astone set fast time with a lap of 25.546, about the same time as the AMA motorcycle record. In the main event, Astone worked his way up from 24th starting position and took the lead at mid-race. He was never challenged after that on his way to victory. During the semi, Mark Radbruch was shaken up when he did a high-speed series of end-over-end flips off of turn three. This was the last time the little cars raced on the half-mile. The 1978 and 1979 Gold Cup was moved to the new quarter-mile track where BCRA Champion Floyd Alvis won both. The only other race on the quarter-mile was held in 1987.

BCRA joined CRA on October 9, 1992, for a twin bill. Terry Tarditti won the race on a questionable track. As Tom Palmer wrote in the *Racing Wheels Newspaper*, "The dusty, slippery, bumpy track caused so many spins and red flags that the 30-lap main event was called at 20 laps."

After racing in San Jose since 1934, the final Midget race was held on May 24, 1997. Marc DeBeaumont won the main event.

See Appendix for complete list of winners.

Marc DeBeaumont won the final Midget race in San Jose history on May 24, 1997. *Dennis Mattish Photo*

Terry Tarditi (above and below) won the Fairgrounds 1992 & 1996 BCRA Midget races. He was also a three-time BCRA champion (1996-1998). Official Davey Munoz makes the trophy presentation. *Dennis Mattish Photo*

Wild BCRA action in 1979 had three cars flip in this crash. Willie Fraser (65), Bill Lindsay (39) and Jerry Merrick (99) were some of the cars involved. *Rich Davis Photo*

Western Dirt Track Nationals

In 1992, former Sportsman and Super Modified driver George Stitze joined forces with Rick Farren and promoted the first Dirt Track Nationals. The three-division (Late Model Stock Car, Grand American Modified and Street Stock) open competition show drew an amazing 165 cars, far too many for a one-day show. Although qualifying began at noon, the program still ran well past the 11p.m. curfew.

The 1993 Dirt Track Nationals was expanded to two days, and 166 cars were vying for the $33,000 purse. The main events were run the following weekend, when rain washed out Saturday night.

October, 1995: the hugely popular Western Dirt Track Nationals drew an unprecedented 220 cars, the largest car count in San Jose racing history. The breakdown was 46 Late Models, 78 Modifieds and 96 Street Stocks. As in the past, the races went past curfew, this time ending in the wee hours of the morning.

Two years later the record was broken again when 229 cars signed into the pits. The 1997 event was run in honor of 1994 rookie of the year, Kimberly Myers, who had died in July from complications caused by cystic fibrosis.

The final Dirt Track Nationals at San Jose took place on October 1 and 2, 1999. The race then moved to Watsonville Speedway for the 2000 edition.

Jim Pettit won the 1999 Modified main event during the Dirt Track National. Presenting the trophy is the founder of the series, George Stitze, and co-promoter Rick Farren.
Dennis Mattish Photo

Richard Pappenhausen (4) and Dave Byrd (7) battle for position during the open compitition Late Model Stock Car main event at the 1995 Dirt Track Nationals. *Dennis Mattish Photo*

Dirt Track National Winners

	Late Model Stock Car	Modified	Street Stock	Car count
1992	Robert Miller	Ken Nott	Dave Hansen	165
1993	Steve Hendren	Bart Reid	Mike Yannone	166
1994	Steve Hendren	Dave Byrd	Darrell Hughes	168
1995	Dan Oliver	Dave Byrd	Randy Hensley	220
1996	Chad Reichenbach	Mark Welch	Doug Hagio	214
1997	Frank Soarie	Dave Byrd	Kurt Slamma	229
1998	Bob Jeffery	Bobby Hogge III	Kurt Slamma	212
1999	Joel Bennett	Jim Pettit	Chris Kearns	162

NARC/Golden State Challenge

Established in 1960, the Northern Auto Racing Club (NARC) became the oldest Sprint Car sanctioning group in California in 1993.

The group ran its first of four races on the half-mile track starting in 1972. The rest of the races were run on the smaller tracks from 1988 through 1999, when both San Jose Fairgrounds Speedway and NARC ceased operations.

NARC also participated, sanctioned and officiated the Golden State Challenge (GSC) series. Points scored in that series applied to the NARC point standings.

GSC held their first race in 1986 and instantly became the top winged Sprint Car series in the West. This unique series runs 410 cubic inch Sprint Car races at six different tracks in California. By incorporating a "lights out" agreement among all the race promoters and sanctioning bodies involved, every GSC event attracts an all-star lineup of talent. At the end of the year, the series champion is crowned the "King of California."

They made their first appearance at San Jose on October 1, 1988, and Brent Kaeding won. At season's end he was crowned the first "King of California."

Baylands Raceway Park held an Annual GSC race called the Gary Patterson Classic, named in honor of the deceased driver. When the track closed, the race moved to the Fairgrounds for the seventh running, which was held on September 30, 1989. Brent Kaeding won the first of six GSC GP Classics held at San Jose.

Every year from 1991 until 1999, NARC held a series of six races at six tracks in six days (more or less) called Speedweek. San Jose became part of Speedweek in 1996, running the July 4th fireworks show every year until the track closed in 1999.

There were a total of 48 NARC/GSC races held at the Fairgrounds from 1972 to 1999. Four races were held on the half-mile, one on the quarter-mile and forty three on the third-mile. Brent was the most dominant driver, picking up 12 wins. His closest challengers were Tim Green with eight victories and Randy Hannagan claiming seven.

1990: (L to R) Brent Kaeding, Tim Green and Steve Kent were the dominant NARC/GSC Sprint Car drivers during the period around 1990. *Dennis Mattish Photo*

One of the West's best. Ronnie Day won four NARC/GSC San Jose main events. He also won both the Johnny Key and Lloyd Beard Classic during 1998. *Dennis Mattish Photo*

GSC parade lap during 1997. Mark Monico (21), Bud Kaeding (29), Lindsey Casto (40) and Randy Tiner (83). *Dennis Mattish Photo*

NARC/GSC Winners

NARC

Date	Winner	
4-30-1972	Rick Goudy	Half-mile
4-29-1973	Leroy Van Connettt	Half-mile
2-27-1977	Leroy Van Connettt	Half-mile
10-11-1986	Jac Haudenschild	Half-mile
10-6-1990	Tim Green	
10-13-1990	Tim Green	
10-12-1990	Tim Green	
3-30-1996	Brent Kaeding	
7-04-1996	Ronnie Day	
3-29-1997	Brent Kaeding	
7-04-1997	Randy Hannagan	
10-18-1997	Randy Hannagan	
7-04-1998	Brent Kaeding	
10-3-1998	Brent Kaeding	
3-27-1999	Randy Hannagan	
7-04-1999	Brent Kaeding	
9-25-1999	Eric Rossi	

GSC

Date	Winner	
10-1-1988	Brent Kaeding	
6-03-1989	Darrell Hanestad	
7-22-1989	Kevin Pylant	
10-28-1989	Brent Kaeding	G. P. Classic VII
6-02-1990	Tim Green	
7-14-1990	Tim Green	
9-29-1990	Terry McCarl	G. P. Classic VIII
6-01-1991	Tim Green	
7-13-1991	Steve Kent	
9-28-1991	Ronnie Day	G. P. Classic IX
6-06-1992	Ronnie Day	
7-11-1992	Ronnie Day	G. P. Classic X
5-22-1993	Steve Kent	
7-10-1993	Tim Green	G. P. Classic XI
4-30-1994	Brent Kaeding	
5-21-1994	Steve Kent	
7-09-1994	Tim Green	G. P. Classic XII
5-20-1995	Brent Kaediing	
7-08-1995	Lee Brewer	
4-27-1996	Steve Kent	
5-18-1996	Paul McMahan	
7-13-1996	Jason Lund	
10-26-1996	Brent Kaeding	
4-26-1997	Brent Kaeding	
5-17-1997	Randy Hannagan	
7-12-1997	Randy Tiner	
4-25-1998	Randy Tiner	
6-13-1998	Randy Hannagan	
8-08-1998	Randy Hannagan	
4-24-1999	Randy Hannagan	
6-12-1999	Brent Kaeding	

Tim Levin gets a face full of Sprint Car during the 1997 Trophy Cup. *Dennis Mattish Photo.*

Dirt flies as cars pile into one another during the 1997 Trophy Cup. Jim Richardson (8), Jeffery Patterson (34ᴾ) and Bud Kaeding were some of the cars that were involved. *Dennis Mattish Photo*

San Jose promoter Rick Farren, who had previously been voted National Promoter of the Year for his successes at San Jose, is shown in 1997. *Dennis Mattish Photo*

(Continued from page 225)

about San Jose Speedway: "This place may have the best grandstands on any stop on the NARC/GSC tour. The sight lines are excellent. The racing is usually of the 'rim riding' variety. If there is a rut in turn one, the racing promises to be very entertaining. Turn two gets real narrow!" He also stated that the track has the "best tenderloin sandwiches and corn on the cob. If you are looking for racing memorabilia, this place is loaded with concessionaires."

1998

The NASCAR Grand American Modifieds became part of the weekly show. They were running for the NASCAR Winston Racing Series, Pacific Coast Region Championship. Bobby Hogge IV far outdistanced his competitors to win the title.

In the 360 Sprint Cars, Charlie Caraccilo became the 10th different driver to win back-to-back championships in the last 53 years.

Early in the year, discussions were underway between the County Board of Supervisors and the Fair Board about building an amphitheater, even going as far as paying a consulting firm $95,000 to come up with a plan for development. The original plan was to tear down the big grandstands and put the amphitheater there.

The plan had problems right from the beginning. Ironically, the same people who spoke out against the racetrack now were doing the same against this idea.

The thought among many was, "Why would you build a multi-million-dollar facility to compete against Shoreline Amphitheater in Mt. View, Concord Pavilion and the San Jose Arena?" It seemed like a bad idea.

Half the Board wanted to move fast; the other half was upset about being pressured to move quickly.

Bobby Hogge IV won seven main events and was crowned 1998 Grand American Modified Champion. Amanda Drake makes the presentation. *Dennis Mattish Photo*

230

NASCAR Grand American Modifieds and Sprint Cars shared equal billing in 1998. They also wheel packed together on occasion as witnessed by Joe Cipparone (44) and Todd Bammer (18). *Dennis Mattish Photo*

Like father like son. Bobby Hogge III pursues his son, Bobby Hogge IV, during a 1998 NASCAR Grand American Modified main event. *Dennis Mattish Photo*

Charlie Caraccilo was the final San Jose Sprint Car Champion, winning back-to-back titles in 1997 & 1998. *Dennis Mattish Photos*

(Above & right) Tim Kaeding (35) had many wins at San Jose driving the Wright One Construction Sprint Car. He also had this spectacular flip during the 1998 Trophy Cup. In a couple of years he would be racing on the WoO circuit where he would win six A Features as of this writing. *Dennis Mattish Photos*

NCMA

The Northern California Modified Association raced a number of times in San Jose. The NCMA is a traveling club that uses older Super Modified and Sprint Cars. A small block engine with a single carburetor powers the cars.

NCMA Winners

1996	Don Hicks
1996	Eddie Rhoades
1996	David McCreary
1997	Del Quinn
1997	Don O'Keefe
1999	Ed Amador

(Left above) Ed Amador and Del Quinn battle for position during NCMA race. (Left) Mark Amador congratulates his dad. *Dennis Mattish Photos*

1999

During the off-season, promoter Rick Farren sent a letter to all San Jose Speedway participants. The letter said because of a 10-year trend in declining attendance, there wasn't enough revenue to support two divisions. The 360 Sprint Cars and Grand American Modifieds would no longer compete on a weekly basis. In 1999, San Jose Speedway would be a "special events track."

The letter also said that they were operating on an extremely restrictive lease agreement with the County Fairgrounds and that the future of the racetrack was uncertain.

The NASCAR Grand American Modifieds did run an abbreviated points season, and Kenny Nott was crowned the champion. He would go down in history as the last San Jose Speedway Champion.

Eric Rossi and Ronnie Day battled wheel to wheel (even banging wheels) through the heavy dust before Rossi emerged victorious in the 46th annual Johnny Key Classic. It was so dusty neither driver knew who won because they never saw the white flag.

(Continued on page 237)

(Above & below) Melissa Rathert (27w) made history when she became the first woman to ever win a main event at San Jose Speedway (from 1946 to 1999). Melissa won the NASCAR American Stock Car main event and Trophy Dash on the same night. NASCAR Official Tim Goulart presented the trophy.
Dennis Mattish Photos

This is the chassis setup that won the 1999 Late Model Stock Car portion of the Dirt Track National for Joel Bennett.
Dennis Mattish Photo

(Above & right) Donnie Hampl's one and only appearance at the San Jose Fairgrounds track resulted in this spectacular flip during qualifying for the 1999 Dirt Track Nationals.
Dennis Mattish Photos

233

Trophy Cup

In 1994 Dave Pusateri and a group of fans came up with a unique idea of having a Sprint Car race in which the winners would have to start at the back of the pack and earn points for each car passed. This was counter to the start-up-front, finish-up-front that was common in Sprint Car racing.

The idea became a reality when the first Trophy Cup was held on October 1, 1994. Ronnie Day won the first main event, and his highest point total placed him starting last in the second main. He proceeded to pass the most cars on his way to finishing seventh, which earned him enough points to claim the Cup. His $11,000 payday was the most lucrative in local Sprint Car history.

Major changes took place for the 1997 event. Originally a race for 410 cubic inch Sprint Cars, the move was made to replace them with 360 cubic inch Sprint Cars. The Trophy Cup also became a two-day show. These changes turned out to be a huge success, as the entry limit of 108 was filled five months before the contest. The event immediately became the biggest, highest-paying 360 Sprint Car race in the World. Drivers from a dozen states participated, with Indiana's Mark Kinser winning the Cup.

The race was so successful that *National Speed Sport News* voted it the #1 short track event in the United States for 1997.

Brent Kaeding became the first repeat winner of the Trophy Cup in 1998, beating Ronnie Day by a mere one point. Finishing two points behind in third was Randy Tiner, making this the closest battle in the five years the race had been run.

The final race in the history of San Jose Fairgrounds Speedway was the Trophy Cup. Thanks to the hard work of Pusateri, the drivers were racing for $100,000. Ninety-four cars signed in on that final night and a good-sized crowd was on hand. Brent Kaeding won his third Trophy Cup, edging out his son Tim by five points. It was only fitting that the final race would have the largest purse ever offered in San Jose Speedway history.

1995 Trophy Cup winner Kevin Pylant (right) joins Dave Pusateri and family in victory lane. *Dennis Mattish Photo*

Trophy Cup winners		Purse
1994	Ronnie Day	$40,000
1995	Kevin Pylant	$50,000
1996	Brent Kaeding	$60,000
1997	Mark Kinser	$70,000
1998	Brent Kaeding	$80,000
1999	Brent Kaeding	$100,000

NASCAR Modifieds, who made their first appearance in San Jose in 1991, were getting top billing for the final season.

Kenny Nott (96) and Bobby Scott (56) battle for the lead of the main event and track championship in 1999. Nott won both while Scott finished third in the final standings. *Dennis Mattish Photo*

Kenny Nott, Jr., won the 1999 NASCAR Grand American Championship, thus becoming the final track champion in San Jose auto racing history. NASCAR official Davey Munoz makes the presentation. *Dennis Mattish Photo*

(Above & below) 1999: NASCAR dirt track Modified racing at its best. *Dennis Mattish Photos*

235

1999: Donny Schatz finished second in the 1998 WoO race held in SJ. He would go on to become one of the greatest Outlaws ever. *Dennis Mattish Photo*

Future NASCAR star Kasey Kahne (23k) spent part of his 1998 season racing in San Jose. *Dennis Mattish Photo*

Sprint Cars are among the most powerful race cars in the world. Jason Statler proves this point with a high speed wheelie. *Steve Lafond/Tear-Off Heaven Foto*

Damien Gardner was another driver who went on to prominence after the Fairgrounds track closed. Besides becoming a USAC Champion, Damien won the world famous Chili Bowl in 2008. *Dennis Mattish Photo*

San Jose Fairgrounds Speedway was a breeding ground for future WoO drivers. Jason Myers was the last of them. As of 2009, Jason had 31 WoO A Feature wins. *Dennis Mattish Photo*

Jac Haudenschild prepares to exit his car after mud packing for the August 28,1999, WoO race. He won the A Feature race that night, the last WoO race ever held in San Jose. *Mattish Photo.*

(Continued from page 233)

As the 1999 season drew to a close, Farren still had no definitive answer about 2000. Art Troyer, Director of Fair Management, said, "Plans to renovate and modernize the Fairgrounds don't include bringing back the Speedway." He further commented, "If things go according to plan, construction will begin next spring." Farren pressed for answers on dates. "He's crazy," Troyer said of Farren for wanting definitive dates for 2000. It was obvious he wanted the racing people out, and he got his wish. There was never another race held at the Speedway–90 years of racing history came to an end, brought on by a handful of people. From Oldfield and Cooper to Kaeding and Kinser, it was over, but what a ride it was.

Days after September 11, 2001, bulldozers moved in and demolished the grandstands. There was no hoopla or publicity; people's attention was on 9-11. No plans or money was ever approved for construction on the site.

Nowadays (2009) you can still see the outline of the San Jose mile from the air. The banked turns from the third–mile oval are still there as well as the back straightaway fence. Absolutely nothing has happened to the ground that the grandstands once occupied. It makes a person scratch his head and wonder why they were in such a hurry to tear the structure down. The amphitheater plan turned into a fiasco that cost the City of San Jose $22 million to settle a lawsuit with the County.

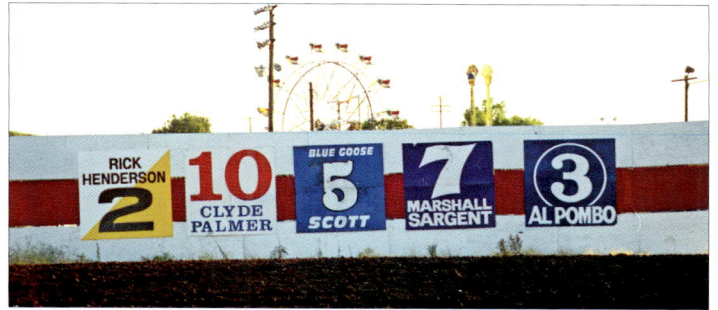

Retired numbers of San Jose racing legends. *Mattish Photo*

The line to get in for the final race. Two million people passed through the turnstiles from 1978 to 1999. *Dennis Mattish Photo*

September, 2001. *Dennis Mattish Photo*

San Jose Fairgrounds Speedway
Final Top 10 Points Standings
1978-1999

1978
Super Modified
1.	Dave Pombo	252
2.	Lloyd Beard	232
3.	George Steitz	195
4.	Mike Parker	153
5.	Mike McCann	144
6.	Art McCarthy	142
7.	Jack Epperson	137
8.	Mike Sargent	134
9.	Mark Sargent	115
10.	Nick Ringo	97

Late Model Stock Car
1.	Larry Lundin	212
2.	Vern Anderson	164
3.	Dave Byrd	163
3.	Dennis Morgan	163
5.	Herb Doxtater	111
6.	Dave Alonzo	95
7.	Dave Thomas	84
8.	Felix DeLeon	82
9.	Jerry Mostek	82
10.	Scott Williamson	82

1979
Super Modified
1.	Mike Sargent	402
2.	Lloyd Beard	395
3.	Howard Kaeding	354
4.	Mark Sargent	287
5.	Mike Parker	269
6.	Bob Bakeman	251
7.	Jerry Freitas	237
8.	Art McCarthy	220
9.	Scott Luhdorff	170
10.	Tom Haylett	160

Late Model Stock Car
1.	Dave Byrd	439
2.	Ray Morgan	383
3.	Dennis Wilson	339
4.	Bob Benge	304
5.	Joe Esperanca	283
6.	John Keldsen	210
7.	Donna Walton	205
8.	Jerry Mostek	204
9.	Bob Burnham	160
10.	Larry Lundin	123

1980
Super Modified
1.	Nick Rescino	541
2.	John Viel	480
3.	Brent Kaeding	423
4.	Mike Sargent	401
5.	Joe Bailey	224
6.	Scott Murray	208
7.	Nick Ringo	196
8.	Billy Yon	182
9.	Bob Bakeman	172
10.	Darrell Dudly	168

Late Model Stock Car
1.	Ray Morgan	357
2.	Vern Anderson	326
3.	Dave Byrd	314
4.	John Keldsen	278
5.	Bob Benge	266
6.	Larry Jackson	205
7.	Jeff Barron	168
7.	Bruce Curl	168
9.	Joe Esperanca	163
10.	Ed Sans Jr.	125

1981
Super Modified
1.	Nick Rescino	538
2.	Mike Sargent	516
3.	John Viel	485
4.	Howard Kaeding	285
5.	Scott Murray	254
6.	Nick Ringo	226
7.	Tom Henry	220
8.	Brent Kaeding	213
9.	Jim Telfer	208
10.	Mark Sargent	186

Late Model Stock Car
1.	Ray Morgan	500
2.	Dave Byrd	420
3.	John Brazil, Jr.	403
4.	John Keldsen	352
5.	Bob Burnham	290
6.	Bob Benge	273
7.	Jim Pettit, Jr.	264
8.	Robert Miller	242
9.	Dave Crocker	206
10.	Joe Garza	128

1982
Super Modified
1.	John Viel	628
2.	Nick Rescino	610
3.	Mike Sargent	516
4.	Ernie Rose	401
5.	Ron Wipperman	334
6.	Jim Telfer	309
7.	Howard Kaeding	305
8.	Tom Henry	281
9.	Rich Voss	180
10.	Pat Holton	179

Late Model Stock Car
1.	Ed Sans	408
2.	Robert Miller	335
3.	John Keldsen	332
4.	Dave Crocker	304
5.	John Van Keuren	256
6.	Larry Lundin	248
7.	Bob Burnham	203
8.	Ken Naber	197
9.	Joe Garza	168
10.	Jim Pettit II	155

1983

Super Modified
1. Nick Rescino — 701
2. John Viel — 638
3. Ernie Rose — 415
4. Rich Voss — 375
5. Chuck Miller — 289
6. Jerry Cecil — 254
7. Johnny Key — 252
8. Ron Wipperman — 246
9. Jim Perry Jr. — 246
10. Mike Sargent — 220

Late Model Stock Car
1. Ed Sans — 393
2. Greg Williams — 383
3. Larry Lundin — 287
4. Robert Miller — 283
5. Mike Williams — 269
6. Dave Crocker — 264
7. Jerry Mostek — 216
8. George Oberle — 209
9. Cliff Reinosa — 191
10. Ken Haskell — 163

Street Stock
1. Dave Collings — 26
2. Kevin Pylant — 24
3. Orval Burke — 22
4. Steven Tatum — 20
5. Roy Large, III — 18
6. Jim Carrell — 16
7. Jim Colendich — 14
8. John Foisy — 12
9. Robert Silveria — 10
10. Brad Barron — 8

1984

Super Modified
1. Nick Rescino — 662
2. Mike Sargent — 628
3. Jerry Cecil — 436
4. Rich Voss — 417
5. Chuck Miller — 336
6. Jim Perry Jr. — 269
7. T.J. Winningham — 260
8. Larry Rudolph — 251
9. Scott Luhdorff — 245
10. Joe McGee — 215

Late Model Stock Car
1. Ed Sans Jr. — 443
2. Johnny Brazil Jr. — 369
3. Larry Lundin — 363
4. John Keldsen — 301
5. Dave Crocker — 288
6. Jerry Mostek — 216
7. Rod Spencer — 216
8. Mark Barron — 212
9. Ray Keldsen — 192
10. Ken Haskell — 169

1985

Super Modified
1. Mike Sargent — 592
2. Chuck Miller — 406
3. John Viel — 385
4. Nick Rescino — 370
5. Jim Perry Jr. — 348
6. Rich Voss — 301
7. Scott Luhdorff — 294
8. Joe McGee — 276
9. Gary Willey — 247
10. Howard Kaeding — 244

Late Model Stock Car
1. Robert Miller — 486
2. Mike Petruzzi — 419
3. Mark Barron — 287
4. Ken Haskell — 254
5. Tom Certo — 234
6. Larry Lundin — 229
7. Bill Wesenberg — 205
8. Cliff Reinosa — 197
9. Mike Williams — 177
10. Mike Cyrus — 146

1986

Super Modified
1. Mike Sargent — 634
2. Jim Perry Jr. — 629
3. John Viel — 602
4. Nick Rescino — 560
5. Rod Spencer — 489
6. Dwane Larson — 289
7. Howard Kaeding — 273
8. John Lott — 242
9. Gary Willey — 233
10. Jerry Freitas — 227

Late Model Stock Car
1. Mike Williams — 490
2. Robert Miller — 375
3. Jerry Bonnema — 327
4. John Keldsen — 305
5. Mike Petruzzi — 282
6. Joe Glade — 281
7. Ray Keldsen — 240
8. Mike Cyrus — 197
9. Joe Esperanca — 184
10. Mike Castellon — 167

1987

Super Modified
1. John Viel — 665
2. Jim Perry Jr. — 586
3. Mike Sargent — 461
4. Rod Spencer — 441
5. Ernie Rose — 426
6. Howard Kaeding — 362
7. Tom Henry — 300
8. Nick Rescino — 284
9. Dwane Larson — 264
10. Johnny Key — 234

Late Model Stock Car
1.	Robert Miller	545
2.	Ed Sans Jr.	476
3.	Mike Williiams	467
4.	John Keldsen	311
5.	Mike Petruzzi	267
6.	Bobby Hogge	204
7.	Kent Potter	198
8.	Guy Pacheco	193
9.	Joe Glade	168
10.	Ken Haskell	164

1988
Super Modified
1.	John Viel	551
2.	Rod Spencer	442
3.	Howard Kaeding	428
4.	Rick Martin	418
5.	Mike Sargent	398
6.	Duane Larson	383
7.	Jerry Miller	368
8.	Nick Rescino	333
9.	Jamie Hood	307
10.	Wayne Katen	264

Late Model Stock Car
1.	Ed Sans Jr.	470
2.	Ken Haskell	347
3.	Tim Balding	307
4.	Mike Petruzzi	240
5.	Mike Larson	224
6.	Todd Souza	188
7.	Guy Pacheco	180
8.	Kent Potter	175
9.	Bill Hall	167
10.	Ray Johnson	160

1989
Super Modified
1.	Rod Spencer	412
2.	Rick Martin	406
3.	Scott Luhdorff	405
4.	Howard Kaeding	355
5.	Dwane Larson	321
6.	Nick Rescino	279
7.	Mark Chaves	263
8.	Dave Thompson	226
9.	Tom Henry	204
10.	Mike Sargent	174

1990
Super Sprint
1.	Rod Spencer	531
2.	Rick Martin	530
3.	Scott Luhdorff	355
4.	Danny Olmstead	340
5.	Randy Hannagan	300
6.	Tom Henry	266
7.	Nick Rescino	261
8.	Mike Sargent	248
9.	Howard Kaeding	238
10.	Mark Chaves	235

1991
Super Sprint
1.	Rick Martin	472
2.	Terry McCarl	464
3.	Danny Olmstead	438
4.	Scott Luhdorff	431
5.	Randy Hannagan	350
6.	Tom Henry	311
7.	Rod Spencer	260
8.	Howard Kaeding	257
9.	Craig Smith	207
10.	Mark Chaves	200

1992
Sprint Car
1.	Pat Rose	344
2.	Scott Luhdorff	316
3.	Rick Martin	309
4.	Tom Henry	298
5.	Randy Hannagan	297
6.	Mark Chaves	175
7.	Lindsey Casto	169
8.	Eric Rossi	151
9.	Charlie Caraccilo	149
10.	Rod Spencer	145

1993
410 Sprint Car
1.	Randy Hannagan	983
2.	Rick Martin	964
3.	Tom Henry	870
4.	Charlie Caraccilo	866
5.	Chuck Miller	811
6.	Mark Chaves	641
7.	Bob Cooney	641
8.	Pat Rose	630
9.	Jason Statler	621
10.	Dave Thompson	581

360 Sprint Car
1.	Randy Hannagan	858
2.	Ivan Worden	652
3.	Sparky Howard	640
4.	Tony Richards	624
5.	Kirk Sargent	537
6.	Jeff Mauldin	531
7.	Jim Perry Jr.	517
8.	Mark Plourde	408
9.	Rob Johnson	401
10.	Don Johnson	360

1994
410 Sprint Car
1.	Rick Martin	1073
2.	Chuck Miller	899
3.	Lindsey Casto	890
4.	Tim Green	868
5.	Pat Rose	791
6.	Bob Cooney	757
7.	Randy Hannagan	734
8.	Ronnie Day	723
9.	Dave Thompson	643
10.	Mark Monico	592

360 Sprint Car

1.	Mark Chaves	838
2.	Joe DeLisle	716
3.	Nick Ringo	663
4.	Kirk Sargent	616
5.	Ryan Bailey	613
6.	Rich Kroll	466
7.	Ken Cox	419
8.	Andy Ferris	410
9.	Mike Doushgounian	402
10.	Johnnie Albanese	394

Late Model Stock Car

1.	Steve Hendren	648
2.	Ed Sans Jr.	565
3.	John Silva	498
4.	Kimberly Myers	490
5.	Vance Beltran	370
6.	Shawn DeForest	280
7.	Ken Haskell	240
8.	Mark Barron	230
9.	Larry Burton	219
10.	Tom Johnson	217

1995
410 Sprint Car

1.	Lindsey Casto	610
2.	Ronnie Day	577
3.	Charlie Caraccilo	551
4.	Scott Luhdorff	539
5.	Chuck Miller	528
6.	Rick Martin	517
7.	George Graham	478
8.	Tom Henry	458
9.	Dave Rule	360
10.	Mark Monico	323

360 Sprint Car

1.	Mark Chaves	479
2.	Mike Doushgounian	375
3.	Ryan Bailey	348
4.	Scott Nail	336
5.	Craig Smith	320
6.	Dave Thompson	313
7.	Howard Fergerson	299
8.	Joey Santos	293
9.	Jim Kaiser Jr.	258
10.	Alan Howell	255

1996
360 Sprint Car

1.	Bud Kaeding	632
2.	Rick Williams	612
3.	John Golobic	577
4.	Charlie Caraccilo	573
5.	Doug Silva	403
6.	Howard Fergerson	358
7.	Dave Schlenz	348
8.	Keith Mohler	326
9.	Jaime Cobby	317
10.	Dave Thompson	295

1997
360 Sprint Car

1.	Charlie Caraccilo	588
2.	Rick Martin	571
3.	Tim Kaeding	555
4.	Craig Smith	486
5.	Mark Monico	483
6.	Lindsey Casto	438
7.	Jeff Mauldin	362
8.	Dave McGourty	355
9.	John Golobic	352
10.	Ray Derby	334

1998
360 Sprint Car

1.	Charlie Caraccilo	850
2.	Mark Monico	831
3.	Craig Dillard	828
4.	Rick Martin	794
5.	Tim Kaeding	548
6.	Craig Smith	545
7.	Cameron Brink	532
8.	Jeff Mauldin	488
9.	Jim Skinner	444
10.	Kirk Organ	411

Grand American Modified

1.	Bobby Hogge IV	982
2.	Chad Chadwick	842
3.	Dave Byrd	831
4.	Phil Torres	677
5.	Chris Wadsworth	652
6.	Troy Shirk	633
7.	Joe Carr	628
8.	Brian Cass	611
9.	Robert Miller	590
10.	Tim Yaeger Jr.	521

1999
Grand American Modified

1.	Kenny Nott Jr.	420
2.	Jeff Decker	395
3.	Bobby Scott	364
4.	Mike Juarez	341
5.	Ed Jacobs	309
6.	Ken Pelphrey	305
7.	Bill Wesenberg	302
8.	Phil Indihar	302
9.	Jim DiGiovanni	239
10.	Tim Yaeger Jr.	234

Santa Clara County Fairgrounds
San Jose Driving Park
One Lap Track Records
1909-1999

One-Mile Oval

1909	W.G. Collins	53.45*
1912	Louis Disbrow	53.21
1912	Barney Oldfield	47.35
1951	Joe Leonard	44.68*
1951	Tony Bettenhausen	36.41
1982	Ricky Graham	36.196*
1990	Scott Parker	36.076*

* = Motorcycle

Hard Top

| 1955 | Ray Raneri | 47.80 |

Horse

| 1941 | | 2:05.00 |

Half-Mile

Sprint Car

1972	Marty Kinrt	24.849
1976	Jimmy Boyd	24.254
1976	Jimmy Boyd	23.257
1977	Jimmy Boyd	21.865
1978	Bobby Allen	21.613
1979	Doug Wolfgang	20.903
1986	Brent Kaeding	19.490
1986	Bobby Allen	18.515

Midget

| 1957 | Mike McGreevy | 27.25 |
| 1977 | Tommy Astone | 25.546 |

Stock Car

| 1987 | Ed Sans | 25.019 |

Tenth-Mile (indoor)

Midget

| 1968 | Larry Mimms | 7.39 |
| 1968 | Gary Koster | 7.383 |

Sixth-Mile

Midget

1970	Tommy Astone	12.60
1971	Duanne Bonini	12.18
1974	Bobby Morrow	12.177

Quarter-Mile

Midget

| 1978 | Ken Nichols | 16.602 |
| 1979 | Wally Pankratz | 15.919 |

Super Modified / Sprint Car

1978	Dave Pombo	16.530
1978	Mark Sargent	16.146
1978	Mike Sargent	16.031
1978	Mike Sargent	15.981
1979	Mike Sargent	15.586
1979	Howard Kaeding	15.265
1979	Mike Sargent	15.230
1979	Mike Sargent	15.196
1979	Art Bigiogni	14.968
1980	Mike Sargent	14.687
1980	Brent Kaeding	14.622
1980	Billy Yon	14.406
1980	Tim Green	13.875*
1983	Nick Rescino	13.665
1984	Nick Rescino	13.379
1987	John Viel	13.151

* = Sprint Car

Stock Car

1978	Nick Foster	19.239
1978	Larry Lundin	19.015
1978	Mitch West	18.947
1978	Ken Naber	18.488
1978	Ken Naber	18.386
1979	Ken Naber	18.133
1979	Dave Byrd	17.812
1979	Ray Morgan	17.785
1984	Larry Lundin	16.928

Third-Mile

Sprint Cars

1988	Rod Spencer	14.442
1988	Tom Henry	14.357
1988	Tom Henry	14.126
1989	Dave Thompson	14.027
1989	Dave Thompson	13.980
1994	Randy Hannagan	13.708
1996	Mark Kinser	13.383

Chapter 13

Miscellaneous

Other Tracks of Interest

1929 - 2007

Gas-powered miniature automobiles, measuring only 18 inches long, were popular before World War II. These little cars were capable of reaching speeds of up to 95 mph.

The San Jose Miniature Car Association held their meets at an oval track located at 17th and Williams Streets. (Another miniature track was later built on Cunningham Ave., opposite Reid Hillview Airport in 1949.) During July, 1941, the California State Miniature Racing Car Championships were held at the Williams Street location. During the meet, Lieutenant Colonel Smith's little roller traveled the half-mile event in 91.74 mph and then repeated with a remarkable 91.83 in the mile run. Both were world records. He covered the half-mile distance in 19.38 seconds. Over 60 of the miniature gas-powered machines participated. This photo was taken at that event. Nowadays, these miniature cars are highly sought after collectables and bring a high price on the market. *Dennis Mattish Collection*

For a number of years during the late 1920s & 1930s, Alviso Harbor was host to Speed Boat races. There were a number of big events, with the fastest boats in the State participating. This *Mercury News* ad from June, 1929, was for such an event.

Silver Creek Raceway was opened in the early 1960s. Built for Go-Karts, the track was located off Loupe Avenue in East San Jose. The first big event was the State Territorial Go-Kart Championship held in 1965. Over 300 riders, some from as far away as Ohio, participated. The track was renamed Snow's Grand Prix Raceway in 1966. The State Championship meet was bigger yet, with the riders racing for a $5,000 purse. The track would remain in use for a few more years before closing.

Go-Kart races were held at the San Jose Flea Market during the 1960 season. The Santa Clara Valley Kart Club sanctioned the events.

The San Jose Arena staged Monster Truck shows for a number of years, sanctioned by the United States Hot Rod Association. This photo of the Dragon Slayer was taken in 2001. *Dennis Mattish Photo.*

As part of the Monster Jam (as it was called), World Wrestling Federation-style Quad races were held pitting Northern California against Los Angeles (blue uniforms). Of course, LA was roundly booed. *Dennis Mattish Photo.*

244

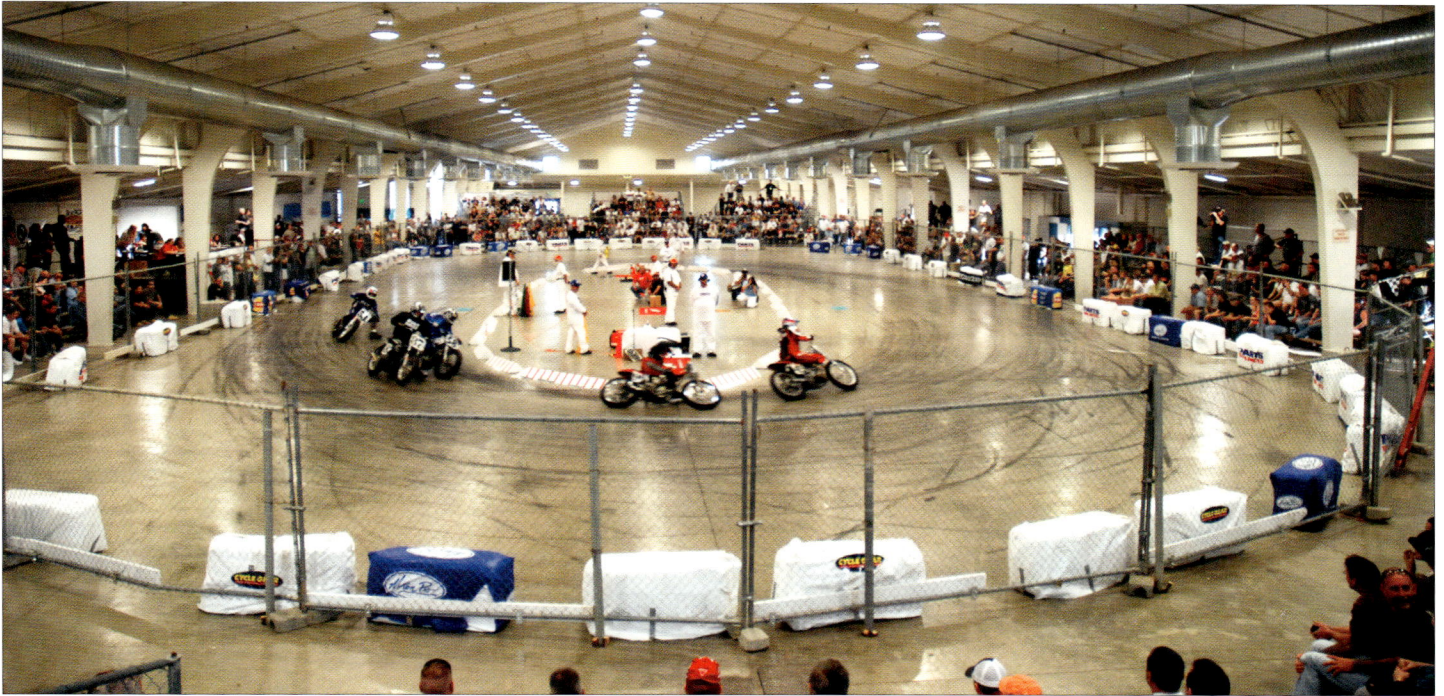

After an absence of three decades, indoor motorcycle racing was revived at the Santa Clara County Fairgrounds in 2007.

Race sponsor Rod Lake, along with promoters Dianne Kanemoto and Pete Francini, are the masterminds behind the event, which was playing before near capacity crowds by 2009 .

This track is narrower (because of Codes) than what the Midgets raced on 40 years earlier.

(Above) 2009: Wide angle view of the clean track and facilities.
(Below) 2009: Typical race action in the pro division. *Photos by Dennis Mattish*

A Quarter-Midget track was built at Trader Lew's Amusement Park in late 1958. The track was Located on Monterey Road, one mile south of the Fairgrounds. The San Jose Quarter-Midget Racing Association started running races there in 1959.

Quarter Midgets during 1958. *Courtesy of onlyclassics*

Dwarf-sized Midget Racers, a craze that was sweeping the country in 1957, held their first race on September 29 at a new racetrack located on Story Road near Bayshore Highway. Young drivers between the ages of four and twelve drove 2 hp, quarter-sized Midgets around a 1/20-mile (88 yards) banked asphalt oval, at speeds of up to 22 mph. The San Jose Quarter Midget Racing Association sanctioned the events, and admission was free to the public.

The California Quarter Midget Championships were held at the track in 1958, and San Jose drivers placed in the top three in every main event. Guy Denofrid set the track record with a time of 7.99. The track had a short history, as the same fate that befell Little Bonneville Drag Strip also happened to the Quarter Midget track in 1959. The land was developed into Tropicana Village.

Local Quarter Midget racing found a new home at Baylands Quarter Midget track in Sunnyvale in 1962. Located on a dumpsite, the track would run for 21 years until it was closed in 1983. The most famous graduates from the track were NASCAR star Jeff Gordon and Open Wheel driver Jimmy Vasser.

In 1985, the Baylands Quarter Midget Club teamed up with the South County Micro Midget and Mini-Sprint Association and built a state-of-the-art racing facility up on Metcalf Road in South San Jose. The track is located in the Santa Clara County Off-Highway Vehicle Park. A 1/20-mile asphalt banked oval was built for the Quarter Midgets, and a 1/9-mile dirt oval was constructed for the Micro Midgets. A combined seating capacity for the two tracks was 1,000. Only the asphalt track remains, but racing continues to this very day.

Baylands champion Tommy McCarthy was one of the dominant Quarter Midget drivers in the state during the 2005-2009 period. *Dennis Mattish Photo*

2008: Quarter Midgets, the "little leagues" of the racing world, battle for position at Metcalf Raceway Park. *Dennis Mattish Photo*

2008: Metcalf Raceway Park is the only racetrack left in San Jose (or Santa Clara County, for that matter). Baylands Quarter Midget Racing Association is the sanctioning body. *Dennis Mattish Photo*

1985 aerial photo of Metcalf Raceway Park. Quarter Midget track is on the left and the Mini Sprint track is on the right. *Courtesy of Mike Manthey*

Mike Manthey leads a trio of Mini Sprints into turn one on the Metcalf Raceway dirt oval during 1985. *Courtesy of Mike Manthey*

Chapter 14

Champ Car

San Jose Grand Prix

2005 - 2007

July 29-31, 2005

During the summer of 2004, negotiations between San Jose and Champ Car commenced. Because weekend attendance for Champ Car races at Laguna Seca Raceway had dropped off substantially in the past few years (133,750 in 2000 to 35,000 in 2004), Champ Car was very interested in what San Jose Sports Authority had to say about moving the race to Silicon Valley. To get the deal done, it had to be approved by the San Jose City Council.

Champ Car, formally known as Championship Auto Racing Teams (CART), was considered a third-string racing circuit (behind NASCAR and the Indy Racing League) and had just spent the previous year fighting for its life in bankruptcy court. Supporting it might prove to be a gamble. But there were many pluses to take into consideration. The event would have a very positive impact on the local economy, it would raise the city profile and the races were for charity.

On November 19, 2004, San Jose officials reached a tentative agreement to stage the Grand Prix race on the streets surrounding HP Pavilion on July 29-31. A five-year agreement was made with the Canary Foundation, a non-profit corporation dedicated to early cancer detection. The foundation would be promoting the event, with proceeds going to charity. The deal was contingent on the City Council approving $650,000 to help shoulder the $3 million needed to put on the race. The city gave its approval on December 7. The races were on.

Taylor Woodrow, builders of homes, was the event sponsor. The race was called the Taylor Woodrow San Jose Grand Prix. Tickets and hospitality packages went on sale in January for a race that was originally going to run around the HP Pavilion (otherwise known as "the Shark Tank" because it is home of the San Jose Sharks). It was

Don Listwin (left), founder of the Canary Fund, and Bob Singleton, General Manager of the San Jose Grand Prix, were the keynote speakers at the Motor Sports Press Association's 42nd Annual Awards Banquet on March 2, 2005. At the time, the planned race course was centered around the HP Pavilion.
Dennis Mattish Photo

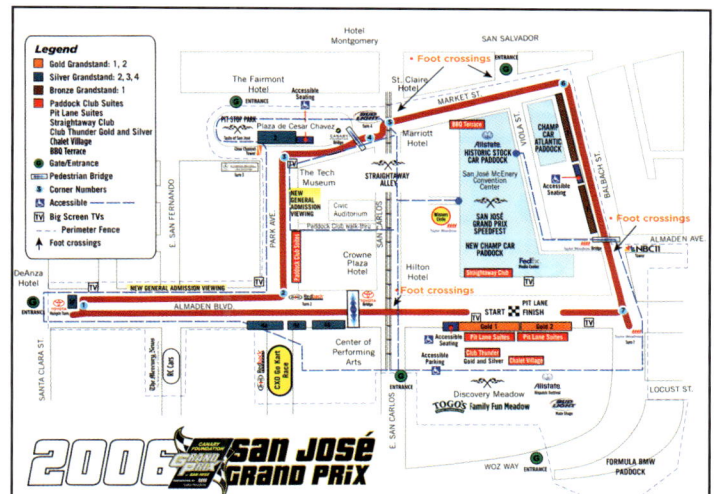

The 1.448-mile street course through downtown San Jose.

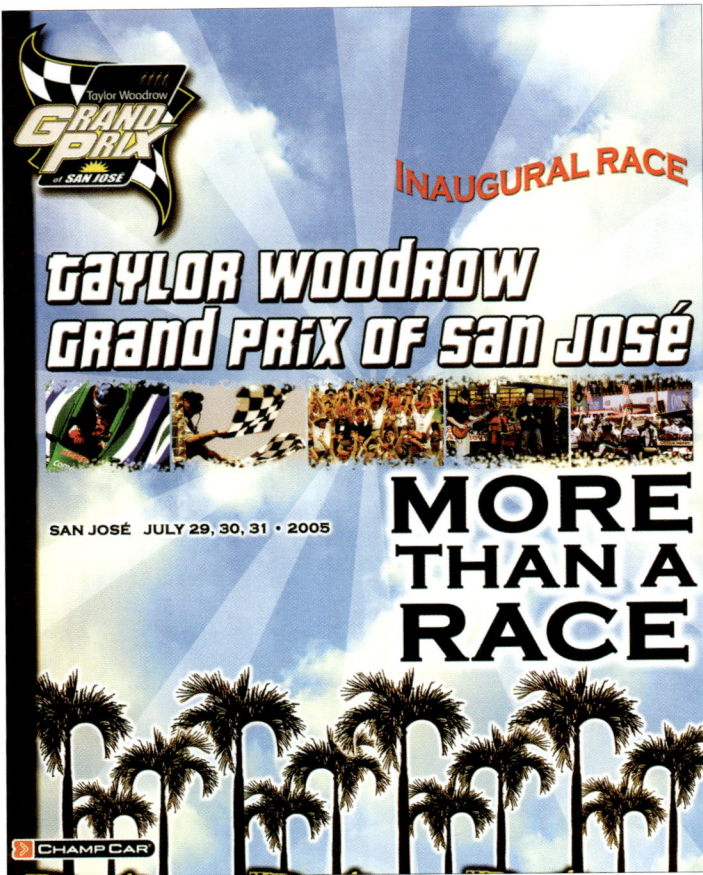

INAUGURAL RACE

TAYLOR WOODROW GRAND PRIX OF SAN JOSÉ

SAN JOSÉ   JULY 29, 30, 31 • 2005

MORE THAN A RACE

soon realized that scaffolding from construction on the Highway 87 overpass, which would have been over the track in two different locations, would interfere with the race course. The organizers quickly found a new, better location, centered on the San Jose McEnery Convention Center in the heart of downtown. The convention center acted as the paddock for the cars and a showroom and entertainment area for the Speedfest activities. There were seven major hotels either inside the track or next to it.

The publicity leading up to the race was as good as any sporting event had ever received in the Bay Area. The TV stations and newspapers were behind the event 100 percent.

Downtown San Jose was abuzz with anticipation and excitement when race weekend arrived. Day one proved to be a challenge for the cars, drivers and fans. The cars

Jimmy Vasser, who grew up in Morgan Hill just a few miles south of San Jose, drives the PKV Racing Champ Car through turn two during the 2005 race. *Dennis Mattish Photo*

Part of the crowded main grandstand with luxury boxes on Almaden Blvd. *Dennis Mattish Photo*

were to start warm ups at 7:45 a.m., but construction was still being done on the pedestrian bridge over the track and fencing was still being installed. Thousands of fans were disappointed when the cars did not get on the track until after noon.

Another problem was the train tracks that ran through two different sections of the track were causing the cars to fly nearly a foot off the ground every time they went over them. Champ Car qualifying would have to wait until the next day.

A huge crowd of 50,962 race fans and curiousity seekers turned out for the Saturday qualifying session and Grand Am race. Receiving a lot of attention was film star and Champ Car owner Paul Newman, who participated in a charity Go-Kart race and wasn't happy when a fellow competitor stuffed him into the hay bales on the first lap.

Champ Car points leader Sebastien Bourdais, who was

British driver Katherine Legge (12) showed the male drivers the fast way around the course when she led the last 16 of 45 laps to win the Toyota Atlantic Series race during 2005. *Dennis Mattish Photo*

Justin Wilson gets air as he flies over the railroad tracks on Almaden Blvd. during the 2005 race. *Dennis Mattish Photo*

With a scenic San Jose skyline as a backdrop, Klaus Graf powers his Jaguar through turn three during the 2005 Trans-Am race. *Dennis Mattish Photo*

Champ Cars head down Park Ave. early in the 2006 race. The Palm trees on the right were relocated to this position after the previous year's race to allow for a wider street. *Dennis Mattish Photo*

Timo Glock of Germany used the San Jose Grand Prix as a stepping-stone to the World Formula 1 circuit. Here he drives the Rocketsports entry through turn two during the 2005 race. *Dennis Mattish Photo*

The San Jose McEnery Convention Center was home to the Speedfest during all three Grands Prix. It also acted as the paddock area for the cars. *Dennis Mattish Photo*

fastest on Friday's practice session, won pole position with a speed of 96.101 mph around the 1.448-mile street course.

Because there was no run-off area at the end of the long straightaway leading into the hairpin turn, a chicane was added to slow down the cars. With stands behind the hairpin and the cars approaching the turn at over 160 mph, this was a wise move.

The train tracks were still a problem for the cars that were traveling 150 mph over them. Champ Car driver Oriol Servia said, "Every time I went over those tracks and the car flew up and then came down so hard, I yelled, 'Aaaaaaaah!' I mean every time. Finally, I told myself, 'Next time, I'm not going to yell.' But I couldn't stop myself. Every time I landed, it was driving my elbows down hard, my back, everything." All the teams were adding extra padding to the cockpits

Boris Said averaged 65.412 mph to win the 75-minute Trans-Am-Cytomax 100 race on July 30, 2005. Afterwards he said, "Never in the world would I ever think I would drive 160 mph through the streets of San Jose." *Dennis Mattish Photo*

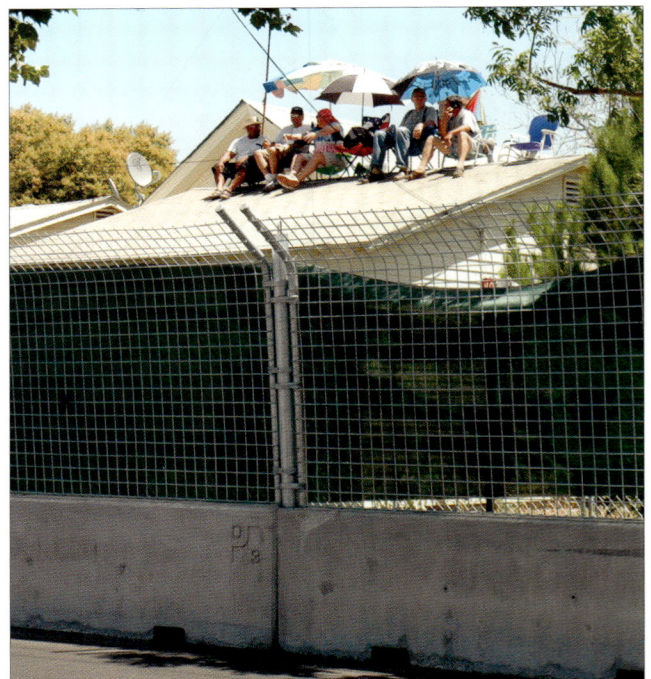

Residents on Balbach Street watch the race from their rooftop during 2005. *Dennis Mattish Photo*

Sebastien Bourdais drove the Newman/Haas entry to victory in both 2005 & 2006. In 2008 he reached the premier circuit of the racing world, Formula 1. *Dennis Mattish Photo*

Car co-owner Paul Newman and a young race fan display the 2006 San Jose Grand Prix trophy. Joining them on the podium are (left to right) Cristiano da Matta (2nd place), car co-owner Carl Haas, race winner Sebastien Bourdais and Justin Wilson (3rd place). *Dennis Mattish Photo*

253

Drifting was one of the most popular events held during the three Grands Prix. *Dennis Mattish Photos*

of the cars to reduce discomfort.

Sunday July 31, 2005, has gone down in the annals of San Jose sports history as the biggest event ever. *San Jose Mercury News* columnist Mark Purdy wrote, "Somehow, it all came together Sunday afternoon for the first Taylor Woodrow Grand Prix, the largest sporting event in city history––and one that created the amazing spectacle of cars whizzing past the Tech Museum and other landmarks at five times the normal speed limit." On Sunday, 62,371 people crowded into the track. The three-day total was 153,767. Attendance-wise, the event was a resounding success.

Bourdais, from France, led the start and finish in the Newman/Hass Ford-Cosworth/Lola and became the first San Jose Grand Prix champion. Finishing four seconds behind was Paul Tracy. Average speed for the 93-lap race was 76.43 mph.

Half the field was eliminated because of shunts with the wall and other cars on the slippery track. Local San Jose driver A.J. Allmendinger slammed into the turn-four wall on lap 12 to end his day early. The most spectacular sight of the day was the cars flying in unison over the train tracks on the opening laps of the race, something you might see at an off-road race.

As can be expected, there were problems in the inaugural event. These problems would be resolved for the next year's event. Unfortunately, some of the people who were not happy because of these problems would not return.

The Historic Stock Car Racing Series participated in all three Grands Prix. They are shown heading down Balbach Street in this photo with crowds lining the rooftops and sidewalks in the background. *Dennis Mattish Photo*

July 28-30, 2006

After the 2005 race, organizers from the Grand Prix approached the San Jose City Council and said they needed money to continue running the race. Behind closed doors, the City agreed to provide a two-year, $4 million subsidy. This would be a hot political issue for the next two years.

Good to their word, the Grand Prix organization, led by President Dale Jantzen and General Manager Bob Singleton, made all the necessary improvements to make this year's event run smoothly. The pedestrian bridges, which the previous year took an hour's wait to get across, were doubled in size, eliminating that problem. The train tracks were smoothed out, making that a non-issue. Sightlines for the general admission patrons were vastly improved. A runoff area in turn one was added, thus eliminating the chicane. Braking into turn one would become the top passing area of the track. The groundwork was set for a highly successful second year.

The three-day event was advertised as more than a race. A good number of people came to just hang out, see the concerts, car shows, and exhibitions and enjoy the food. One couple stated, "We have no idea who's racing, it's just the fact that this event is here is the reason we are here."

With the elimination of the chicane and the widening of the track in certain areas, the track record took

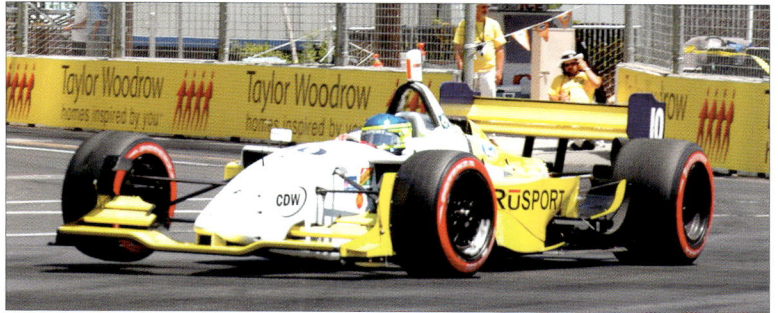

Brazilian Cristiano da Matta hikes his right front rounding turn seven during the 2006 race. He finished second. *Dennis Mattish Photo*

Oriol Servia had two third-place finishes during the three-year history of the race. He is shown in 2006 driving the PKV entry. *Dennis Mattish Photo*

A. J. Allmendinger (who grew up and went to school in San Jose) negotiates the hairpin turn in the Forsythe Ford-Cosworth-powered Lola in 2006. The following year he joined the NASCAR circuit. *Dennis Mattish Photo*

Paul Tracy prepares to exit his mount moments after a collision with Alex Tagliani during the 2006 race. *Dennis Mattish Photo*

Alexander Rossi won the 2007 Formula BMW USA race held on Saturday. *Dennis Mattish Photo*

a major beating on Saturday. Sebastien Bourdais went a full 10 mph faster than the previous year to win his second pole position in a row. He toured the 1.443-mile track in 48.989 seconds at a speed of 106.040 mph. San Jose's A. J. Allmendinger was second fastest with a lap at 105.448 mph.

Formula BMW USA held the only race on Saturday, and Reed Stevens of Palo Alto won that. The following day, BMW points leader Robert Wickens won race #2.

On Sunday, the Champ Car Atlantic Series race had a wild start as a multi-car pile-up took place in turn one on the opening lap. The crash happened behind pole-sitter Raphael Matos and 17-year-old Graham Rahal, who pulled away from the pack. Rahal chased Matos for 26 laps before hitting the tire barrier in turn six. Matos went unchallenged the rest of the way to win the 45-lap race. This was his first Atlantic win.

"A SMOOTHER RIDE THIS TIME AROUND" shouted the headlines on page one of the *San Jose Mercury News* the following day. "Miles better than a year ago, this race should stay in San Jose," said Sports Columnist and sometimes Critic Mark Purdy of the *Mercury News*. The announced crowd was 67,128; the three-day total of 155,934, which would later prove to be an inflated figure, saw a wild, madcap and occasional riveting

The hairpin turn on the first lap of the 2006 Atlantic race saw James Hinchcliffe drive over the top of Alan Sciuto. *Dennis Mattish Photo*

race. At the drop of the green, Bourdais led the pack into turn one (hairpin) and was tagged from behind by Allmendinger. Bourdais continued with no damage, but Allmendinger had to go to the pits for a new nosepiece. His day was a struggle and he would eventually finish seventh. Bourdais set the pace, leading 69 of the race's 97 laps with an average speed of 85.694 mph to post an easy win over second-placed Cristiano da Matta. Sebastien was two-for-two in SJ Grand Prix wins.

On lap 52, Paul Tracy, who was running in third position, overshot turn six and went into the run-off area. He then made a dangerous move, trying to get back on the track ahead of a speeding fourth-placed Alex Tagliani. The two Canadians then collided, sending parts flying through the air. Tracy's car came to a halt at the end of Balbach Street and Tagliani limped into the pits. As Tracy came walking into the pits, Tagliani confronted and then grabbed him. The pair was separated, but then more angry words were exchanged. Then a fight broke out with punches being thrown. The smaller Tagliani ended up on the ground.

There was plenty of other action on the track. "It was

Movie legend Paul Newman was a regular in the charity Go-Kart races. *Dennis Mattish Photo*

Sebastien Bourdais leads the pack into the turn-one hairpin at the start of the 2007 race. *Dennis Mattish Photos*

Jonathan Bomarito of Monterey, Ca., had the fastest ride in the 2007 Champ Car Atlantic competition as he dominated the race from pole. *Dennis Mattish Photo*

Will Power is pursued by Dan Clarke during 2007. *Dennis Mattish Photo*

2006 San Jose Atlantic winner Raphael Matos clinched the 2007 Atlantic series championship at San Jose. *Dennis Mattish Photo*

Neel Jani glances at his mirror as he exits turn seven in 2007. He would finish a career best second place driving the Red Bull entry. *Dennis Mattish Photo*

crazy out there," said Katherine Legge, who was involved in three incidents before finishing 12th. "There were mistakes being made everywhere and people driving into each other. I was getting hit so much that I felt I was driving a Stock Car."

After the race, drivers who one year earlier had condemned the street course had nothing but praise for it. Bourdais said, "There really is no comparison between this year's track and last year's." But the San Jose Grand Prix still lost money.

July 27-29, 2007

The event picked up a new sponsor and was now called the San Jose Grand Prix at Redback Raceway.

Another good crowd turned out for the third edition of the downtown street race.

England's Justin Wilson turned a lap of 49.039 at

105.932 mph to win pole position, ending Sebastien Bourdais' two-year claim to that position. Champ Car adopted the World Formula 1 style of standing starts for the 2007 season. At the drop of the green flag, the field got away cleanly as Bourdais beat Wilson into the turn-one hairpin. Back in the bunched-up pack, Robert Doornbos went airborne as he climbed over the back of Jan Heylen's car. The Dutchman lost track positions in the pits while his pit crew replaced the nose section. He re-entered the track in last place, where he would methodically start working his way up through the field.

Bourdais was trying to save fuel when he stalled his car during the yellow flag created by the hairpin pile-up. This cost him the lead and he would struggle his way to a fifth-place finish. The two-time San Jose Grand Prix and four-time Champ Car Champion left the series at the end of the year and moved up to World F1 Grand Prix cars. During a lap-four yellow, race leader Wilson was idling behind the pace car when, for some unknown reason, Dan Clarke, who was running second, accelerated into the back of Wilson, damaging both cars. A seething Wilson sat in the pits for 21 laps while repairs were made.

(Left & above)17-year-old, second-generation driver Graham Rahal drove the Newman/Hass car to a sixth-place finish in 2007. *Dennis Mattish Photo*

Clarke went into the pits and had his nose wing replaced. Ten seconds after re-entering the track, he ran into Katherine Legge, knocking both out of the race.

Doornbos, who clearly had the fastest car on the track, passed Neel Jani for the lead on lap 96 of 107 and pulled away for a seven-second victory. His average speed was a record 88.127 mph in a time of 1hour 45minutes and 7.617 seconds.

In the Formula BMW support race, 15-year-old rookie driver Alexander Rossi won from pole position.

The successful three-day race festival was attended by 120,000 (81,538 paid). The following day the San Jose Grand Prix ran a full-page ad in the *San Jose Mercury News* thanking the sponsors, the City of San Jose and the fans. They ended the ad with "We look forward to seeing you again next year."

Two months later

On September 12 the headlines in the local paper screamed "SAN JOSE GRAND PRIX FINISHED." The subheadline stated, "Unpopular city subsidy undercut support for event." It went on to read: "After exhausting a $4 million taxpayer subsidy, the 3-year-old San Jose Grand Prix abruptly called it quits Tuesday." Reactions to the sudden announcement were as polarized as the political debate that raged over the subsidy itself.

Mark Purdy wrote, "Such a coincidence. As soon as the city's heavy financial subsidy for the event stopped, so did the event. The Grand Prix promoters took $4 million of taxpayers' money over the past two years and made promises. Never mind." John Kelly, editor of *MotoRacing*, wrote in his column: "We suspect the reason for the departure of the street race is the event has run out of OPM (other people's money)."

The reason stated by Dale Jantzen in the *Mercury News* was the event was "no longer viable in it's current location" because of plans by developer Boston Properties to move forward on a three-tower office development on Almaden Boulevard, where the race had set up its main spectator grandstands." Purdy wrote "There was no confir-

mation that ground will be broken on the Almaden Blvd. lot anytime soon. Probably because it won't. If Champ Car and Don Listwin had wanted the GP to continue, it would have. It could have moved back to the original configuration around HP Pavilion."

It is ironic that if the San Jose Grand Prix organization had waited a few months, it would have had a graceful exit from its commitment to the city and race fans. With the merger of Champ Car and the Indy Racing League (IRL), the race would have been cancelled anyway.

During the three years the event was held, the Grand Prix raised $3.4 million for the Canary Foundation. This is a subject that was rarely, if ever, brought up in the debate caused by the subsidy uproar.

The biggest losers besides the taxpayers and charity were the race fans. For one weekend a year, the Grand Prix turned downtown San Jose into an adrenalin rush of action, a loud, crazy place of activity, a place to be seen at, a grand spectacle and a place where you could see cars screaming past the Center for the Performing Arts at 170 mph. San Jose was a wonderful place to be on the last weekend of July for race fans.

Final San Jose victory photo featured (left to right) second place Neel Jani, race winner Robert Doornbos and third place finisher Oriol Servia. *Dennis Mattish Photo*

San Jose Grand Prix Results

2005

Champ Car
1. Sebastien Bourdais
2. Paul Tracy
3. Oriol Servia
4. Justin Wilson
5. Mario Dominguez
6. Timo Glock
7. Ronnie Bremer
8. Bjorn Wirdheim
9. Alex Tagliani
10. Cristiano da Matta
11. Jimmy Vasser
12. Marcus Marshall
13. Rodolfo Lavin
14. Ryan Hunter-Reay
15. Nelson Philippe
16. Andrew Ranger
17. A.J. Allmendinger
18. Ricardo Sperafico

Trans-Am
1. Boris Said
2. Greg Pickett
3. Klaus Graf
4. Randy Ruhiman
5. Hima Maher
6. Rudy Revak
7. Steve Kelso
8. Art Muncheryan
9. Guy Dreier
10. Tim Barber

Toyota Atlantic
1. Katherine Legge
2. David Martinez
3. Charles Zwoisman
4. Allan Scito
5. Andreas Wirth
6. Al Unser III
7. Grant Ryley
8. Phil Giebler
9. Justin Sofio
10. Dan Seiznick

2006

Champ Car
1. Sebastien Bourdais
2. Cristiano da Matta
3. Justin Wilson
4. Nelson Philippe
5. Mario Dominquez
6. Will Power
7. A.J. Allmendinger
8. Oriol Servia
9. Charles Zwolsman
10. Nicky Pastorelli
11. Jan Heylen
12. Katherine Legge
13. Andrew Ranger
14. Alex Tagliani
15. Paul Tracy
16. Dan Clarke
17. Bruno Junqueira

Atlantic
1. Raphael Matos
2. Ryan Lewis
3. Danilo Dirani
4. Tim Bridgman
5. Leonardo Maia
6. David Martinez
7. James Davison
8. Simon Pagenaud
9. Justin Sofio
10. Carlos Mastretta

Formula BMW USA
Race #1
1. Reed Stevens
2. Tom Sutherland
3. David Garza
4. Simona de Silvestro
5. Race Johnson

Race #2
1. Robert Wickens
2. Matt Lee
3. Reed Stevens
4. Simona de Silvestro
5. Daniel Morad

2007

Champ Car
1. Robert Doornbos
2. Neel Jani
3. Oriol Servia
4. Will Power
5. Sebastien Bourdais
6. Graham Rahal
7. Bruno Junqueira
8. Tristan Gommendy
9. Jan Heylen
10. Simon Pagenaud
11. Paul Tracy
12. Mario Dominguez
13. Justin Wilson
14. Alex Figge
15. Alex Tagliani
16. Katherine Legge
17. Dan Clarke

Atlantic
1. Jonathan Bomarito
2. Franck Perera
3. Robert Wickens
4. Raphael Matos
5. Junior Strous
6. Adrian Carrio
7. Alan Sciuto
8. Justin Sofio
9. Ronnie Bremer
10. Simona De Silvestro

Formula BMW USA
Race #1
1. Alexander Rossi
2. Maxime Pelletier
3. Robert Thorne
4. Ricardo Favoretto
5. Yannick Hofman

Race #2
1. Esteban Gutierrez
2. Daniel Morad
3. Ricardo Favoretto
4. Maxime Pelletier
5. Philip Major

Appendix

Note: For track records and final point standings, see back of individual chapters.

**AAA Sanction
Complete List of
San Jose Winners**

Date	Track	Winner
11-28-1909	San Jose Driving Park	W.H. Turner
5-13-1910	San Jose Driving Park	W.T. Warren
9-3-1911	San Jose Driving Park	Earl Cooper
3-17-1912	San Jose Driving Park	Earl Cooper
4-14-1912	San Jose Driving Park	Louis Disbrow
11-12-1912	San Jose Driving Park	Earl Cooper
7-4-1915	San Jose Driving Park	Thomas
7-4-1923	San Jose Speedway	Red Murray
8-12-1923	San Jose Speedway	Fred Luelling
8-19-1923	San Jose Speedway	Gene Rapp
9- 23-1923	San Jose Speedway	Fred Lyons
11-11-1923	San Jose Speedway	Adolph Gusti
12-2-1923	San Jose Speedway	Fred Lyons
6-29-1924	San Jose Speedway	Fred Luelling
7-27-1924	San Jose Speedway	Adolph Gusti
9-1-1924	San Jose Speedway	Ralph De Palma
10-18-1924	San Jose Speedway	Ralph De Palma
10-26-1924	San Jose Speedway	Fred Luelling
11-27-1924	San Jose Speedway	Babe Stapp
3-15-1925	San Jose Speedway	Jack Petticord
5-24-1925	San Jose Speedway	Fred Lyon
6-14-1925	San Jose Speedway	Babe Stapp
2-17-1929	San Jose Speedway	Johnny Sawyer
7-28-1929	San Jose Speedway	Walter May
9-15-1929	San Jose Speedway	Mel Keneally
10-27-1929	San Jose Speedway	Speed Hinkley
5-11-1930	San Jose Speedway	Jimmy Sharp
6-8-1930	San Jose Speedway	Jimmy Sharp
7-13-1930	San Jose Speedway	Jimmy Sharp
8-17-1930	San Jose Speedway	Jimmy Sharp
9-21-1930	San Jose Speedway	Mel Kenealy
10-19-1930	San Jose Speedway	Francis Quinn
11-30-1930	San Jose Speedway	Babe Stapp
12-28-1930	San Jose Speedway	Francis Quinn

Date	Track	Winner
3-15-1931	San Jose Speedway	Stubby Stubblefield
4-5-1931	San Jose Speedway	Stubby Stubblefield
6-7-1931	San Jose Speedway	Chet Gardner
6-21-1931	San Jose Speedway	Speed Hinkley
7-12-1931	San Jose Speedway	Stubby Stubblefield
8-16-1931	San Jose Speedway	Ernie Triplett
9-13-1931	San Jose Speedway	Ernie Triplett
10-4-1931	San Jose Speedway	Arvol Brunmier
11-29-1931	San Jose Speedway	Babe Stapp
8-28-1932	San Jose Speedway	Les Spangler
9-25-1932	San Jose Speedway	Babe Stapp
10-16-1932	San Jose Speedway	Les Spangler
6-4-1933	San Jose Speedway	Swede Smith
7-16-1933	San Jose Speedway	Herb Balmer
9-10-1933	San Jose Speedway	Al Chasteen
10-8-1933	San Jose Speedway	Les Dresback
8-20-1950	San Jose Speedway Tully Road	George Amick
10-21-1951	Santa Clara County Fairgrounds	Tony Bettenhausen
11- 2-1952	Santa Clara County Fairgrounds	Bobby Ball

1958: Jim Abreu Photo

Midget Race Cars Complete List of
San Jose Main Event Winners.
Compiled by Jim Montgomery & Author

Date	Track	Driver	Car Owner	Sanction
4-27-1934	New Alviso Speedway	Leo Faulkner	Leo Faulkner	MARA
5-4-1934	New Alviso Speedway	Leo Faulkner	Leo Faulkner	MARA
5-11-1934	New Alviso Speedway	Bill Betteridge	Bill Betteridge	MARA
5-18-1934	New Alviso Speedway	Bill Betteridge	Charlie Allen	MARA
5-25-1934	New Alviso Speedway	Leo Faulkner	Leo Faulkner	MARA
6-1-1934	New Alviso Speedway	Bill Betteridge	Bill Betteridge	MARA
6-8-1934	New Alviso Speedway	Al Sherman	Charlie Allen	MARA
6-15-1934	New Alviso Speedway	Curly Mills	Bert Krause	MARA
6-22-1934	New Alviso Speedway	Bill Betteridge	Bill Betteridge	MARA
6-29-1934	New Alviso Speedway	Hap Woodman	Hap Woodman	MARA
7-6-1934	New Alviso Speedway	Bill Betteridge	Bill Betteridge	MARA
7-13-1934	New Alviso Speedway	Leo Faulkner	Leo Faulkner	MARA
7-20-1934	New Alviso Speedway	Leo Faulkner	Leo Faulkner	MARA
7-26-1935	New Alviso Speedway	Les Dreisbach	Ken Brennaman	MARA
8-2-1935	New Alviso Speedway	Les Dreisbach	Ken Brennaman	MARA
8-9-1935	New Alviso Speedway	Les Dreisbach	Ken Brennaman	MARA
8-16-1935	New Alviso Speedway	Les Dreisbach	Ken Brennaman	MARA
8-23-1935	New Alviso Speedway	"Skeets" Jones	Casey Jones	MARA
9-28-1941	San Jose Motordrome	Gene Figone	George Bignotti	None
10-19-1941	San Jose Motordrome	Buck Whitmer	George Bignotti	None
5-19-1946	San Jose Speedway	Swede Lindskog	Walt Seyerie	URA
6-9-1946	San Jose Speedway	Ed Haddad	Johnny Balch	URA
6-16-1946	San Jose Speedway	Lyle Dickey	Ray Gardner	URA
7-4-1946	San Jose Speedway	Ed Normi	George Bignotti	BCRA
7-11-1946	San Jose Speedway	Fred Friday	Fred Friday	BCRA
7-18-1946	San Jose Speedway	Fred Agabashian	Jack London	BCRA
7-25-1946	San Jose Speedway	Buck Whitmer	George Bignotti	BCRA
8-1-1946	San Jose Speedway	Jerry Piper	Les Dreisbach	BCRA
8-8-1946	San Jose Speedway	Bob Barkhimer	Rudy Hennig	BCRA
8-15-1946	San Jose Speedway	Fred Agabashian	Jack London	BCRA
8-22-1946	San Jose Speedway	Jerry Piper	Jerry Piper	BCRA
8-29-1946	San Jose Speedway	Jerry Piper	Jerry Piper	BCRA
9-5-1946	San Jose Speedway	Jerry Piper	Bob Feehan	BCRA
9-12-1946	San Jose Speedway	Jerry Piper	Bob Feehan	BCRA
9-19-1946	San Jose Speedway	Johnny Smith	Les Dreisbach	BCRA
9-26-1946	San Jose Speedway	Fred Agabashian	Jack London	BCRA
10-3-1946	San Jose Speedway	Johnny Smith	Les Dreisbach	BCRA
10-10-1946	San Jose Speedway	Fred Agabashian	Jack London	BCRA
10-17-1946	San Jose Speedway	Fred Agabashian	Jack London	BCRA
10-21-1946	San Jose Speedway	Johnny Smith	Les Dreisbach	BCRA
4-24-1947	San Jose Speedway	Andy Guthrie	Fred DeOrian	BCRA
5-1-1947	San Jose Speedway	Bob Barkhimer	Harry Schilling	BCRA
5-8-1947	San Jose Speedway	Bill Evans	George Naruo	BCRA
5-15-1947	San Jose Speedway	Woody Brown	Jack London	BCRA
5-22-1947	San Jose Speedway	Eddie Bennett	Jack London	BCRA
5-29-1947	San Jose Speedway	Woody Brown	Jack London	BCRA
6-5-1947	San Jose Speedway	Woody Brown	Jack London	BCRA
6-12-1947	San Jose Speedway	Eddie Bennett	Jack London	BCRA
6-19-1947	San Jose Speedway	Fred Friday	Fred Friday	BCRA
6-26-1947	San Jose Speedway	Fred Agabashian	George Bignotti	BCRA
7-3-1947	San Jose Speedway	Johnny Smith	Ike Baumbach	BCRA
7-10-1947	San Jose Speedway	Marvin Burke	Lenny Gonsel	BCRA
7-17-1947	San Jose Speedway	Frank Cavanagh	Frank Vogel	BCRA
8-21-1947	San Jose Speedway	Johnny Soares	Harry Schilling	BCRA
8-28-1947	San Jose Speedway	Marvin Burke	Lenny Gonsel	BCRA
9-4-1947	San Jose Speedway	Fred Agabashian	George Bignotti	BCRA

Date	Track	Driver	Car Owner	Sanction
9-11-1947	San Jose Speedway	Johnny Smith	Ike Baumbach	BCRA
9-18-1947	San Jose Speedway	Fred Agabashian	George Bignotti	BCRA
9-25-1947	San Jose Speedway	Fred Agabashian	George Bignotti	BCRA
10-5-1947	San Jose Speedway	Norm Holtkamp	Jack London	BCRA
10-12-1947	San Jose Speedway	Fred Agabashian	George Bignotti	BCRA
11-9-1947	San Jose Speedway	Jerry Piper	Ed Pippo	BCRA
5-6-1948	San Jose Speedway	Norm Holtkamp	Eddie Meyer	BCRA
5-13-1948	San Jose Speedway	Fred Agabashian	George Bignotti	BCRA
5-27-1948	San Jose Speedway	Johnny Soares	Harry Schilling	BCRA
6-3-1948	San Jose Speedway	Johnny Boyd	Fred DeOrian	BCRA
6-10-1948	San Jose Speedway	Jerry Piper	Rudy Hennig	BCRA
7-22-1948	San Jose Speedway	Fred Agabashian	George Bignotti	BCRA
5-8-1949	San Jose Speedway	Chuck Stevenson	Ike Baumbach	BCRA
5-15-1949	San Jose Speedway	Woody Brown	Harry Schilling	BCRA
5-22-1949	San Jose Speedway	Woody Brown	Harry Schilling	BCRA
6-5-1949	San Jose Speedway	Jerry Piper	George Naruo	BCRA
6-12-1949	San Jose Speedway	Fred Friday	Fred Friday	BCRA
6-19-1949	San Jose Speedway	Fred Agabashian	George Bignotti	BCRA
6-26-1949	San Jose Speedway	Johnny Smith	Walt Land	BCRA
7-3-1949	San Jose Speedway	Marvin Burke	George Bignotti	BCRA
7-10-1949	San Jose Speedway	Jerry Piper	George Naruo	BCRA
10-23-1949	San Jose Speedway	Marvin Burke	George Bignotti	BCRA
7-3-1950	San Jose Speedway	Dickie Reese	Al Dean	BCRA
8-20-1950	San Jose Speedway	George Amick	Lysle Greenman	AAA
11-5-1950	San Jose Speedway	Mike McGreevy	Al Dean	BCRA
8-26-1951	San Jose Speedway	Ed Elisian	Buzz Balfour	BCRA
10-5-1951	San Jose Speedway	Johnny Boyd	George Bignotti	BCRA
3-30-1952	San Jose Speedway	Johnny Boyd	George Bignotti	BCRA
5-2-1952	San Jose Speedway	Dickie Reese	Frank Cavazza	BCRA
7-3-1952	San Jose Speedway	Ed Elisian	George Bignotti	BCRA
8-31-1952	San Jose Speedway	Bob Veith	Stan Brooks	BCRA
11-23-1952	San Jose Speedway	Tommy Copp	Merrit Groulx	BCRA
5-29-1953	San Jose Speedway	Johnny Baldwin	Jess Beene	BCRA
7-4-1953	San Jose Speedway	Earl Motter	Frank Magarian	BCRA
8-9-1953	San Jose Speedway	Earl Motter	Frank Magarian	BCRA
5-30-1954	San Jose Speedway	Bob Machin	Stan Brooks	BCRA
6-27-1954	San Jose Speedway	Bob Machin	Stan Brooks	BCRA
9-5-1954	San Jose Speedway	Johnny Baldwin	Jess Beene	BCRA
5-29-1955	San Jose Speedway	Johnny Baldwin	Jess Beene	BCRA
8-27-1955	San Jose Speedway	Bob Machin	Stan Brooks	BCRA
9-10-1955	San Jose Speedway	Bob Machin	Stan Brooks	BCRA
9-24-1955	San Jose Speedway	Bob Machin	Stan Brooks	BCRA
4-21-1956	San Jose Speedway	Bob Machin	Stan Brooks	BCRA
5-29-1956	San Jose Speedway	Tommy Morrow	Iver Hoerle	BCRA
6-23-1956	San Jose Speedway	Norm Rapp	Norm Rapp	BCRA
7-21-1956	San Jose Speedway	Johnny Boyd	George Bignotti	BCRA
9-8-1956	San Jose Speedway	Norm Rapp	Stan Brooks	BCRA
10-14-1956	San Jose Speedway	Bob Ramage	Howard Segur	BCRA
2-10-1957	San Jose Speedway	Shorty Templeman	Jack Whelan	USAC
4-7-1957	San Jose Speedway	Bob Machin	Lloyd Ridge	BCRA
5-29-1957	San Jose Speedway	Bob Cortner	Gene Cox	BCRA
7-3-1957	San Jose Speedway	Bob Cortner	Bob Cortner	BCRA
8-24-1957	San Jose Speedway	Bob Cortner	Gene Cox	BCRA
9-14-1957	Fairgrounds ½-mile	Tommy Copp	Sim Clark	BCRA
3-9-1958	San Jose Speedway	Billy Garrett	Gus Linhares	USAC
4-19-1958	San Jose Speedway	Johnny Baldwin	Stan Brooks	BCRA
5-10-1958	San Jose Speedway	Mike McGreevy	Adolph Bonini	BCRA
5-29-1958	San Jose Speedway	Mike McGreevy	Adolph Bonini	BCRA
8-16-1958	San Jose Speedway	Johnny Baldwin	Harold Guidi	BCRA

Date	Track	Driver	Car Owner	Sanction
5-29-1959	San Jose Speedway	Mike McGreevy	Lloyd Ridge	BCRA
9-29-1959	San Jose Speedway	Dave Moses	Len Esposto	BCRA
10-31-1959	San Jose Speedway	Cliff Spalding	Don Harmon	USAC
5-29-1960	San Jose Speedway	Mike McGreevy	Lloyd Ridge	BCRA
7-3-1960	San Jose Speedway	Ed Andrews	Charlie Nelson	BCRA
10-23-1960	San Jose Speedway	Harry Beck	Harry Beck	BCRA
5-12-1961	San Jose Speedway	Norm Rapp	Norm Rapp	BCRA
5-29-1961	San Jose Speedway	Johnny Baldwin	Lloyd Ridge	BCRA
6-30-1961	San Jose Speedway	Dean Holden	Floyd Hughes	BCRA
9-3-1961	San Jose Speedway	George Benson	George Benson	BCRA
5-29-1962	San Jose Speedway	Bob DeJong	Sim Clark	BCRA
9-3-1962	Alviso Speedway	Mike McGreevy	Porter Goff	BCRA
10-5-1962	Alviso Speedway	Charlie Lawlor	Harry Stryker	BCRA
10-21-1962	San Jose Speedway	Bob Wente	Bob Higman	USAC
5-29-1963	San Jose Speedway	Bob Burbridge	Porter Goff	BCRA
7-4-1963	Alviso Speedway	Bob Burbridge	Porter Goff	BCRA
9-1-1963	San Jose Speedway	Mike McGreevy	Porter Goff	BCRA
2-9-1964	San Jose Speedway	Johnny Baldwin	Glen Dennee	USAC
5-29-1964	San Jose Speedway	Dee Hileman	Moe Goff	BCRA
11-8-1964	San Jose Speedway	Parnelli Jones	Marv Edwards	USAC
5-30-1965	San Jose Speedway	George Benson	Ollie Johnson	BCRA
9-5-1965	San Jose Speedway	Dick Atkins	John Pestana	BCRA
5-29-1966	San Jose Speedway	Rick Henderson	Jack London	BCRA
7-3-1966	San Jose Speedway	George Benson	Ollie Johnson	BCRA
8-6-1966	San Jose Speedway	Dave Strickland	Bob Rosen	BCRA
9-4-1966	San Jose Speedway	Burt Foland	Jack London	BCRA
2-19-1967	San Jose Speedway	Bill Vukovich	Bob Consani	USAC
5-29-1967	San Jose Speedway	Burt Foland	Jack London	BCRA
7-3-1967	San Jose Speedway	Burt Foland	Jack London	BCRA
8-5-1967	San Jose Speedway	Burt Foland	Jack London	BCRA
9-3-1967	San Jose Speedway	Rick Henderson	Ollie Johnson	BCRA
1-6-1968	Fairgrounds-Indoors	Dick Deis	Myron Caves	BCRA
1-20-1968	Fairgrounds-Indoors	Gary Ponzini	Duane Kastor	BCRA
2-3-1968	Fairgrounds-Indoors	Hank Butcher	Jim Montgomery	BCRA
2-10-1968	Fairgrounds-Indoors	Burt Foland	Mason Cook	BCRA
2-18-1968	San Jose Speedway	Bill Vukovich	Doug Caruthers	USAC
5-29-1968	San Jose Speedway	Dewayne Woodward	Lloyd Del Nero	BCRA
7-12-1968	San Jose Speedway	Burt Foland	Jack London	BCRA
7-19-1968	San Jose Speedway	Burt Foland	Jack London	BCRA
7-26-1968	San Jose Speedway	Burt Foland	Burt Foland	BCRA
8-2-1968	San Jose Speedway	Dick Deis	Myron Caves	BCRA
8-9-1968	San Jose Speedway	Burt Foland	Burt Foland	BCRA
8-16-1968	San Jose Speedway	Burt Foland	Burt Foland	BCRA
8-23-1968	San Jose Speedway	Burt Foland	Burt Foland	BCRA
8-30-1968	San Jose Speedway	Burt Foland	Burt Foland	BCRA
10-26-1968	San Jose Speedway	Dick Whalen	Jerry O'Connell	BCRA
12-6-1968	Fairgrounds-Indoors	Bob DeJong	Fino Saccullo	BCRA
2-16-1969	San Jose Speedway	George Benson	Ollie Johnson	USAC
7-4-1969	San Jose Speedway	George Benson	Ollie Johnson	USAC
8-2-1969	San Jose Speedway	Burt Foland	Jerry O'Connell	BCRA
8-31-1969	San Jose Speedway	Burt Foland	Jerry O'Connell	BCRA
9-26-1969	San Jose Speedway	Burt Foland	Burt Foland	USAC
2-22-1970	San Jose Speedway	Johnny Parsons Jr.	Leonard Faas	USAC
3-22-1970	San Jose Speedway	Bob DeJong	Sim Clark	BCRA
7-3-1970*	San Jose Speedway	Tommy Astone Jr.	Jack London	BCRA
7-3-1970	San Jose Speedway	Tommy Astone Jr.	Jack London	BCRA
8-17-1970	Fairgrounds 1/6-mile	Bill McCormick	Bob Sousa	BCRA
11-1-1970	San Jose Speedway	Burt Foland	Jack London	USAC
2-14-1971	San Jose Speedway	Burt Foland	Ollie Johnson	USAC

Date	Track	Driver	Car Owner	Sanction
7-4-1971	San Jose Speedway	Tommy Astone Jr.	Jack London	BCRA
8-16-1971	Fairgrounds 1/6-mile	Bob DeJong	Bill Roberts	BCRA
8-17-1971	Fairgrounds 1/6-mile	Hank Butcher	Walt Rore	BCRA
10-1-1971	San Jose Speedway	Jimmy Caruthers	Doug Caruthers	USAC
2-20-1972	San Jose Speedway	Gary Bettenhausen	Caruthers	USAC
5-28-1972	San Jose Speedway	Burt Foland	Jack London	BCRA
8-21-1972	Fairgrounds 1/6-mile	Ronnie Hulse	Bob Valencia	BCRA
8-22-1972	Fairgrounds 1/6-mile	Hank Butcher	Bill Eskesen	BCRA
9-3-1972	San Jose Speedway	Burt Foland	Jack London	BCRA
10-1-1972	San Jose Speedway	Nick Rescino	Tom Dupont	BCRA
2-25-1973	San Jose Speedway	Gary Bettenhausen	Caruthers	USAC
5-27-1973	San Jose Speedway	Chuck Gurney	Art Shanoian	BCRA
8-20-1973	Fairgrounds 1/6-mile	Floyd Alvis	Floyd Alvis	BCRA
8-21-1973	Fairgrounds 1/6-mile	Rich Govan	Jim Montgomery	BCRA
9-30-1973	San Jose Speedway	Johnny Anderson	Lenny Gonsel	BCRA
11-3-1973	Fairgrounds-Indoors	Ken Nichols	Bill Nichols	BCRA
2-17-1974	San Jose Speedway	Jimmy Caruthers	Caruthers	USAC
5-26-1974	San Jose Speedway	Hank Butcher	Tom Dupont	BCRA
8-20-1974	Fairgrounds 1/6-mile	Hank Butcher	Harry Stryker	BCRA
8-21-1974	Fairgrounds 1/6-mile	Hank Butcher	Harry Stryker	BCRA
9-29-1974	San Jose Speedway	Johnny Anderson	Lenny Gonsel	BCRA
2-23-1975	San Jose Speedway	Bobby Olivero	LTC Research	USAC
5-25-1975	San Jose Speedway	Bob DeJong	Bob Miller	BCRA
6-14-1975	San Jose Speedway	Danny O'Neill	Ray Bussell	BCRA
9-28-1975	San Jose Speedway	Johnny Anderson	Lenny Gonsel	BCRA
2-15-1976	San Jose Speedway	"Sleepy" Tripp	Ed Koster	USAC
2-22-1976	San Jose Speedway	Chuck Gurney	Sam Hucke	BCRA
3-20-1976	San Jose Speedway	Harry Stryker Jr.	Harry Stryker	BCRA
5-31-1976	San Jose Speedway	Larry Patton	Sam Hucke	BCRA
6-6-1976	San Jose Speedway	Hank Butcher	Tom Dupont	BCRA
6-6-1976*	San Jose Speedway	Hank Butcher	Tom Dupont	BCRA
6-13-1976	San Jose Speedway	Wheeler Gresham	Ken Wilton	BCRA
6-13-1976*	San Jose Speedway	Hank Butcher	Tom Dupont	BCRA
6-27-1976	San Jose Speedway	Ken Molica	Ken Molica	BCRA
6-27-1976*	San Jose Speedway	Ken Molica	Ken Molica	BCRA
7-2-1976	San Jose Speedway	Hank Butcher	Tom Dupont	BCRA
7-9-1976	San Jose Speedway	Hank Butcher	Tom Dupont	BCRA
7-16-1976	San Jose Speedway	Hank Butcher	Tom Dupont	BCRA
7-23-1976	San Jose Speedway	Johnny Anderson	Lenny Gonsel	BCRA
7-30-1976	San Jose Speedway	Danny O'Neill	Ray Bussell	BCRA
2-20-1977	San Jose Speedway	Hank Butcher	Jim Dour	USAC
4-16-1977	San Jose Speedway	Ron Vines	Jim Montgomery	BCRA
5-30-1977	San Jose Speedway	Danny O'Neill	Ray Bussell	BCRA
7-2-1977	San Jose Speedway	Danny O'Neill	Ray Bussell	BCRA
8-6-1977	San Jose Speedway	Hank Butcher	Jim Dour	BCRA
9-4-1977	Fairgrounds ½-mile	Tommy Astone Jr.	Mason Cook	BCRA
9-3-1978	Fairgrounds ¼-mile	Floyd Alvis	Floyd Alvis	BCRA
10-13-1979	Fairgrounds ¼-mile	Floyd Alvis	Floyd Alvis	BCRA
10-10-1987	Fairgrounds ¼-mile	Joe Winters	Al Winters	BCRA
10-9-1992	Fairgrounds 1/3-mile	Terry Tarditi	Terry Tarditi	BCRA
9-3-1994	Fairgrounds 1/3-mile	Craig Dillard	Martin Hagopian	BCRA
8-10-1996	Fairgrounds 1/3-mile	Terry Tarditi	Terry Tarditi	BCRA
5-24-1997	Fairgrounds 1/3-mile	Marc DeBeaumont	Jim DeBeaumont	BCRA

* Two main events were held on this night.

MARA: Midget Auto Racing Association
URA: United Racing Association
BCRA: Bay Cities Racing Association
AAA: American Automobile Association
USAC: United States Auto Club

The Greatest

Greatest San Jose Drivers
Joe Leonard
Earl Cooper
Babe Stapp
Howard, Brent, Tim & Bud Kaeding
Marshall & Mike Sargent
Adolph Gusti
A.J. Allmendinger
Willy T. Ribbs
Scott Speed

Greatest Drivers to Race in San Jose
Barney Oldfield
Ralph DePalma
Bill Cummings
Wilbur Shaw
Sam Hanks
Ted Horn
Troy Ruttman
Bob Sweikert
A.J. Foyt
Parnelli Jones
Roger Ward
Rick Mears
Tony & Gary Bettenhausen
Billy & Bill Vuckovich
Duane and Poncho Carter
Johnnie Parsons Jr. & Sr.
Art Pollard
Gene & Norm Rapp
Freddie Agabashian
Mel Kenyon
Al and Dave Pombo
Burt Foland
Rick Henderson
George Snider
Johnny Boyd
Johnny Key
Jan Opperman
Steve Kinser
Sammy Swindell
Donny Schatz
Doug Wolfgang
Dave Blaney
Ernie Irvan
Nick Rescino
Kasey Kahne
Sebastien Bourdais
Timo Glock
and many more

San Jose Racing Deaths

San Jose Driving Park
1912   Reed Orr
1912   W.T. Baker
1915   Paul Brasher

San Jose Speedway (Alum Rock Ave.)
1923   Paul Arrighi
1924   Al Mulford
1924   Adolph Gusti
1924   Jess Soares
1925   Jack Kemp
1925   Henry Beal
1931   Walt May
1934   Howard Ordrop
1935   Eugene McCarthy

San Jose Speedway (Tully Road)
1950   Russ Margolati
1961   James Williamson
1967   Cliff Rogalsky
1969   Lloyd Nygren
1974   Stephen Tarigo
1975   Bob Zwemke

Santa Clara County Fairgrounds
1952   Joe James
1955   Reco Whitton
1973   Lloyd Allen Houchins
1989   Frank Carlotta

Bibliography

Brown, Allan E. *The History of American Speedway*. Comstock Park, MI: Allan E. Brown, 1994.

Burrill, Robert and Rogers, Lynn. *Alviso, San Jose*. Charleston SC: Arcadia Publishing, 2006.

Busby, Floyd P. *BCRA Yearbooks*. Concord, CA: Buzco Enterprises, 2000-2004.

Barkhimer, Robert. *Speed, Northern California's Auto Racing Magazine*. Berkeley, CA: Motor Speedway, 1946 - 1955.

Clark, Shannon E. *The Alameda*. San Jose, CA: Alameda Business Association, 2006.

Cole, Dermot. *Hard Driving*. New York, NY: Paragon House, 1991.

Fenster, Julie M. *Race of the Century*. New York, NY: Three Rivers Press, 2005.

Fox, Jack. *BCRA Yearbooks*. San Jose, CA: Jack C. Fox Graphics and Publications, 1964-1975.

Fox, Jack C. *The Mighty Midgets*. Speedway, IN: Carl Hungness, 1977.

Gilbert, Lauren M. and Bob Johnson. San Jose Public Library. *San Jose's Historic Downtown*. San Jose, CA: Arcadia, 2004.

Hungness, Carl. *USAC Sprint History-1956-1980*. Speedway, IN: Carl Hungness, 1981.

Lucero, John R. *Legion Ascot Speedway*. Huntington Park, CA: Orecul Publishing Company, 1982.

McCoy, Jack. *Racing's Real McCoy*. Modesto, CA: Mcracebk Publishing, 2000.

McDonald, Johnny . *San Diego Motorsports-100 Racing Years*. San Diego, CA: Ramona Home Journal, 2006.

Motter, Tom. *A History of the Oakland Speedway*. Rancho Cordova, CA: Vintage Images, 2002.

Motter, Tom. *BCRA-The first 50 Years*. Pleasant Hill, CA: Bay Cities Racing Association, 1990.

Motter, Tom. *Indoors*. Rancho Cordova, CA: Vintage Images, 2004.

Montgomery, Bill. *BCRA Yearbook*. Fremont,CA: Bill Montgomery, 1980.

Nolan, William F. *Barney Oldfield*. Carpinteria, CA: Brown Fox Books, 1961.

Pearce, Ralph M. *Asahi to Zebras*. San Jose, CA: Japanese American Museum of San Jose, 2005.

Radbruch, Don. *Dirt Track Auto Racing 1919-1941*. Jefferson, NC: McFarland & Company, Inc. Publishers, 2004.

Radbruch, Don. *Roaring Roadsters. Driggs, ID:* Tex Smith Publishing, 1994.

Radbruch, Don. *Roaring Roadsters #2. Driggs, ID:* Tex Smith Publishing, 2000.

Rose, Buzz . *Kings of the Hills*. Glendale, AZ: Rose Racing Publications, 2006.

Shiels, Jim. *WAR in California*. Stockton, CA: Jim Shiels, 1998.

Spalding, John E. *A Century of Sports in Santa Clara County 1900-1999*. San Jose CA: AG Press, 2000.

USAC. *The AAA/USAC National Midget Auto Racing Hall of Fame*. Marshall, IN: Whitness Productions, 1995.

USAC. *USAC Yearbooks*. Speedway, IN: USAC, 1956-2005.

Weltch, Andrew. *Oval Racing in Devon and Cornwall*. Wales, GB: Tempus Publishing Limited, 2003.

White, Gordon Eliot. *Lost Race Tracks*. Hudson, Wisconsin: Iconografix, 2002.

Yasukawa, Jane M. *Tales of the Oval*. New York, NY: RJ Communications LLC, 2002.

Index

1959: Ray Coupland

Hardtop

1963: Bruce Brown

1963: Archie Tucker (28), Al Pombo (3), Herman Hutton

1964: Les Levi   **Super Modified Hardtop**

1965: Stan Luhdorff

1971: Bill Scott

1972: Ted Witt - Nick Rescino

Ha
Sp
The
Pho

De

The first H.
Jose was he
next fifty ye
evolve into
Super Modi
Modified, Su
a Sprint Car.
time-line of

1981: Mike Sargent   **Super Modified**

1982: John Viel

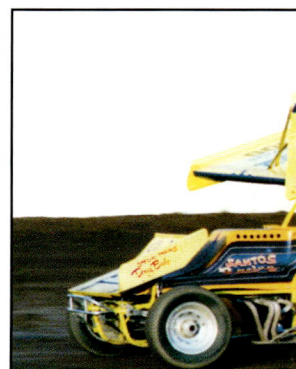
1985: Joe